THE

SYMBOLISM OF FREEMASONRY

ILLUSTRATING AND EXPLAINING

Its Science and Philosophy, its Legends,

Myths, and Symbols

BY

Albert G. Mackey, M.D.

STONE GUILD PUBLISHING
PLANO, TEXAS
HTTP://WWW.STONEGUILDPUBLISHING.COM/

2009

Originally Published By:
CLARK AND MAYNARD
1882

This Edition Copyright © 2008
Stone Guild Publishing, Inc.
Plano, Texas
http://www.stoneguildpublishing.com/

First Paperback Edition 2009

ISBN-13 978-1-60532-050-2
ISBN-10 1-60532-050-1

10 9 8 7 6 5 4 3 2

TO

GENERAL JOHN C. FREMONT.

My Dear Sir:

While any American might be proud of associating his name with that of one who has done so much to increase the renown of his country, and to enlarge the sum of human knowledge, this book is dedicated to you as a slight testimonial of regard for your personal character, and in grateful recollection of acts of friendship.

Yours very truly,

A. G. MACKEY.

PREFACE.

Of the various modes of communicating instruction to the uninformed, the masonic student is particularly interested in two; namely, the instruction by legends and that by symbols. It is to these two, almost exclusively, that he is indebted for all that he knows, and for all that he can know, of the philosophic system which is taught in the institution. All its mysteries and its dogmas, which constitute its philosophy, are intrusted for communication to the neophyte, sometimes to one, sometimes to the other of these two methods of instruction, and sometimes to both of them combined. The Freemason has no way of reaching any of the esoteric teachings of the Order except through the medium of a legend or a symbol.

A legend differs from an historical narrative only in this—that it is without documentary evidence of authenticity. It is the offspring solely of tradition. Its details may be true in part or in whole. There may be no internal evidence to the contrary, or there may be internal evidence that they are altogether false. But neither the possibility of truth in the one case, nor the certainty of falsehood in the other, can remove the traditional narrative

3

from the class of legends. It is a legend simply because it rests on no written foundation. It is oral, and therefore legendary.

In grave problems of history, such as the establishment of empires, the discovery and settlement of countries, or the rise and fall of dynasties, the knowledge of the truth or falsity of the legendary narrative will be of importance, because the value of history is impaired by the imputation of doubt. But it is not so in Freemasonry. Here there need be no absolute question of the truth or falsity of the legend. The object of the masonic legends is not to establish historical facts, but to convey philosophical doctrines. They are a method by which esoteric instruction is communicated, and the student accepts them with reference to nothing else except their positive use and meaning as developing masonic dogmas. Take, for instance, the Hiramic legend of the third degree. Of what importance is it to the disciple of Masonry whether it is true or false? All that he wants to know is its internal signification; and when he learns that it is intended to illustrate the doctrine of the immortality of the soul, he is content with that interpretation, and he does not deem it necessary, except as a matter of curious or antiquarian inquiry, to investigate its historical accuracy, or to reconcile any of its apparent contradictions. So of the lost keystone; so of the second temple; so of the hidden ark: these are to him legendary narratives, which, like the casket, would be of no value, were it not for the precious jewel contained within. Each of these legends is the expression of a philosophical idea.

But there is another method of masonic instruction, and that is by symbols. No science is more ancient than that of symbolism. At one time, nearly all the learning of the world was conveyed in symbols. And although modern philosophy now deals only in abstract propositions, Freemasonry still cleaves to the ancient method, and has preserved it in its primitive importance as a means of communicating knowledge.

According to the derivation of the word from the Greek, "to symbolize" signifies "to compare one thing with another." Hence a symbol is the expression of an idea that has been derived from the comparison or contrast of some object with a moral conception or attribute. Thus we say that the plumb is a symbol of rectitude of conduct. The physical qualities of the plumb are here compared or contrasted with the moral conception of virtue, or rectitude. Then to the Speculative Mason it becomes, after he has been taught its symbolic meaning, the visible expression of the idea of moral uprightness.

But although there are these two modes of instruction in Freemasonry, —by legends and by symbols,—there really is no radical difference between the two methods. The symbol is a visible, and the legend an audible representation of some contrasted idea —of some moral conception produced from a comparison. Both the legend and the symbol relate to dogmas of a deep religious character; both of them convey moral sentiments in the same peculiar method, and both of them are designed by this method to illustrate the philosophy of Speculative Masonry.

To investigate the recondite meaning of these legends and symbols, and to elicit from them the moral and philosophical lessons which they were intended to teach, is to withdraw the veil with which ignorance and indifference seek to conceal the true philosophy of Freemasonry.

To study the symbolism of Masonry is the only way to investigate its philosophy. This is the portal of its temple, through which alone we can gain access to the sacellum where its aporrheta are concealed.

Its philosophy is engaged in the consideration of propositions relating to God and man, to the present and the future life. Its science is the symbolism by which these propositions are presented to the mind.

The work now offered to the public is an effort to develop and explain this philosophy and science. It will show that there are in Freemasonry the germs of profound speculation. If it does not interest the learned, it may instruct the ignorant. If so, I shall not regret the labor and research that have been bestowed upon its composition.

ALBERT G. MACKEY, M. D.

CONTENTS.

I.

PRELIMINARY.

THE ORIGIN AND PROGRESS OF FREEMASONRY.

ANY inquiry into the symbolism and philosophy of Freemasonry must necessarily be preceded by a brief investigation of the origin and history of the institution. Ancient and universal as it is, whence did it arise? What were the accidents connected with its birth? From what kindred or similar association did it spring? Or was it original and autochthonic, independent, in its inception, of any external influences, and unconnected with any other institution? These are questions which an intelligent investigator will be disposed to propound in the very commencement of the inquiry; and they are questions which must be distinctly answered before he can be expected to comprehend its true character as a symbolic institution. He must know something of its antecedents before he can appreciate its character.

But he who expects to arrive at a satisfactory solution of this inquiry must first—as a preliminary absolutely necessary to success—release himself from the influence of an error into which novices in Masonic philosophy are too apt to fall. He must not confound the doctrine of Freemasonry with its outward and extrinsic form. He must not suppose that certain usages and ceremonies, which exist at this day, but which, even now, are subject to extensive variations in different countries, constitute the sum and substance of Freemasonry. "Prudent antiquity," says Lord Coke, "did for more solemnity and better memory and observation of that which is to be done, express substances under ceremonies." But it must be always remembered that the ceremony is not the substance. It is but the outer garment which covers and perhaps adorns it, as clothing does the human figure. But divest man of that outward apparel, and you still have the microcosm, the wondrous creation, with all his nerves, and bones, and muscles, and, above all, with his brain, and thoughts, and feelings. And so take from Masonry these external ceremonies, and you still have remaining its philosophy and science. These have, of course, always continued the same, while the ceremonies have varied in different ages, and still vary in different countries.

The definition of Freemasonry that it is "a science of morality, veiled in allegory, and illustrated by symbols," has been so often quoted, that, were it not for its beauty, it would become wearisome. But this definition contains the exact principle that has just been enunciated. Freemasonry is a science—a philosophy—a system of doctrines which is taught, in a manner peculiar to itself, by allegories and symbols. This is its internal character. Its ceremonies are external additions, which affect not its substance.

Now, when we are about to institute an inquiry into the origin of Freemasonry, it is of this peculiar system of philosophy that we are to inquire, and not of the ceremonies which have been foisted on it. If we pursue any other course we shall assuredly fall into error.

Thus, if we seek the origin and first beginning of the Masonic philosophy, we must go away back into the ages of remote antiquity, when we shall find this beginning in the bosom of kindred associations, where the same philosophy was maintained and taught. But if we confound the ceremonies of Masonry with the philosophy of Masonry, and seek the origin of the institution, moulded into outward form as it is to-day, we can scarcely be required to look farther back than the beginning of the eighteenth century, and, indeed, not quite so far. For many important modifications have been made in its rituals since that period.

Having, then, arrived at the conclusion that it is not the Masonic ritual, but the Masonic philosophy, whose origin we are to investigate, the next question naturally relates to the peculiar nature of that philosophy.

Now, then, I contend that the philosophy of Freemasonry is engaged in the contemplation of the divine and human character; of GOD as one eternal, self-existent being, in contradiction to the mythology of the ancient peoples, which was burdened with a multitude of gods and goddesses, of demigods and heroes; of MAN as an immortal being, preparing in the present life for an eternal future, in like contradiction to the ancient philosophy, which circumscribed the existence of man to the present life.

These two doctrines, then, of the unity of God and the

immortality of the soul, constitute the philosophy of Freemasonry. When we wish to define it succinctly, we say that it is an ancient system of philosophy which teaches these two dogmas. And hence, if, amid the intellectual darkness and debasement of the old polytheistic religions, we find interspersed here and there, in all ages, certain institutions or associations which taught these truths, and that, in a particular way, allegorically and symbolically, then we have a right to say that such institutions or associations were the incunabula—the predecessors— of the Masonic institution as it now exists.

With these preliminary remarks the reader will be enabled to enter upon the consideration of that theory of the origin of Freemasonry which I advance in the following propositions:—

1. In the first place, I contend that in the very earliest ages of the world there were existent certain truths of vast importance to the welfare and happiness of humanity, which had been communicated,—no matter how, but,—most probably, by direct inspiration from God to man.

2. These truths principally consisted in the abstract propositions of the unity of God and the immortality of the soul. Of the truth of these two propositions there cannot be a reasonable doubt. The belief in these truths is a necessary consequence of that religious sentiment which has always formed an essential feature of human nature. Man is, emphatically, and in distinction from all other creatures, a religious animal. Gross commences his interesting work on "The Heathen Religion in its Popular and Symbolical Development" by the statement that "one of the most remarkable phenomena of the

human race is the universal existence of religious ideas— a belief in something supernatural and divine, and a worship corresponding to it." As nature had implanted the religious sentiment, the same nature must have directed it in a proper channel. The belief and the worship must at first have been as pure as the fountain whence they flowed, although, in subsequent times, and before the advent of Christian light, they may both have been corrupted by the influence of the priests and the poets over an ignorant and superstitious people. The first and second propositions of my theory refer only to that primeval period which was antecedent to these corruptions, of which I shall hereafter speak.

3. These truths of God and immortality were most probably handed down through the line of patriarchs of the race of Seth, but were, at all events, known to Noah, and were by him communicated to his immediate descendants.

4. In consequence of this communication, the true worship of God continued, for some time after the subsidence of the deluge, to be cultivated by the Noachidæ, the Noachites, or the descendants of Noah.

5. At a subsequent period (no matter when, but the biblical record places it at the attempted building of the tower of Babel), there was a secession of a large number of the human race from the Noachites.

6. These seceders rapidly lost sight of the divine truths which had been communicated to them from their common ancestor, and fell into the most grievous theological errors, corrupting the purity of the worship and the orthodoxy of the religious faith which they had primarily received.

7. These truths were preserved in their integrity by but a very few in the patriarchal line, while still fewer were enabled to retain only dim and glimmering portions of the true light.

8. The first class was confined to the direct descendants of Noah, and the second was to be found among the priests and philosophers, and, perhaps, still later, among the poets of the heathen nations, and among those whom they initiated into the secrets of these truths. Of the prevalence of these religious truths among the patriarchal descendants of Noah, we have ample evidence in the sacred records. As to their existence among a body of learned heathens, we have the testimony of many intelligent writers who have devoted their energies to this subject. Thus the learned Grote, in his "History of Greece," says, "The allegorical interpretation of the myths has been, by several learned investigators, especially by Creuzer, connected with the hypothesis of *an ancient and highly instructed body of priests,* having their origin either in Egypt or in the East, and communicating to the rude and barbarous Greeks religious, physical, and historical knowledge, *under the veil of symbols."* What is here said only of the Greeks is equally applicable to every other intellectual nation of antiquity.

9. The system or doctrine of the former class has been called by Masonic writers the "Pure or Primitive Freemasonry" of antiquity, and that of the latter class the "Spurious Freemasonry" of the same period. These terms were first used, if I mistake not, by Dr. Oliver, and are intended to refer—the word *pure* to the doctrines taught by the descendants of Noah in the Jewish

line, and the word *spurious* to his descendants in the
heathen or Gentile line.

10. The masses of the people, among the Gentiles
especially, were totally unacquainted with this divine
truth, which was the foundation stone of both species of
Freemasonry, the pure and the spurious, and were
deeply immersed in the errors and falsities of heathen
belief and worship.

11. These errors of the heathen religions were not the
voluntary inventions of the peoples who cultivated them,
but were gradual and almost unavoidable corruptions of
the truths which had been at first taught by Noah; and,
indeed, so palpable are these corruptions, that they can
be readily detected and traced to the original form from
which, however much they might vary among different
peoples, they had, at one time or another, deviated. Thus,
in the life and achievements of Bacchus or Dionysus, we
find the travestied counterpart of the career of Moses,
and in the name of Vulcan, the blacksmith god, we
evidently see an etymological corruption of the
appellation of Tubal Cain, the first artificer in metals.
For *Vul-can* is but a modified form of *Baal-Cain,* the
god Cain.

12. But those among the masses—and there were
some —who were made acquainted with the truth,
received their knowledge by means of an initiation into
certain sacred Mysteries, in the bosom of which it was
concealed from the public gaze.

13. These Mysteries existed in every country of
heathendom, in each under a different name, and to some
extent under a different form, but always and everywhere
with the same design of inculcating, by allegorical and

symbolic teachings, the great Masonic doctrines of the unity of God and the immortality of the soul. This is an important proposition, and the fact which it enunciates must never be lost sight of in any inquiry into the origin of Freemasonry; for the pagan Mysteries were to the spurious Freemasonry of antiquity precisely what the Masters' lodges are to the Freemasonry of the present day. It is needless to offer any proof of their existence, since this is admitted and continually referred to by all historians, ancient and modern; and to discuss minutely their character and organization would occupy a distinct treatise. The Baron de Sainte Croix has written two large volumes on the subject, and yet left it unexhausted.

14. These two divisions of the Masonic Institution which were defined in the 9th proposition, namely, the pure or primitive Freemasonry among the Jewish descendants of the patriarchs, who are called, by way of distinction, the Noachites, or descendants of Noah, because they had not forgotten nor abandoned the teachings of their great ancestor, and the spurious Freemasonry practised among the pagan nations, flowed down the stream of time in parallel currents, often near together, but never commingling.

15. But these two currents were not always to be kept apart, for, springing, in the long anterior ages, from one common fountain,—that ancient priesthood of whom I have already spoken in the 8th proposition,—and then dividing into the pure and spurious Freemasonry of antiquity, and remaining separated for centuries upon centuries, they at length met at the building of the great temple of Jerusalem, and were united, in the instance of the Israelites under King Solomon, and the Tyrians

under Hiram, King of Tyre, and Hiram Abif. The spurious Freemasonry, it is true, did not then and there cease to exist. On the contrary, it lasted for centuries subsequent to this period; for it was not until long after, and in the reign of the Emperor Theodosius, that the pagan Mysteries was finally and totally abolished. But by the union of the Jewish or pure Freemasons and the Tyrian or spurious Freemasons at Jerusalem, there was a mutual infusion of their respective doctrines and ceremonies, which eventually terminated in the abolition of the two distinctive systems and the establishment of a new one, that may be considered as the immediate prototype of the present institution. Hence many Masonic students, going no farther back in their investigations than the facts announced in this 15th proposition, are content to find the origin of Freemasonry at the temple of Solomon. But if my theory be correct, the truth is, that it there received, not its birth, but only a new modification of its character. The legend of the third degree—the golden legend, the *legenda aurea*—of Masonry was there adopted by pure Freemasonry, which before had no such legend, from spurious Freemasonry. But the legend had existed under other names and forms, in all the Mysteries, for ages before. The doctrine of immortality, which had hitherto been taught by the Noachites simply as an abstract proposition, was thenceforth to be inculcated by a symbolic lesson—the symbol of Hiram the Builder was to become forever after the distinctive feature of Freemasonry.

16. But another important modification was effected in the Masonic system at the building of the temple. Previous to the union which then took place, the pure Freemasonry

of the Noachites had always been speculative, but resembled the present organization in no other way than in the cultivation of the same abstract principles of divine truth.

17. The Tyrians, on the contrary, were architects by profession, and, as their leaders were disciples of the school of the spurious Freemasonry, they, for the first time, at the temple of Solomon, when they united with their Jewish contemporaries, infused into the speculative science, which was practised by the latter, the elements of an operative art.

18. Therefore the system continued thenceforward, for ages, to present the commingled elements of operative and speculative Masonry. We see this in the *Collegia Fabrorum,* or Colleges of Artificers, first established at Rome by Numa, and which were certainly of a Masonic form in their organization; in the Jewish sect of the Essenes, who wrought as well as prayed, and who are claimed to have been the descendants of the temple builders, and also, and still more prominently, in the Travelling Freemasons of the middle ages, who identify themselves by their very name with their modern successors, and whose societies were composed of learned men who thought and wrote, and of workmen who labored and built. And so for a long time Freemasonry continued to be both operative and speculative.

19. But another change was to be effected in the institution to make it precisely what it now is, and, therefore, at a very recent period (comparatively speaking), the operative feature was abandoned, and Freemasonry became wholly speculative. The exact time of this change is not left to conjecture. It took place in the reign of Queen Anne, of England, in the beginning of the

eighteenth century. Preston gives us the very words of the decree which established this change, for he says that at that time it was agreed to "that the privileges of Masonry should no longer be restricted to operative Masons, but extend to men of various professions, provided they were regularly approved and initiated into the order."

The nineteen propositions here announced contain a brief but succinct view of the progress of Freemasonry from its origin in the early ages of the world, simply as a system of religious philosophy, through all the modifications to which it was submitted in the Jewish and Gentile races, until at length it was developed in its present perfected form. During all this time it preserved unchangeably certain features that may hence be considered as its specific characteristics, by which it has always been distinguished from every other contemporaneous association, however such association may have simulated it in outward form. These characteristics are, first, the doctrines which it has constantly taught, namely, that of the unity of God and that of the immortality of the soul; and, secondly, the manner in which these doctrines have been taught, namely, by symbols and allegories.

Taking these characteristics as the exponents of what Freemasonry is, we cannot help arriving at the conclusion that the speculative Masonry of the present day exhibits abundant evidence of the identity of its origin with the spurious Freemasonry of the ante-Solomonic period, both systems coming from the same pure source, but the one always preserving, and the other continually corrupting, the purity of the common fountain. This is also the necessary conclusion as a corollary from the propositions advanced in this essay.

There is also abundant evidence in the history, of which these propositions are but a meagre outline, that a manifest influence was exerted on the pure or primitive Freemasonry of the Noachites by the Tyrian branch of the spurious system, in the symbols, myths, and legends which the former received from the latter, but which it so modified and interpreted as to make them consistent with its own religious system. One thing, at least, is incapable of refutation; and that is, that we are indebted to the Tyrian Masons for the introduction of the symbol of Hiram Abif. The idea of the symbol, although modified by the Jewish Masons, is not Jewish in its inception. It was evidently borrowed from the pagan mysteries, where Bacchus, Adonis, Proserpine, and a host of other apotheosized beings play the same role that Hiram does in the Masonic mysteries.

And lastly, we find in the technical terms of Masonry, in its working tools, in the names of its grades, and in a large majority of its symbols, ample testimony of the strong infusion into its religious philosophy of the elements of an operative art. And history again explains this fact by referring to the connection of the institution with the Dionysiac Fraternity of Artificers, who was engaged in building the temple of Solomon, with the Workmen's Colleges of Numa, and with the Travelling Freemasons of the middle ages, who constructed all the great buildings of that period.

These nineteen propositions, which have been submitted in the present essay, constitute a brief summary or outline of a theory of the true origin of Freemasonry, which long and patient investigation has led me to adopt. To attempt to prove the truth of each of these propositions in its order by logical demonstration, or by historical evidence, would involve the writing of an elaborate treatise. They are now offered simply as suggestions on which the Masonic student may ponder. They are but intended as guide-posts, which may direct him in his journey should he undertake the pleasant although difficult task of instituting an inquiry into the origin and progress of Freemasonry from its birth to its present state of full-grown manhood.

But even in this abridged form they are absolutely necessary as preliminary to any true understanding of the symbolism of Freemasonry.

II.

THE NOACHIDÆ

IPROCEED, then, to inquire into the historical origin of Freemasonry, as a necessary introduction to any inquiry into the character of its symbolism. To do this, with any expectation of rendering justice to the subject, it is evident that I shall have to take my point of departure at a very remote era. I shall, however, review the early and antecedent history of the institution with as much brevity as a distinct understanding of the subject will admit.

Passing over all that is within the antediluvian history of the world, as something that exerted, so far as our subject is concerned, no influence on the new world which sprang forth from the ruins of the old, we find, soon after the cataclysm, the immediate descendants of Noah in the possession of at least two religious truths, which they received from their common father, and which he must have derived from the line of patriarchs who preceded him. These truths were the doctrine of the existence of a Supreme Intelligence, the Creator, Preserver, and Ruler of the Universe, and, as a necessary corollary, the belief in the immortality of the soul,* which, as an emanation from that primal cause, was to be distinguished, by a future and eternal life, from the vile and perishable dust which forms its earthly tabernacle.

The assertion that these doctrines were known to and recognized by Noah will not appear as an assumption to the believer in divine revelation. But any philosophic mind must, I conceive, come to the same conclusion, independently of any other authority than that of reason.

The religious sentiment, so far, at least, as it relates to the belief in the existence of God, appears to be in some sense innate, or instinctive, and consequently universal in the human mind.† There is no record of any nation, however intellectually and morally debased, that has not given some evidence of a tendency to such belief. The sentiment may be perverted, the idea may be grossly corrupted, but it is nevertheless there, and shows the source whence it sprang.‡

* "The doctrine of the immortality of the soul, if it is a real advantage, follows unavoidably from the idea of God. The *best* Being, he must *will* the best of good things; the *wisest,* he must devise plans for that effect; the *most powerful,* he must bring it about. None can deny this." — THEO. PARKER, *Discourse of Matters pertaining to Religion,* b. ii. ch. viii. p. 205.

† "This institution of religion, like society, friendship, and marriage, comes out of a principle, deep and permanent in the heart: as humble, and transient, and partial institutions come out of humble, transient, and partial wants, and are to be traced to the senses and the phenomena of life, so this sublime, permanent, and useful institution came out from sublime, permanent, and universal wants, and must be referred to the soul, and the unchanging realities of life." — PARKER, *Discourse of Religion,* b. i. ch. i. p. 14.

‡ "The sages of all nations, ages, and religions had some ideas of these sublime doctrines, though more or less degraded, adulterated

Even in the most debased forms of fetichism, where the negro kneels in reverential awe before the shrine of some uncouth and misshapen idol, which his own hands, perhaps, have made, the act of adoration, degrading as the object may be, is nevertheless an acknowledgment of the longing need of the worshipper to throw himself upon the support of some unknown power higher than his own sphere. And this unknown power, be it what it may, is to him a God.*

But just as universal has been the belief in the immortality of the soul. This arises from the same longing in man for the infinite; and although, like the former doctrine, it has been perverted and corrupted, there exists among all nations a tendency to its acknowledgment. Every people, from the remotest times, have wandered involuntarily into the ideal of another world, and sought to find a place for their departed spirits. The deification of the dead, man-worship, or hero-worship, the next development of the religious idea after fetichism, was simply an acknowledgment of the belief in a future life;

and obscured; and these scattered hints and vestiges of the most sacred and exalted truths were originally rays and emanations of ancient and primitive traditions, handed down from generation to generation, since the beginning of the world, or at least since the fall of man, to all mankind." — CHEV. RAMSAY, *Philos. Princ. of Nat. and Rev. Relig.,* vol. ii. p. 8.

* "In this form, not only the common objects above enumerated, but gems, metals, stones that fell from heaven, images, carved bits of wood, stuffed skins of beasts, like the medicine-bags of the North American Indians, are reckoned as divinities, and so become objects of adoration. But in this case, the visible object is idealized; not worshipped as the brute thing really is, but as the type and symbol of God." — PARKER, *Disc. of Relig.,* b. i. ch. v. p. 50.

for the dead could not have been deified unless after death they had continued to live. The adoration of a putrid carcass would have been a form of fetichism lower and more degrading than any that has yet been discovered. But man-worship came after fetichism. It was a higher development of the religious sentiment, and included a possible hope for, if not a positive belief in, a future life.

Reason, then, as well as revelation, leads us irresistibly to the conclusion that these two doctrines prevailed among the descendants of Noah, immediately after the deluge. They were believed, too, in all their purity and integrity, because they were derived from the highest and purest source.

These are the doctrines which still constitute the creed of Freemasonry; and hence one of the names bestowed upon the Freemasons from the earliest times was that of the *"Noachidæ,"* or *"Noachites,"* that is to say, the descendants of Noah, and the transmitters of his religious dogmas.

III.

THE PRIMITIVE FREEMASONRY OF ANTIQUITY.

THE next important historical epoch which demands our attention is that connected with what, in sacred history, is known as the dispersion at Babel. The brightness of truth, as it had been communicated by Noah, became covered, as it were, with a cloud. The dogmas of the unity of God and the immortality of the soul were lost sight of, and the first deviation from the true worship occurred in the establishment of Sabianism, or the worship of the sun, moon, and stars, among some peoples, and the deification of men among others. Of these two deviations, Sabianism, or sun-worship, was both the earlier and the more generally diffused.* "It seems," says the learned Owen, "to have had

---

* A recent writer thus eloquently refers to the universality, in ancient times, of sun-worship: "Sabaism, the worship of light, prevailed amongst all the leading nations of the early world. By the rivers of India, on the mountains of Persia, in the plains of Assyria, early mankind thus adored, the higher spirits in each country rising in spiritual thought from the solar orb up to Him whose vicegerent it seems — to the Sun of all being, whose divine light irradiates and purifies the world of soul, as the solar

its rise from some broken traditions conveyed by the patriarchs touching the dominion of the sun by day and of the moon by night." The mode in which this old system has been modified and spiritually symbolized by Freemasonry will be the subject of future consideration.

But Sabianism, while it was the most ancient of the religious corruptions, was, I have said, also the most generally diffused; and hence, even among nations which afterwards adopted the polytheistic creed of deified men and factitious gods, this ancient sun-worship is seen to be continually exerting its influences. Thus, among the Greeks, the most refined people that cultivated heroworship, Hercules was the sun, and the mythologic fable of his destroying with his arrows the many-headed hydra of the Lernæan marshes was but an allegory to denote the dissipation of paludal malaria by the purifying rays of the orb of day. Among the Egyptians, too, the chief deity, Osiris, was but another name for the sun,

radiance does the world of sense. Egypt, too, though its faith be but dimly known to us, joined in this worship; Syria raised her grand temples to the sun; the joyous Greeks sported with the thought while feeling it, almost hiding it under the mythic individuality which their lively fancy superimposed upon it. Even prosaic China makes offerings to the yellow orb of day; the wandering Celts and Teutons held feasts to it, amidst the primeval forests of Northern Europe; and, with a savagery characteristic of the American aborigines, the sun temples of Mexico streamed with human blood in honor of the beneficent orb."— *The Castes and Creeds of India,* Blackw. Mag., vol. lxxxi. p. 317.— "There is no people whose religion is known to us," says the Abbé Banier, "neither in our own continent nor in that of America, that has not paid the sun a religious worship, if we except some inhabitants of the torrid zone, who are continually cursing the sun for scorching them with his beams."—*Mythology,* lib. iii. ch. iii.— Macrobius, in his *Saturnalia,* undertakes to prove that all the gods of Paganism may be reduced to the sun.

while his arch-enemy and destroyer, Typhon, was the typification of night, or darkness. And lastly, among the Hindus, the three manifestations of their supreme deity, Brahma, Siva, and Vishnu, were symbols of the rising, meridian, and setting sun.

This early and very general prevalence of the sentiment of sun-worship is worthy of especial attention on account of the influence that it exercised over the spurious Freemasonry of antiquity, of which I am soon to speak, and which is still felt, although modified and Christianized in our modern system. Many, indeed nearly all, of the masonic symbols of the present day can only be thoroughly comprehended and properly appreciated by this reference to sun-worship.

This divine truth, then, of the existence of one Supreme God, the Grand Architect of the Universe, symbolized in Freemasonry as the TRUE WORD, was lost to the Sabians and to the polytheists who arose after the dispersion at Babel, and with it also disappeared the doctrine of a future life; and hence, in one portion of the masonic ritual, in allusion to this historic fact, we speak of "the lofty tower of Babel, where language was confounded and Masonry lost."

There were, however, some of the builders on the plain of Shinar who preserved these great religious and masonic doctrines of the unity of God and the immortality of the soul in their pristine purity. These were the patriarchs, in whose venerable line they continued to be taught. Hence, years after the dispersion of the nations at Babel, the world presented two great religious sects, passing onward down the stream of time, side by side, yet as diverse from each other as light from darkness, and truth from falsehood.

One of these lines of religious thought and sentiment was the idolatrous and pagan world. With it all masonic doctrine, at least in its purity, was extinct, although there mingled with it, and at times to some extent influenced it, an offshoot from the other line, to which attention will be soon directed.

The second of these lines consisted, as has already been said, of the patriarchs and priests, who preserved in all their purity the two great masonic doctrines of the unity of God and the immortality of the soul.

This line embraced, then, what, in the language of recent masonic writers, has been designated as the *Primitive Freemasonry of Antiquity.*

Now, it is by no means intended to advance any such gratuitous and untenable theory as that proposed by some imaginative writers, that the Freemasonry of the patriarchs was in its organization, its ritual, or its symbolism, like the system which now exists. We know not, indeed, that it had a ritual, or even a symbolism. I am inclined to think that it was made up of abstract propositions, derived from antediluvian traditions. Dr. Oliver thinks it probable that there were a few symbols among these Primitive and Pure Freemasons, and he enumerates among them the serpent, the triangle, and the point within a circle; but I can find no authority for the supposition, nor do I think it fair to claim for the order more than it is fairly entitled to, nor more than it can be fairly proved to possess. When Anderson calls Moses a Grand Master, Joshua his Deputy, and Aholiab and Bezaleel

Grand Wardens, the expression is to be looked upon simply as a *façon de parler,* a mode of speech entirely figurative in its character, and by no means intended to convey the idea which is entertained in respect to officers of that character in the present system. It would, undoubtedly, however, have been better that such language should not have been used.

All that can be claimed for the system of Primitive Freemasonry, as practised by the patriarchs, is, that it embraced and taught the two great dogmas of Freemasonry, namely, the unity of God, and the immortality of the soul. It may be, and indeed it is highly probable, that there was a secret doctrine, and this doctrine was not indiscriminately communicated. We know that Moses, who was necessarily the recipient of the knowledge of his predecessors, did not publicly teach the doctrine of the immortality of the soul. But there was among the Jews an oral or secret law which was never committed to writing until after the captivity; and this law, I suppose, may have contained the recognition of those dogmas of the Primitive Freemasonry.

Briefly, then, this system of Primitive Freemasonry, — without ritual or symbolism, that has come down to us, at least, — consisting solely of traditionary legends, teaching only the two great truths already alluded to, and being wholly speculative in its character, without the slightest infusion of an operative element, was regularly transmitted through the Jewish line of patriarchs, priests, and kings, without alteration, increase, or diminution, to the time of Solomon, and the building of the temple at Jerusalem.

Leaving it, then, to pursue this even course of descent,

let us refer once more to that other line of religious history, the one passing through the idolatrous and polytheistic nations of antiquity, and trace from it the regular rise and progress of another division of the masonic institution, which, by way of distinction, has been called the *Spurious Freemasonry of Antiquity.*

IV.

THE SPURIOUS FREEMASONRY OF ANTIQUITY.

IN the vast but barren desert of polytheism—dark and dreary as were its gloomy domains—there were still, however, to be found some few oases of truth. The philosophers and sages of antiquity had, in the course of their learned researches, aided by the light of nature, discovered something of those inestimable truths in relation to God and a future state which their patriarchal contemporaries had received as a revelation made to their common ancestry before the flood, and which had been retained and promulgated after that event by Noah.

They were, with these dim but still purifying perceptions, unwilling to degrade the majesty of the First Great Cause by sharing his attributes with a Zeus and a Hera in Greece, a Jupiter and a Juno in Rome, an Osiris and an Isis in Egypt; and they did not believe that the thinking, feeling, reasoning soul, the guest and companion of the body, would, at the hour of that body's dissolution, be consigned, with it, to total annihilation.

Hence, in the earliest ages after the era of the dispersion, there were some among the heathen who believed in the unity of God and the immortality of the soul. But these doctrines they durst not publicly teach. The minds of the people, grovelling in superstition, and devoted, as St. Paul testifies of the Athenians, to the worship of unknown gods, were not prepared for the philosophic teachings of a pure theology. It was, indeed, an axiom unhesitatingly enunciated and frequently repeated by their writers, that "there are many truths with which it is useless for the people to be made acquainted, and many fables which it is not expedient that they should know to be false." * Such is the language of Varro, as preserved by St. Augustine; and Strabo, another of their writers, exclaims, "It is not possible for a philosopher to conduct a multitude of women and ignorant people by a method of reasoning, and thus to invite them to piety, holiness, and faith; but the philosopher must also make use of superstition, and not omit the invention of fables and the performance of wonders."†

While, therefore, in those early ages of the world, we find the masses grovelling in the intellectual debasement of a polytheistic and idolatrous religion, with no support for the present, no hope for the future, — living without the knowledge of a supreme and superintending Providence,

---

* "Varro de religionibus loquens, evidenter dicit, multa esse vera, quæ vulgo scire non sit utile; multaque, quæ tametsi falsa sint, aliter existimare populum expediat."— St. AUGUSTINE, *De Civit. Dei.*— We must regret, with the learned Valloisin, that the sixteen books of Varro, on the religious antiquities of the ancients, have been lost; and the regret is enhanced by the reflection that they existed until the beginning of the fourteenth century, and disappeared only when their preservation for less than two centuries more would, by the discovery of printing, have secured their perpetuity.

† Strabo, Geog., lib. i.

and dying without the expectation of a blissful immortality, —we shall at the same time find ample testimony that these consoling doctrines were secretly believed by the philosophers and their disciples.

But though believed, they were not publicly taught. They were heresies which it would have been impolitic and dangerous to have broached to the public ear; they were truths which might have led to a contempt of the established system and to the overthrow of the popular superstition. Socrates, the Athenian sage, is an illustrious instance of the punishment that was meted out to the bold innovator who attempted to insult the gods and to poison the minds of youth with the heresies of a philosophic religion. "They permitted, therefore," says a learned writer on this subject,* "the multitude to remain plunged as they were in the depth of a gross and complicated idolatry; but for those philosophic few who could bear the light of truth without being confounded by the blaze, they removed the mysterious veil, and displayed to them the Deity in the radiant glory of his unity. From the vulgar eye, however, these doctrines were kept inviolably sacred, and wrapped in the veil of impenetrable mystery."

The consequence of all this was, that no one was permitted to be invested with the knowledge of these sublime truths, until by a course of severe and arduous trials, by a long and painful initiation, and by a formal series of gradual preparations, he had proved himself worthy and capable of receiving the full light of wisdom. For this purpose, therefore, those peculiar religious institutions

* Maurice, Indian Antiquities, vol. ii. p. 297.

were organized which the ancients designated as the MYSTERIES, and which, from the resemblance of their organization, their objects, and their doctrines, have by masonic writers been called the "Spurious Freemasonry of Antiquity."

Warburton,* in giving a definition of what these Mysteries were, says, "Each of the pagan gods had (besides the public and open) a secret worship paid unto him, to which none were admitted but those who had been selected by preparatory ceremonies, called initiation. This secret worship was termed the Mysteries." I shall now endeavor briefly to trace the connection between these Mysteries and the institution of Freemasonry; and to do so, it will be necessary to enter upon some details of the constitution of those mystic assemblies.

Almost every country of the ancient world had its peculiar Mysteries, dedicated to the occult worship of some especial and favorite god, and to the inculcation of a secret doctrine, very different from that which was taught in the public ceremonial of devotion. Thus in Persia the Mysteries were dedicated to Mithras, or the Sun; in Egypt, to Isis and Osiris; in Greece, to Demeter; in Samothracia, to the gods Cabiri, the Mighty Ones; in Syria, to Dionysus; while in the more northern nations of Europe, such as Gaul and Britain, the initiations were dedicated to their peculiar deities, and were celebrated under the general name of the Druidical rites. But no matter where or how instituted, whether ostensibly in honor of the effeminate Adonis, the favorite of Venus, or of the implacable Odin, the Scandinavian god of war and carnage;

* Div. Leg., vol. i. b. ii. § iv. p. 193, Ioth Lond. edit.

whether dedicated to Demeter, the type of the earth, or to Mithras, and the symbol of all that fructifies that earth, —the great object and design of the secret instruction were identical in all places, and the Mysteries constituted a school of religion in which the errors and absurdities of polytheism were revealed to the initiated. The candidate was taught that the multitudinous deities of the popular theology were but hidden symbols of the various attributes of the supreme god, — a spirit invisible and indivisible, — and that the soul, as an emanation from his essence, could "never see corruption," but must, after the death of the body, be raised to an eternal life.*

That this was the doctrine and the object of the Mysteries is evident from the concurrent testimony both of those ancient writers who flourished contemporaneously with the practice of them, and of those modern scholars who have devoted themselves to their investigation.

Thus Isocrates, speaking of them in his Panegyric, says, "Those who have been initiated in the Mysteries of Ceres entertain better hopes both as to the end of life and the whole of futurity."†

Epictetus‡ declares that everything in these Mysteries was instituted by the ancients for the instruction and amendment of life.

And Plato§ says that the design of initiation was to restore the soul to that state of perfection from which it had originally fallen.

---

* The hidden doctrines of the unity of the Deity and the immortality of the soul were taught originally in all the Mysteries, even those of Cupid and Bacchus. — WARBURTON, apud Spence's *Anecdotes,* p. 309.

† Isoc. Paneg., p. 59.

‡ Apud Arrian. Dissert., lib. iii. c. xxi.

§ Phædo.

Thomas Taylor, the celebrated Platonist, who possessed an unusual acquaintance with the character of these ancient rites, asserts that they "obscurely intimated, by mystic and splendid visions, the felicity of the soul, both here and hereafter, when purified from the defilements of a material nature, and constantly elevated to the realities of intellectual vision."*

Creuzer,† a distinguished German writer, who has examined the subject of the ancient Mysteries with great judgment and elaboration, gives a theory on their nature and design which is well worth consideration.

This theory is, that when there had been placed under the eyes of the initiated symbolical representations of the creation of the universe, and the origin of things, the migrations and purifications of the soul, the beginning and progress of civilization and agriculture, there was drawn from these symbols and these scenes in the Mysteries an instruction destined only for the more perfect, or the epopts, to whom were communicated the doctrines of the existence of a single and eternal God, and the destination of the universe and of man.

Creuzer here, however, refers rather to the general object of the instructions, than to the character of the rites and ceremonies by which they were impressed upon the mind; for in the Mysteries, as in Freemasonry, the Hierophant, whom we would now call the Master of the Lodge, often, as Lobeck observes, delivered a mystical lecture, or discourse, on some moral subject.

Faber, who, notwithstanding the predominance in his

* Dissert. on the Eleusinian and Bacchic Mysteries, in the Pamphleteer, vol. viii. p. 53.

† Symbol. und Mythol. der Alt. Völk.

mind of a theory which referred every rite and symbol of the ancient world to the traditions of Noah, the ark, and the deluge, has given a generally correct view of the systems of ancient religion, describes the initiation into the Mysteries as a scenic representation of the mythic descent into Hades, or the grave, and the return from thence to the light of day.

In a few words, then, the object of instruction in all these Mysteries was the unity of God, and the intention of the ceremonies of initiation into them was, by a scenic representation of death, and subsequent restoration to life,* to impress the great truths of the resurrection of the dead and the immortality of the soul.

I need scarcely here advert to the great similarity in design and conformation which existed between these ancient rites and the third or Master's degree of Masonry. Like it they were all funereal in their character: they began in sorrow and lamentation, they ended in joy; there was an aphanism, or burial; a pastos, or grave; a euresis, or discovery of what had been lost; and a legend, or mythical relation, — all of which were entirely and profoundly symbolical in their character.

And hence, looking to this strange identity of design and form, between the initiations of the ancients and those of the modern Masons, writers have been disposed to designate these mysteries as the SPURIOUS FREEMASONRY OF ANTIQUITY.

---

*In these Mysteries, after the people had for a long time bewailed the loss of a particular person, he was at last supposed to be restored to life. —BRYANT, *Anal. of Anc. Mythology,* vol. iii. p. 176.

V.

THE ANCIENT MYSTERIES.

I NOW propose, for the purpose of illustrating these views, and of familiarizing the reader with the coincidences between Freemasonry and the ancient Mysteries, so that he may be better enabled to appreciate the mutual influences of each on the other as they are hereafter to be developed, to present a more detailed relation of one or more of these ancient systems of initiation.

As the first illustration, let us select the Mysteries of Osiris, as they were practised in Egypt, the birthplace of all that is wonderful in the arts or sciences, or mysterious in the religion, of the ancient world.

It was on the Lake of Sais that the solemn ceremonies of the Osirian initiation were performed. "On this lake," says Herodotus, "it is that the Egyptians represent by night his sufferings whose name I refrain from mentioning; and this representation they call their Mysteries."*

Osiris, the husband of Isis, was an ancient king of the Egyptians. Having been slain by Typhon, his body was

---

* Herod. Hist., lib. iii. c. clxxi.

cut into pieces* by his murderer, and the mangled remains cast upon the waters of the Nile, to be dispersed to the four winds of heaven. His wife, Isis, mourning for the death and the mutilation of her husband, for many days searched diligently with her companions for the portions of the body, and having at length found them, united them together, and bestowed upon them decent interment, — while Osiris, thus restored, became the chief deity of his subjects, and his worship was united with that of Isis, as the fecundating and fertilizing powers of nature. The candidate in these initiations was made to pass through a mimic repetition of the conflict and destruction of Osiris, and his eventual recovery; and the explanations made to him, after he had received the full share of light to which the painful and solemn ceremonies through which he had passed had entitled him, constituted the secret doctrine of which I have already spoken, as the object of all the Mysteries. Osiris, — a real and personal god to the people, — to be worshipped with fear and with trembling, and to be propitiated with sacrifices and burnt offerings, became to the initiate but a symbol of the

"Great first cause, least understood,"

while his death, and the wailing of Isis, with the recovery of the body, his translation to the rank of a celestial being, and the consequent rejoicing of his spouse, were but a

---

* The legend says it was cut into *fourteen* pieces. Compare this with the *fourteen* days of burial in the masonic legend of the third degree. Why the particular number in each? It has been thought by some, that in the latter legend there was a reference to the half of the moon's age, or its dark period, symbolic of the darkness of death, followed by the fourteen days of bright moon, or restoration to life.

tropical mode of teaching that after death comes eternal life, and that though the body is destroyed, the soul shall still live.

"Can we doubt," says the Baron Sainte Croix, "that such ceremonies as those practised in the Mysteries of Osiris had been originally instituted to impress more profoundly on the mind the dogma of future rewards and punishments?"*

"The sufferings and death of Osiris," says Mr. Wilkinson,† "were the great Mystery of the Egyptian religion; and some traces of it are perceptible among other people of antiquity. His being the divine goodness and the abstract idea of 'good,' his manifestation upon earth (like an Indian god), his death and resurrection, and his office as judge of the dead in a future state, look like the early revelation of a future manifestation of the deity converted into a mythological fable."

A similar legend and similar ceremonies, varied only as to time, and place, and unimportant details, were to be found in all the initiations of the ancient Mysteries. The dogma was the same, — future life, — and the method of inculcating it was the same. The coincidences between the design of these rites and that of Freemasonry, which must already begin to appear, will enable us to give its full value to the expression of Hutchinson, when he says that "the Master Mason represents a man under

* Mystères du Paganisme, tom. i. p. 6.

† Notes to Rawlinson's Herodotus, b. ii. ch. clxxi. Mr. Bryant expresses the same opinion: "The principal rites in Egypt were confessedly for a person lost and consigned for a time to darkness, who was at last found. This person I have mentioned to have been described under the character of Osiris."—*Analysis of Ancient Mythology,* vol. iii. p. 177.

the Christian doctrine saved from the grave of iniquity and rose to the faith of salvation."*

In Phœnicia similar Mysteries were celebrated in honor of Adonis, the favorite lover of Venus, who, having, while hunting, been slain by a wild boar on Mount Lebanon, was restored to life by Proserpine. The mythological story is familiar to every classical scholar. In the popular theology, Adonis was the son of Cinyras, king of Cyrus, whose untimely death was wept by Venus and her attendant nymphs: in the physical theology of the philosophers,† he was a symbol of the sun, alternately present to and absent from the earth; but in the initiation into the Mysteries of his worship, his resurrection and return from Hades were adopted as a type of the immortality of the soul. The ceremonies of initiation in the Adonia began with lamentation for his loss, — or, as the prophet Ezekiel expresses it, "Behold, there sat women weeping for Thammuz," — for such was the name under which his worship was introduced among the Jews; and they ended with the most extravagant demonstrations of joy at the representation of his return to life,‡ while the hierophant exclaimed, in a congratulatory strain,—

> "Trust, ye initiates; the god is safe,
> And from our grief salvation shall arise."

* Spirit of Masonry, p. 100.

† Varro, according to St. Augustine (De Civ. Dei, vi. 5), says that among the ancients there were three kinds of theology — a *mythical,* which was used by the poets; a *physical,* by the philosophers, and a *civil,* by the people.

‡ "Tous les ans," says Sainte Croix, "pendant les jours consacrés au souvenir de sa mort, tout étoit plongé dans la tristesse: on ne cessoit de pousser des gémissemens; on alloit même jusquà se flageller et se donner des coups. Le dernier jour de ce deuil,

Before proceeding to an examination of those Mysteries which are the most closely connected with the masonic institution, it will be as well to take a brief view of their general organization.

The secret worship, or Mysteries, of the ancients were always divided into the lesser and the greater; the former being intended only to awaken curiosity, to test the capacity and disposition of the candidate, and by symbolical purifications to prepare him for his introduction into the greater Mysteries.

The candidate was at first called an aspirant, or seeker of the truth, and the initial ceremony which he underwent was a lustration or purification by water. In this condition he may be compared to the Entered Apprentice of the masonic rites, and it is here worth adverting to the fact (which will be hereafter more fully developed) that all the ceremonies in the first degree of masonry are symbolic of an internal purification.

In the lesser Mysteries* the candidate took an oath of secrecy, which was administered to him by the mystagogue, and then received a preparatory instruction,†

on faisoit des sacrifices funèbres en l'honneur de ce dieu. Le jour suivant, on recevoit la nouvelle qu'Adonis venoit d'être rappelé à la vie, qui mettoit fin à leur deuil." — *Recherches sur les Myst. du Paganisme,* tom. ii. p. 105.

* Clement of Alexandria calls them μυστήρια τὰ πρὸ μυστηρίων, "the mysteries before the mysteries."

† Les petits mystères ne consistoient qu'en cérémonies préparatoires. — *Sainte Croix,* i. 297. — As to the oath of secrecy, Bryant says, "The first thing at these awful meetings was to offer an oath of secrecy to all who were to be initiated, after which they proceeded to the ceremonies." —*Anal. of Anc. Myth.,* vol. iii. p. 174. —The Orphic Argonautics allude to the oath: μετὰ δ' ὁρχια Μύσταις, χ.τ.λ., "after the oath was administered to the mystes," &c. — *Orph. Argon.,* v. 11.

which enabled him afterwards to understand the developments of the higher and subsequent division. He was now called a *Mystes,* or initiate, and may be compared to the Fellow Craft of Freemasonry.

In the greater Mysteries the whole knowledge of the divine truths, which was the object of initiation, was communicated. Here we find, among the various ceremonies which assimilated these rites to Freemasonry, the *aphanism,* which was the disappearance or death; the *pastos,* the couch, coffin, or grave; the *euresis,* or the discovery of the body; and the *autopsy,* or full sight of everything, that is, the complete communication of the secrets. The candidate was here called an *epopt,* or eyewitness, because nothing was now hidden from him; and hence he may be compared to the Master Mason, of whom Hutchinson says that "he has discovered the knowledge of God and his salvation, and been redeemed from the death of sin and the sepulchre of pollution and unrighteousness."

VI.

THE DIONYSIAC ARTIFICERS.

AFTER this general view of the religious Mysteries of the ancient world, let us now proceed to a closer examination of those which are more intimately connected with the history of Freemasonry, and whose influence is, to this day, most evidently felt in its organization.

Of all the pagan Mysteries instituted by the ancients none were more extensively diffused than those of the Grecian god Dionysus. They were established in Greece, Rome, Syria, and all Asia Minor. Among the Greeks, and still more among the Romans, the rites celebrated on the Dionysiac festival were, it must be confessed, of a dissolute and licentious character.* But in Asia they

---

* The satirical pen of Aristophanes has not spared the Dionysiac festivals. But the raillery and sarcasm of a comic writer must always be received with many grains of allowance. He has, at least, been candid enough to confess that no one could be initiated who had been guilty of any crime against his country or the public security. —*Ranæ*, v. 360-365.—Euripides makes the chorus in his Bacchæ proclaim that the Mysteries were practised only for virtuous purposes. In Rome, however, there can be little

assumed a different form. There   , as elsewhere, the legend (for it has already been said that each Mystery had its legend) recounted, and the ceremonies represented, the murder of Dionysus by the Titans. The secret doctrine, too, among the Asiatics, was not different from that among the western nations, but there was something peculiar in the organization of the system. The Mysteries of Dionysus in Syria, more especially, were not simply of a theological character. There the disciples joined to the indulgence in their speculative and secret opinions as to the unity of God and the immortality of the soul, which were common to all the Mysteries, the practice of an operative and architectural art, and occupied themselves as well in the construction of temples and public buildings as in the pursuit of divine truth.

I can account for the greater purity of these Syrian rites only by adopting the ingenious theory of Thirwall,[*] that all the Mysteries "were the remains of a worship which preceded the rise of the Hellenic mythology, and its attendant rites, grounded on a view of nature less fanciful, more earnest, and better fitted to awaken both philosophical thought and religious feeling," and by supposing that the Asiatics, not being, from their geographical

doubt that the initiations partook at length of a licentious character. "On ne peut douter," says Ste. Croix, "que l'introduction des fêtes de Bacchus en Italie n'ait accéléré les progrès du libertinage et de la débauche dans cette contrée." — *Myst. du Pag.,* tom. ii. p. 91. — St. Augustine (De Civ. Dei, lib. vii. c. xxi.) inveighs against the impurity of the ceremonies in Italy of the sacred rites of Bacchus. But even he does not deny that the motive with which they were performed was of a religious, or at least superstitious nature —"Sic videlicet Liber deus placandus fuerat." The propitiation of a deity was certainly a religious act.

   * Hist. Greece, vol. ii. p. 140.

position, so early imbued with the errors of Hellenism, had been better able to preserve the purity and philosophy of the old Pelasgic faith, which, itself, was undoubtedly a direct emanation from the patriarchal religion, or, as it has been called, the Pure Freemasonry of the antediluvian world.

Be this, however, as it may, we know that "the Dionysiacs of Asia Minor were undoubtedly an association of architects and engineers, who had the exclusive privilege of building temples, stadia, and theatres, under the mysterious tutelage of Bacchus, and were distinguished from the uninitiated or profane inhabitants by the science which they possessed, and by many private signs and tokens by which they recognized each other."[*]

This speculative and operative society[†] — speculative in the esoteric, theologic lessons which were taught in its initiations, and operative in the labors of its members as architects — was distinguished by many peculiarities that closely assimilate it to the institution of Freemasonry. In the practice of charity, the more opulent were bound to relieve the wants and contribute to the support of the poorer brethren. They were divided, for the conveniences of labor and the advantages of government, into smaller bodies, which, like our lodges, were directed by superintending officers. They employed, in their ceremonial

[*] This language is quoted from Robison (Proofs of a Conspiracy, p. 20, Lond. edit. 1797), whom none will suspect or accuse of an undue veneration for the antiquity or the morality of the masonic order.

[†] We must not confound these Asiatic builders with the playactors, who were subsequently called by the Greeks, as we learn from Aulus Gellius (lib. xx. cap. 4), "artificers of Dionysus" — Διονυσιαχοι τεχνιται.

observances, many of the implements of operative Masonry, and used, like the Masons, a universal language, and conventional modes of recognition, by which *one brother might know another in the dark as well as the light,* and which served to unite the whole body, wheresoever they might be dispersed, in one common brotherhood.*

I have said that in the mysteries of Dionysus the legend recounted the death of that hero-god, and the subsequent discovery of his body. Some further details of the nature of the Dionysiac ritual are, therefore, necessary for a thorough appreciation of the points to which I propose directly to invite attention.

In these mystic rites, the aspirant was made to represent, symbolically and in a dramatic form, the events connected with the slaying of the god from whom the Mysteries derived their name. After a variety of preparatory ceremonies, intended to call forth all his courage and fortitude, the aphanism or mystical death of Dionysus

---

* There is abundant evidence, among ancient authors, of the existence of signs and passwords in the Mysteries. Thus Apuleius, in his Apology, says, "Si qui forte adest eorundem Solemnium mihi particeps, signum dato," etc.; that is, "If any one happens to be present who has been initiated into the same rites as myself, if he will give me the sign, he shall then be at liberty to hear what it is that I keep with so much care." Plautus also alludes to this usage, when, in his "Miles Gloriosus," act iv. sc. 2, he makes Milphidippa say to Pyrgopolonices, "Cedo signum, si harunc Baccharum es;" i. e., "Give the sign if you are one of these Bacchæ," or initiates into the Mysteries of Bacchus. Clemens Alexandrinus calls these modes of recognition σωθηυατα, as if *means of safety.* Apuleius elsewhere uses *memoracula,* I think to denote passwords, when he says, "sanctissimè sacrorum signa et memoracula custodire," which I am inclined to translate, "most scrupulously to preserve the signs and passwords of the sacred rites."

was figured out in the ceremonies, and the shrieks and lamentations of the initiates, with the confinement or burial of the candidate on the pastos, couch, or coffin, constituted the first part of the ceremony of initiation. Then began the search of Rhea for the remains of Dionysus, which was continued amid scenes of the greatest confusion and tumult, until, at last, the search having been successful, the mourning was turned into joy, light succeeded to darkness, and the candidate was invested with the knowledge of the secret doctrine of the Mysteries — the belief in the existence of one God, and a future state of rewards and punishments.*

Such were the mysteries that were practised by the architects—the Freemasons, so to speak — of Asia Minor. At Tyre, the richest and most important city of that region, a city memorable for the splendor and magnificence of the buildings with which it was decorated, there were colonies or lodges of these mystic architects; and this fact I request that you will bear in mind, as it forms an important link in the chain that connects the Dionysiacs with the Freemasons.

But to make every link in this chain of connection complete, it is necessary that the mystic artists of Tyre should be proved to be at least contemporaneous with the

* The Baron de Sainte Croix gives this brief view of the ceremonies: "Dans ces mystères on employoit, pour remplir l'âme des assistans d'une sainte horreur, les mêmes moyens qu'à Eleusis. L'apparition de fantômes et de divers objets propres à effrayer, sembloit disposer les esprits à la crédulité. Ils en avoient sans doute besoin, pour ajouter foi à toutes les explications des mystagogues: elles rouloient sur le massacre de Bacchus par les Titans," &c. — *Recherches sur les Mystères du Paganisme,* tom. ii. sect. vii. art. iii. p. 89.

building of King Solomon's temple; and the evidence of that fact I shall now attempt to produce.

Lawrie, whose elaborate researches into this subject leave us nothing further to discover, places the arrival of the Dionysiacs in Asia Minor at the time of the Ionic migration, when "the inhabitants of Attica, complaining of the narrowness of their territory and the unfruitfulness of its soil, went in quest of more extensive and fertile settlements. Being joined by a number of the inhabitants of surrounding provinces, they sailed to Asia Minor, drove out the original inhabitants, and seized upon the most eligible situations, and united them under the name of Ionia, because the greatest number of the refugees were natives of that Grecian province."* With their knowledge of the arts of sculpture and architecture, in which the Greeks had already made some progress, the emigrants brought over to their new settlements their religious customs also, and introduced into Asia the mysteries of Athene and Dionysus long before they had been corrupted by the licentiousness of the mother country.

Now, Playfair places the Ionic migration in the year 1044 B. C., Gillies in 1055, and the Abbé Barthelemy in 1076. But the latest of these periods will extend as far back as forty-four years before the commencement of the temple of Solomon at Jerusalem, and will give ample time for the establishment of the Dionysiac fraternity at the city of Tyre, and the initiation of "Hiram the Builder" into its mysteries.

Let us now pursue the chain of historical events which

---

* Lawrie, Hist. of Freemasonry, p. 27.

finally united this purest branch of the Spurious Freemasonry of the pagan nations with the Primitive Freemasonry of the Jews at Jerusalem.

When Solomon, king of Israel, was about to build, in accordance with the purposes of his father, David, "a house unto the name of Jehovah, his God," he made his intention known to Hiram, king of Tyre, his friend and ally; and because he was well aware of the architectural skill of the Tyrian Dionysiacs, he besought that monarch's assistance to enable him to carry his pious design into execution. Scripture informs us that Hiram complied with the request of Solomon, and sent him the necessary workmen to assist him in the glorious undertaking. Among others, he sent an architect, who is briefly described, in the First Book of Kings, as "a widow's son, of the tribe of Naphtali, and his father a man of Tyre, a worker in brass, a man filled with wisdom and understanding and cunning to work all works in brass;" and more fully, in the Second Book of Chronicles, as "a cunning man, endued with understanding of Hiram my father's, the son of a woman of the daughters of Dan, and his father, a man of Tyre, skilful to work in gold, and in silver, in brass, in iron, in stone, and in timber, in purple, in blue, and in fine linen and in crimson, also to grave any manner of graving, and to find out any device which shall be put to him."

To this man—this widow's son (as Scripture history, as well as masonic tradition informs us)—was intrusted by King Solomon an important position among the workmen at the sacred edifice, which was constructed on Mount Moriah. His knowledge and experience as an artificer, and his eminent skill in every kind of "curious and cunning workmanship," readily placed him at the head of both the Jewish and Tyrian craftsmen, as the chief builder and principal conductor of the works; and it is to him, by means of the large authority which this position gave him, that we attribute the union of two people, so antagonistical in race, so dissimilar in manners, and so opposed in religion, as the Jews and Tyrians, in one common brotherhood, which resulted in the organization of the institution of Freemasonry. This Hiram, as a Tyrian and an artificer, must have been connected with the Dionysiac fraternity; nor could he have been a very humble or inconspicuous member, if we may judge of his rank in the society, from the amount of talent which he is said to have possessed, and from the elevated position that he held in the affections, and at the court, of the king of Tyre. He must, therefore, have been well acquainted with all the ceremonial usages of the Dionysiac artificers, and must have enjoyed a long experience of the advantages of the government and discipline which they practised in the erection of the many sacred edifices in which they were engaged. A portion of these ceremonial usages and of this discipline he would naturally be inclined to introduce among the workmen at Jerusalem. He therefore united them in a society, similar in many respects to that of the Dionysiac artificers. He inculcated lessons of charity and brotherly love; he established a ceremony of initiation, to test experimentally the fortitude and worth of the candidate; adopted modes of recognition; and impressed the obligations of duty and principles of morality by means of symbols and allegories.

To the laborers and men of burden, the Ish Sabal,

and to the craftsmen, corresponding with the first and second degrees of more modern Masonry, but little secret knowledge was confided. Like the aspirants in the lesser Mysteries of paganism, their instructions were simply to purify and prepare them for a more solemn ordeal, and for the knowledge of the sublimest truths. These were to be found only in the Master's degree, which it was intended should be in imitation of the greater Mysteries; and in it were to be unfolded, explained, and enforced the great doctrines of the unity of God and the immortality of the soul. But here there must have at once arisen an apparently insurmountable obstacle to the further continuation of the resemblance of Masonry to the Mysteries of Dionysus. In the pagan Mysteries, I have already said that these lessons were allegorically taught by means of a legend. Now, in the Mysteries of Dionysus, the legend was that of the death and subsequent resuscitation of the god Dionysus. But it would have been utterly impossible to introduce such a legend as the basis of any instructions to be communicated to Jewish candidates. Any allusion to the mythological fables of their Gentile neighbors, any celebration of the myths of pagan theology, would have been equally offensive to the taste and repugnant to the religious prejudices of a nation educated, from generation to generation, in the worship of a divine being jealous of his prerogatives, and who had made himself known to his people as the JEHOVAH, the God of time present, past, and future. How this obstacle would have been surmounted by the Israelitish founder of the order I am unable to say: a substitute would, no doubt, have been invented, which would have met all the symbolic requirements of the legend of the

Mysteries, or Spurious Freemasonry, without violating the religious principles of the Primitive Freemasoury of the Jews; but the necessity for such invention never existed, and before the completion of the temple a melancholy event is said to have occurred, which served to cut the Gordian knot, and the death of its chief architect has supplied Freemasonry with its appropriate legend—a legend which, like the legends of all the Mysteries, is used to testify our faith in the resurrection of the body and the immortality of the soul.

Before concluding this part of the subject, it is proper that something should be said of the authenticity of the legend of the third degree. Some distinguished Masons are disposed to give it full credence as an historical fact, while others look upon it only as a beautiful allegory. So far as the question has any bearing upon the symbolism of Freemasonry it is not of importance; but those who contend for its historical character assert that they do so on the following grounds: —

First. Because the character of the legend is such as to meet all the requirements of the well-known axiom of Vincentius Lirinensis, as to what we are to believe in traditionary matters.*

"Luod semper, quod ubique, quod ab omnibus traditum est."

* Vincentius Lirinensis or Vincent of Lirens, who lived in the fifth century of the Christian era, wrote a controversial treatise entitled "Commonitorium," remarkable for the blind veneration which it pays to the voice of tradition. The rule which he there lays down, and which is cited in the text, may be considered, in a modified application, as an axiom by which we may test the *probability,* at least, of all sorts of traditions. None out of the pale of Vincent's church will go so far as he did in making it the criterion of positive truth.

That is, we are to believe whatever tradition has been at all times, in all places, and by all persons handed down.

With this rule the legend of Hiram Abif, they say, agrees in every respect. It has been universally received, and almost universally credited, among Freemasons from the earliest times. We have no record of any Masonry having ever existed since the time of the temple without it; and, indeed, it is so closely interwoven into the whole system, forming the most essential part of it, and giving it its most determinative character, that it is evident that the institution could no more exist without the legend, than the legend could have been retained without the institution. This, therefore, the advocates of the historical character of the legend think, gives probability at least to its truth.

Secondly. It is not contradicted by the scriptural history of the transactions at the temple, and therefore, in the absence of the only existing written authority on the subject, we are at liberty to depend on traditional information, provided the tradition be, as it is contended that in this instance it is, reasonable, probable, and supported by uninterrupted succession.

Thirdly. It is contended that the very silence of Scripture in relation to the death of Hiram, the Builder, is an argument in favor of the mysterious nature of that death. A man so important in his position as to have been called the favorite of two kings, —sent by one and received by the other as a gift of surpassing value, and the donation thought worthy of a special record, would hardly have passed into oblivion, when his labor was finished, without the memento of a single line, unless his death had taken place in such a way as to render a public account of it improper. And this is supposed to have been the fact. It had become the legend of the new Mysteries, and, like those of the old ones, was only to be divulged when accompanied with the symbolic instructions which it was intended to impress upon the minds of the aspirants.

But if, on the other hand, it be admitted that the legend of the third degree is a fiction,—that the whole masonic and extra-scriptural account of Hiram Abif is simply a myth, — it could not, in the slightest degree, affect the theory which it is my object to establish. For since, in a mythic relation, as the learned Müller* has observed, fact and imagination, the real and the ideal, are very closely united, and since the myth itself always arises, according to the same author, out of a necessity and unconsciousness on the part of its framers, and by impulses which act alike on all, we must go back to the Spurious Freemasonry of the Dionysiacs for the principle which led to the involuntary formation of this Hiramic myth; and then we arrive at the same result, which has been already indicated, namely, that the necessity of the religious sentiment in the Jewish mind, to which the introduction of the legend of Dionysus would have been abhorrent, led to the substitution for it of that of Hiram, in which the ideal parts of the narrative have been intimately blended with real transactions. Thus, that there was such a man as Hiram Abif; that he was the chief builder at the temple of Jerusalem; that he was the confidential friend of the kings of Israel and Tyre, which is indicated by his title of *Ab,* or father; and that he is not heard of after the completion of the temple,—are all historical facts. That

---

* Proleg. zu einer wissenshaftlich. Mythologie.

he died by violence, and in the way described in the masonic legend, may be also true, or may be merely mythical elements incorporated into the historical narrative.

But whether this be so or not, — whether the legend be a fact or a fiction, a history or a myth,—this, at least, is certain: that it was adopted by the Solomonic Masons of the temple as a substitute for the idolatrous legend of the death of Dionysus which belonged to the Dionysiac Mysteries of the Tyrian workmen.

VII.

THE UNION OF SPECULATIVE AND OPERATIVE
MASONRY AT THE TEMPLE OF SOLOMON.

THUS, then, we arrive at another important epoch in the history of the origin of Freemasonry.

I have shown how the Primitive Freemasonry, originating in this new world, with Noah, was handed down to his descendants as a purely speculative institution, embracing certain traditions of the nature of God and of the soul.

I have shown how, soon after the deluge, the descendants of Noah separated, one portion, losing their traditions, and substituting in their place idolatrous and polytheistic religions, while the other and smaller portion retained and communicated those original traditions under the name of the Primitive Freemasonry of antiquity.

I have shown how, among the polytheistic nations, there were a few persons who still had a dim and clouded understanding of these traditions, and that they taught them in certain secret institutions, known as the "Mysteries," thus establishing another branch of the speculative science which is known under the name of the Spurious Freemasonry of antiquity.

Again, I have shown how one sect or division of these Spurious Freemasons existed at Tyre about the time of the building of King Solomon's temple, and added to their speculative science, which was much purer than that of their contemporary Gentile mystics, the practice of the arts of architecture and sculpture, under the name of the Dionysiac Fraternity of Artificers.

And, lastly, I have shown how, at the building of the Solomonic temple, on the invitation of the king of Israel, a large body of these architects repaired from Tyre to Jerusalem, organized a new institution, or, rather, a modification of the two old ones, the Primitive Freemasons among the Israelites yielding something, and the Spurious Freemasons among the Tyrians yielding more; the former purifying the speculative science, and the latter introducing the operative art, together with the mystical ceremonies with which they accompanied its administration.

It is at this epoch, then, that I place the first union of speculative and operative Masonry,—a union which continued uninterruptedly to exist until a comparatively recent period, to which I shall have occasion hereafter briefly to advert.

The other branches of the Spurious Freemasonry were not, however, altogether and at once abolished by this union, but continued also to exist and teach their halftruthful dogmas, for ages after, with interrupted success and diminished influence, until, in the fifth century of the Christian era, the whole of them were proscribed by the Emperor Theodosius. From time to time, however, other partial unions took place, as in the instance of

Pythagoras, who, originally a member of the school of Spurious Freemasonry, was, during his visit to Babylon, about four hundred and fifty years after the union at the temple of Jerusalem, initiated by the captive Israelites into the rites of Temple Masonry, whence the instructions of that sage approximate much more nearly to the principles of Freemasonry, both in spirit and in letter, than those of any other of the philosophers of antiquity; for which reason he is familiarly called, in the modern masonic lectures, "an ancient friend and brother," and an important symbol of the order, the forty-seventh problem of Euclid, has been consecrated to his memory.

I do not now propose to enter upon so extensive a task as to trace the history of the institution from the completion of the first temple to its destruction by Nebuchadnezzar; through the seventy-two years of Babylonish captivity to the rebuilding of the second temple by Zerubbabel; thence to the devastation of Jerusalem by Titus, when it was first introduced into Europe; through all its struggles in the middle ages, sometimes protected and sometimes persecuted by the church, sometimes forbidden by the law and oftener encouraged by the monarch; until, in the beginning of the sixteenth century, it assumed its present organization. The details would require more time for their recapitulation than the limits of the present work will permit.

But my object is not so much to give a connected history of the progress of Freemasonry as to present a rational view of its origin and an examination of those important modifications which, from time to time, were impressed upon it by external influences, so as to enable us the more readily to appreciate the true character and design of its symbolism.

Two salient points, at least, in its subsequent history, especially invite attention, because they have an important bearing on its organization, as a combined speculative and operative institution.

VIII.

THE TRAVELING FREEMASONS OF THE MIDDLE AGES.

THE first of these points to which I refer is the establishment of a body of architects, widely disseminated throughout Europe during the middle ages under the avowed name of *Travelling Freemasons.* This association of workmen, said to have been the descendants of the Temple Masons, may be traced by the massive monuments of their skill at as early a period as the ninth or tenth century; although, according to the authority of Mr. Hope, who has written elaborately on the subject, some historians have found the evidence of their existence in the seventh century, and have traced a peculiar masonic language in the reigns of Charlemagne of France and Alfred of England.

It is to these men, to their preëminent skill in architecture, and to their well-organized system as a class of workmen, that the world is indebted for those magnificent edifices which sprang up in such undeviating principles of architectural form during the middle ages.

"Wherever they came," says Mr. Hope, "in the suite of missionaries, or were called by the natives, or arrived of their own accord, to seek employment, they appeared headed by a chief surveyor, who governed the whole troop, and named one man out of every ten, under the name of warden, to overlook the nine others, set themselves to building temporary huts * for their habitation around the spot where the work was to be carried on, regularly organized their different departments, fell to work, sent for fresh supplies of their brethren as the object demanded, and, when all was finished, again raised their encampment, and went elsewhere to undertake other jobs." †

This society continued to preserve the commingled features of operative and speculative masonry, as they had been practised at the temple of Solomon. Admission to the community was not restricted to professional artisans, but men of eminence, and particularly ecclesiastics, were numbered among its members. "These latter," says Mr. Hope, "were especially anxious, themselves, to direct the improvement and erection of their churches and monasteries, and to manage the expenses of their buildings, and became members of an establishment which had so high and sacred a destination, was so entirely exempt from all local, civil jurisdiction, acknowledged the pope alone as its direct chief, and only worked under his immediate authority; and thence we read of so many ecclesiastics of the highest rank —abbots, prelates, bishops— conferring additional weight and respectability on the order of Freemasonry by becoming its members

---

* In German *hutten,* in English *lodges,* whence the masonic term.
† Historical Essay on Architecture, ch. xxi.

—themselves giving the designs and superintending the construction of their churches, and employing the manual labor of their own monks in the edification of them."

Thus in England, in the tenth century, the Masons are said to have received the special protection of King Athelstan; in the eleventh century, Edward the Confessor declared himself their patron; and in the twelfth, Henry I. gave them his protection.

Into Scotland the Freemasons penetrated as early as the beginning of the twelfth century, and erected the Abbey of Kilwinning, which afterwards became the cradle of Scottish Masonry under the government of King Robert Bruce.

Of the magnificent edifices which they erected, and of their exalted condition under both ecclesiastical and lay patronage in other countries, it is not necessary to give a minute detail. It is sufficient to say that in every part of Europe evidences are to be found of the existence of Freemasonry, practised by an organized body of workmen, and with whom men of learning were united; or, in other words, of a combined operative and speculative institution.

What the nature of this speculative science continued to be, we may learn from that very curious, if authentic, document, dated at Cologne, in the year 1535, and hence designated as the "Charter of Cologne." In that instrument, which purports to have been issued by the heads of the order in nineteen different and important cities of Europe, and is addressed to their brethren as a defence against the calumnies of their enemies, it is announced that the order took its origin at a time "when a few adepts, distinguished by their life, their moral doctrine, and their sacred interpretation of the arcanic truths, withdrew themselves from the multitude in order more effectually to preserve uncontaminated the moral precepts of that religion which is implanted in the mind of man."

We thus, then, have before us an aspect of Freemasonry as it existed in the middle ages, when it presents itself to our view as both operative and speculative in its character. The operative element that had been infused into it by the Dionysiac artificers of Tyre, at the building of the Solomonic temple, was not yet dissevered from the pure speculative element which had prevailed in it anterior to that period.

IX.

DISSEVERANCE OF THE OPERATIVE ELEMENT.

THE next point to which our attention is to be directed is when, a few centuries later, the operative character of the institution began to be less prominent, and the speculative to assume a preeminence which eventually ended in the total separation of the two.

At what precise period the speculative began to predominate over the operative element of the society, it is impossible to say. The change was undoubtedly gradual, and is to be attributed, in all probability, to the increased number of literary and scientific men who were admitted into the ranks of the fraternity.

The Charter of Cologne, to which I have just alluded, speaks of "learned and enlightened men" as constituting the society long before the date of that document, which was 1535; but the authenticity of this work has, it must be confessed, been impugned, and I will not, therefore, press the argument on its doubtful authority. But the diary of that celebrated antiquary, Elias Ashmole, which is admitted to be authentic, describes his admission in the year 1646 into the order, when there is no doubt that the operative character was fast giving way to the speculative. Preston tells us that about thirty years before, when the Earl of Pembroke assumed the Grand Mastership of England, "many eminent, wealthy, and learned men were admitted."

In the year 1663 an assembly of the Freemasons of England was held at London, and the Earl of St. Albans was elected Grand Master. At this assembly certain regulations were adopted, in which the qualifications prescribed for candidates clearly allude to the speculative character of the institution.

And, finally, at the commencement of the eighteenth century, and during the reign of Queen Anne, who died, it will be remembered, in 1714, a proposition was agreed to by the society "that the privileges of Masonry should no longer be restricted to operative masons, but extend to men of various professions, provided that they were regularly approved and initiated into the order."

Accordingly the records of the society show that from the year 1717, at least, the era commonly, but improperly, distinguished as the restoration of Masonry, the operative element of the institution has been completely discarded, except so far as its influence is exhibited in the choice and arrangement of symbols, and the typical use of its technical language.

The history of the origin of the order is here concluded; and in briefly recapitulating, I may say that in its first inception, from the time of Noah to the building of the temple of Solomon, it was entirely speculative in its character; that at the construction of that edifice, an operative element was infused into it by the Tyrian builders; that it continued to retain this compound operative and speculative organization until about the middle of the seventeenth century, when the latter element began to predominate; and finally, that at the commencement of the eighteenth century, the operative element wholly disappeared, and the society has ever since presented itself in the character of a simply speculative association.

The history that I have thus briefly sketched, will elicit from every reflecting mind at least two deductions of some importance to the intelligent Mason.

In the first place, we may observe, that ascending, as the institution does, away up the stream of time, almost to the very fountains of history, for its source, it comes down to us, at this day, with so venerable an appearance of antiquity, that for that cause and on that claim alone it demands the respect of the world. It is no recent invention of human genius, whose vitality has yet to be tested by the wear and tear of time and opposition, and no sudden growth of short-lived enthusiasm, whose existence may be as ephemeral as its birth was recent. One of the oldest of these modern institutions, the Carbonarism of Italy, boasts an age that scarcely amounts to the half of a century, and has not been able to extend its progress beyond the countries of Southern Europe, immediately adjacent to the place of its birth; while it and every other society of our own times that have sought to simulate the outward appearance of Freemasonry, seem to him who has examined the history of this ancient institution to have sprung around it, like mushrooms bursting from between the roots and vegetating under the shade of some mighty and venerable oak, the patriarch of the forest, whose huge trunk and wide-extended branches have protected them from the sun and the gale, and whose fruit, thrown off in autumn, has enriched and fattened the soil that gives these humbler plants their power of life and growth.

But there is a more important deduction to be drawn from this narrative. In tracing the progress of Freemasonry, we shall find it so intimately connected with the history of philosophy, of religion, and of art in all ages of the world, that it is evident that no Mason can expect thoroughly to understand the nature of the institution, or to appreciate its character, unless he shall carefully study its annals, and make himself conversant with the facts of history, to which and from which it gives and receives a mutual influence. The brother who unfortunately supposes that the only requisites of a skilful Mason consist in repeating with fluency the ordinary lectures, or in correctly opening and closing the lodge, or in giving with sufficient accuracy the modes of recognition, will hardly credit the assertion, that he whose knowledge of the "royal art" extends no farther than these preliminaries has scarcely advanced beyond the rudiments of our science. There is a far nobler series of doctrines with which Freemasonry is connected, and which no student ever began to investigate who did not find himself insensibly led on, from step to step in his researches, his love and admiration of the order increasing with the augmentation of his acquaintance with its character. It is this which constitutes the science and the philosophy of Freemasonry, and it is this alone which will return the scholar who devotes himself to the task a sevenfold reward for his labor.

With this view I propose, in the next place, to enter upon an examination of that science and philosophy as they are developed in the system of symbolism, which owes its existence to this peculiar origin and organization of the order, and without a knowledge of which, such as I have attempted to portray it in this preliminary inquiry, the science itself could never be understood.

X.

THE SYSTEM OF SYMBOLIC INSTRUCTION.

THE lectures of the English lodges, which are far more philosophical than our own, — although I do not believe that the system itself is in general as philosophically studied by our English brethren as by ourselves, —have beautifully defined Freemasonry to be "a science of morality veiled in allegory and illustrated by symbols." But allegory itself is nothing else but verbal symbolism; it is the symbol of an idea, or of a series of ideas, not presented to the mind in an objective and visible form, but clothed in language, and exhibited in the form of a narrative. And therefore the English definition amounts, in fact, to this: that *Freemasonry is a science of morality, developed and inculcated by the ancient method of symbolism.* It is this peculiar character as a symbolic institution, this entire adoption of the method of instruction by symbolism, which gives its whole identity to Freemasonry, and has caused it to differ from every other association that the ingenuity of man has devised. It is this that has bestowed upon it that attractive form which has always secured the attachment of its disciples and its own perpetuity.

The Roman Catholic church * is, perhaps, the only contemporaneous institution which continues to cultivate, in any degree, the beautiful system of symbolism. But that which, in the Catholic church, is, in a great measure, incidental, and the fruit of development, is, in Freemasonry, the very life-blood and soul of the institution, born with it at its birth, or, rather, the germ from which the tree has sprung, and still giving it support, nourishment, and even existence. Withdraw from Freemasonry its symbolism, and you take from the body its soul, leaving behind nothing but a lifeless mass of effete matter, fitted only for a rapid decay.

Since, then, the science of symbolism forms so important a part of the system of Freemasonry, it will be well to commence any discussion of that subject by an investigation of the nature of symbols in general.

There is no science so ancient as that of symbolism,† and no mode of instruction has ever been so general as

---

* Bishop England, in his "Explanation of the Mass," says that in every ceremony we must look for three meanings: "the first, the literal, natural, and, it may be said, the original meaning; the second, the figurative or emblematic signification; and thirdly, the pious or religious meaning: frequently the two last will be found the same; sometimes all three will be found combined." Here lies the true difference between the symbolism of the church and that of Masonry. In the former, the symbolic meaning was an afterthought applied to the original, literal one; in the latter, the symbolic was always the original signification of every ceremony.

† "Was not all the knowledge
Of the Egyptians writ in mystic symbols?
Speak not the Scriptures oft in parables?
Are not the choicest fables of the poets,
That were the fountains and first springs of wisdom,
Wrapped in perplexed allegories?"
BEN JONSON, *Alchemist*, act ii. sc. i.

was the symbolic in former ages. "The first learning in the world," says the great antiquary, Dr. Stukely, "consisted chiefly of symbols. The wisdom of the Chaldeans, Phœnicians, Egyptians, Jews, of Zoroaster, Sanchoniathon, Pherecydes, Syrus, Pythagoras, Socrates, Plato, of all the ancients that is come to our hand, is symbolic." And the learned Faber remarks, that "allegory and personification were peculiarly agreeable to the genius of antiquity, and the simplicity of truth was continually sacrificed at the shrine of poetical decoration."

In fact, man's earliest instruction was by symbols.* The objective character of a symbol is best calculated to be grasped by the infant mind, whether the infancy of that mind be considered *nationally* or *individually*. And hence, in the first ages of the world, in its infancy, all propositions, theological, political, or scientific, were expressed in the form of symbols. Thus the first religions were eminently symbolical, because, as that great philosophical historian, Grote, has remarked, "At a time when language was yet in its infancy, visible symbols were the most vivid means of acting upon the minds of ignorant hearers."

Again: children receive their elementary teaching in symbols. "A was an Archer;" what is this but symbolism? The archer becomes to the infant mind the symbol of the letter A, just as, in after life, the letter becomes, to the more advanced mind, the symbol of a certain sound

---

* The distinguished German mythologist Müller defines a symbol to be "an eternal, visible sign, with which a spiritual feeling, emotion, or idea is connected." I am not aware of a more comprehensive, and at the same time distinctive, definition.

of the human voice.* The first lesson received by a child in acquiring his alphabet is thus conveyed by symbolism. Even in the very formation of language, the medium of communication between man and man, and which must hence have been an elementary step in the progress of human improvement, it was found necessary to have recourse to symbols, for words are only and truly certain arbitrary symbols by which and through which we give an utterance to our ideas. The construction of language was, therefore, one of the first products of the science of symbolism.

We must constantly bear in mind this fact, of the primary existence and predominance of symbolism in the earliest times.† when we are investigating the nature of the ancient religions, with which the history of Freemasonry is so intimately connected. The older the religion, the more the symbolism abounds. Modern religions may convey their dogmas in abstract propositions; ancient religions always conveyed them in symbols. Thus there is more symbolism in the Egyptian religion than in the

* And it may be added, that the word becomes a symbol of an idea; and hence, Harris, in his "Hermes," defines language to be "a system of articulate voices, the symbols of our ideas, but of those principally which are general or universal."—*Hermes,* book iii. ch. 3.

† "Symbols," says Müller, "are evidently coeval with the human race; they result from the union of the soul with the body in man; nature has implanted the feeling for them in the human heart."—*Introduction to a Scientific System of Mythology,* p. 196, Leitch's translation.—R. W. Mackay says, "The earliest instruments of education were symbols, the most universal symbols of the multitudinously present Deity, being earth or heaven, or some selected object, such as the sun or moon, a tree or a stone, familiarly seen in either of them."—*Progress of the Intellect,* vol. i. p. 134.

Jewish, more in the Jewish than in the Christian, more in the Christian than in the Mohammedan, and, lastly, more in the Roman than in the Protestant.

But symbolism is not only the most ancient and general, but it is also the most practically useful, of sciences. We have already seen how actively it operates in the early stages of life and of society. We have seen how the first ideas of men and of nations are impressed upon their minds by means of symbols. It was thus that the ancient peoples were almost wholly educated.

"In the simpler stages of society," says one writer on this subject, "mankind can be instructed in the abstract knowledge of truths only by symbols and parables. Hence we find most heathen religions becoming mythic, or explaining their mysteries by allegories, or instructive incidents. Nay, God himself, knowing the nature of the creatures formed by him, has condescended, in the earlier revelations that he made of himself, to teach by symbols; and the greatest of all teachers instructed the multitudes by parables.* The great exemplar of the ancient philosophy and the grand archetype of modern philosophy were alike distinguished by their possessing this faculty

* Between the allegory, or parable, and the symbol, there is, as I have said, no essential difference. The Greek verb $\pi\alpha\rho\alpha\beta\alpha\lambda\lambda\omega$, whence comes the word *parable,* and the verb $\sigma\upsilon\mu\beta\alpha\lambda\lambda\omega$ in the same language, which is the root of the word *symbol,* both have the synonymous meaning "to compare." A parable is only a spoken symbol. The definition of a parable given by Adam Clarke is equally applicable to a symbol, viz.: "A comparison or similitude, in which one thing is compared with another, especially spiritual things with natural, by which means these spiritual things are better understood, and make a deeper impression on the attentive mind."

in a high degree, and have told us that man was best instructed by similitudes." *

Such is the system adopted in Freemasonry for the development and inculcation of the great religious and philosophical truths, of which it was, for so many years, the sole conservator. And it is for this reason that I have already remarked, that any inquiry into the symbolic character of Freemasonry, must be preceded by an investigation of the nature of symbolism in general, if we would properly appreciate its particular use in the organization of the masonic institution.

* North British Review, August, 1851. Faber passes a similar encomium. "Hence the language of symbolism, being so purely a language of ideas, is, in one respect, more perfect than any ordinary language can be: it possesses the variegated elegance of synonymes without any of the obscurity which arises from the use of ambiguous terms."—*On the Prophecies,* ii. p. 63.

XI.

THE SPECULATIVE SCIENCE AND THE OPERATIVE ART.

AND now, let us apply this doctrine of symbolism to an investigation of the nature of a speculative science, as derived from an operative art; for the fact is familiar to every one that Freemasonry is of two kinds. We work, it is true, in speculative Masonry only, but our ancient brethren wrought in both operative and speculative; and it is now well understood that the two branches are widely apart in design and in character—the one a mere useful art, intended for the protection and convenience of man and the gratification of his physical wants, the other a profound science, entering into abstruse investigations of the soul and a future existence, and originating in the craving need of humanity to know something that is above and beyond the mere outward life that surrounds us with its gross atmosphere here below.* Indeed, the only bond or link that unites

---

* "By speculative Masonry we learn to subdue our passions, to act upon the square, to keep a tongue of good report, to

speculative and operative Masonry is the symbolism that belongs altogether to the former, but which, throughout its whole extent, is derived from the latter.

Our first inquiry, then, will be into the nature of the symbolism which operative gives to speculative Masonry; and thoroughly to understand this—to know its origin, and its necessity, and its mode of application—we must begin with a reference to the condition of a long past period of time.

Thousands of years ago, this science of symbolism was adopted by the sagacious priesthood of Egypt to convey the lessons of worldly wisdom and religious knowledge, which they thus communicated to their disciples.* Their science, their history, and their philosophy were thus concealed beneath an impenetrable veil from all the profane, and only the few who had passed through the severe ordeal of initiation were put in possession of the key which enabled them to decipher and read with ease those mystic lessons

maintain secrecy, and practise charity."—*Lect. of Fel. Craft.* But this is a very meagre definition, unworthy of the place it occupies in the lecture of the second degree.

* "Animal worship among the Egyptians was the natural and unavoidable consequence of the misconception, by the vulgar, of those emblematical figures invented by the priests to record their own philosophical conception of absurd ideas. As the pictures and effigies suspended in early Christian churches, to commemorate a person or an event, became in time objects of worship to the vulgar, so, in Egypt, the esoteric or spiritual meaning of the emblems was lost in the gross materialism of the beholder. This esoteric and allegorical meaning was, however, preserved by the priests, and communicated in the mysteries alone to the initiated, while the uninstructed retained only the grosser conception."—GLIDDON, *Otia Ægyptiaca*, p. 94.

which we still see engraved upon the obelisks, the tombs, and the sarcophagi, which lie scattered,at this day, in endless profusion along the banks of the Nile.

From the Egyptians the same method of symbolic instruction was diffused among all the pagan nations of antiquity, and was used in all the ancient Mysteries* as the medium of communicating to the initiated the esoteric and secret doctrines for whose preservation and promulgation these singular associations were formed.

Moses, who, as Holy Writ informs us, was skilled in all the learning of Egypt, brought with him, from that cradle of the sciences, a perfect knowledge of the science of symbolism, as it was taught by the priests of Isis and Osiris, and applied it to the ceremonies with which he invested the purer religion of the people for whom he had been appointed to legislate.†

Hence we learn, from the great Jewish historian, that, in the construction of the tabernacle, which gave the first model for the temple at Jerusalem, and afterwards for every masonic lodge, this principle of symbolism was applied to every part of it. Thus it was divided into three parts, to represent the three great elementary divisions of the universe—the

* "To perpetuate the esoteric signification of these symbols to the initiated, there were established the Mysteries, of which institution we have still a trace in Freemasonry."—GLIDDON,*Otia Ægyp.* p. 95.

† Philo Judæus says, that "Moses had been initiated by the Egyptians into the philosophy of symbols and hieroglyphics, as well as into the ritual of the holy animals." And Hengstenberg, in his learned work on "Egypt and the Books of Moses," conclusively shows, by numerous examples, how direct were the Egyptian references of the Pentateuch; in which fact, indeed, he recognizes "one of the most powerful arguments for its credibility and for its composition by Moses."—HENGSTENBERG, p. 239, Robbins's trans.

land, the sea, and the air. The first two, or exterior portions, which were accessible to the priests and the people, were symbolic of the land and the sea, which all men might inhabit; while the third, or interior division,—the holy of holies,—whose threshold no mortal dared to cross, and which was peculiarly consecrated to GOD, was emblematic of heaven, his dwelling-place. The veils, too, according to Josephus, were intended for symbolic instruction in their color and their materials. Collectively, they represented the four elements of the universe; and, in passing, it may be observed that this notion of symbolizing the universe characterized all the ancient systems, both the true and the false, and that the remains of the principle are to be found everywhere, even at this day, pervading Masonry, which is but a development of these systems. In the four veils of the tabernacle, the white or fine linen signified the earth, from which flax was produced; the scarlet signified fire, appropriately represented by its flaming color; the purple typified the sea, in allusion to the shell-fish murex, from which the tint was obtained; and the blue, the color of the firmament, was emblematic of air.*

It is not necessary to enter into a detail of the whole system of religious symbolism, as developed in the Mosaic ritual. It was but an application of the same principles of instruction, that pervaded all the surrounding Gentile nations, to the inculcation of truth. The very idea of the ark itself† was borrowed, as the discoveries of the modern

* Josephus, *Antiq.* book iii. ch. 7.

† The ark, or sacred boat, of the Egyptians frequently occurs on the walls of the temples. It was carried in great pomp by the priests on the occasion of the "procession of the shrines," by

Egyptologists have shown us, from the banks of the Nile; and the breastplate of the high priest, with its Urim and Thummim,* was indebted for its origin to a similar ornament worn by the Egyptian judge. The system was the same; in its application, only, did it differ.

With the tabernacle of Moses the temple of King Solomon is closely connected: the one was the archetype of the other. Now, it is at the building of that temple that we must place the origin of Freemasonry in its present organization: not that the system did not exist before, but that the union of its operative and speculative character, and the mutual dependence of one upon the other, were there first established.

At the construction of this stupendous edifice— stupendous, not in magnitude, for many a parish church has since excelled it in size,† but stupendous in the wealth and magnificence of its ornaments—the wise king of Israel, with all that sagacity for which he was so eminently distinguished, and aided and counselled by the Gentile experience of the king of Tyre, and that immortal architect who superintended his workmen, saw at once the excellence and beauty of this method of inculcating moral and religious truth, and gave, therefore, the impulse to that symbolic reference of material things to a

means of staves passed through metal rings in its side. It was thus conducted into the temple, and deposited on a stand. The representations we have of it bear a striking resemblance to the Jewish ark, of which it is now admitted to have been the prototype.

* "The Egyptian reference in the Urim and Thummim is especially distinct and incontrovertible." — HENGSTENBERG, p. 158.

† According to the estimate of Bishop Cumberland, it was only one hundred and nine feet in length, thirty-six in breadth, and fifty-four in height.

spiritual sense, which has ever since distinguished the institution of which he was the founder.

If I deemed it necessary to substantiate the truth of the assertion that the mind of King Solomon was eminently symbolic in its propensities, I might easily refer to his writings, filled as they are to profusion with tropes and figures. Passing over the Book of Canticles, — that great lyrical drama, whose abstruse symbolism has not yet been fully evolved or explained, notwithstanding the vast number of commentators who have labored at the task, — I might simply refer to that beautiful passage in the twelfth chapter of Ecclesiastes, so familiar to every Mason as being appropriated, in the ritual, to the ceremonies of the third degree, and in which a dilapidated building is metaphorically made to represent the decays and infirmities of old age in the human body. This brief but eloquent description is itself an embodiment of much of our masonic symbolism, both as to the mode and the subject matter.

In attempting any investigation into the symbolism of Freemasonry, the first thing that should engage our attention is the general purport of the institution, and the mode in which its symbolism is developed. Let us first examine it as a whole, before we investigate its parts, just as we would first view, as critics, the general effect of a building, before we began to inquire into its architectural details.

Looking, then, in this way, at the institution—coming down to us, as it has, from a remote age—having passed unaltered and unscathed through a thousand revolutions of nations—and engaging, as disciples in its school of mental labor, the intellectual of all times—the first thing that must naturally arrest the attention is the singular combination that it presents of an operative with a speculative organization—an art with a science—the technical terms and language of a mechanical profession with the abstruse teachings of a profound philosophy.

Here it is before us—a venerable school, discoursing of the deepest subjects of wisdom, in which sages might alone find themselves appropriately employed, and yet having its birth and deriving its first life from a society of artisans, whose only object was, apparently, the construction of material edifices of stone and mortar.

The nature, then, of this operative and speculative combination, is the first problem to be solved, and the symbolism which depends upon it is the first feature of the institution which is to be developed.

Freemasonry, in its character as an operative art, is familiar to every one. As such, it is engaged in the application of the rules and principles of architecture to the construction of edifices for private and public use—houses for the dwelling-place of man, and temples for the worship of Deity. It abounds, like every other art, in the use of technical terms, and employs, in practice, an abundance of implements and materials which are peculiar to itself.

Now, if the ends of operative Masonry had here ceased,—if this technical dialect and these technical implements had never been used for any other purpose, nor appropriated to any other object, than that of enabling its disciples to pursue their artistic labors with greater convenience to themselves,—Freemasonry would never have existed. The same principles might, and in all probability would, have been developed in some other way; but the organization, the name, the mode of instruction, would all have most materially differed.

But the operative Masons, who founded the order, were

not content with the mere material and manual part of their profession: they adjoined to it, under the wise instructions of their leaders, a correlative branch of study.

And hence, to the Freemason, this operative art has been symbolized in that intellectual deduction from it, which has been correctly called Speculative Masonry. At one time, each was an integrant part of one undivided system. Not that the period ever existed when every operative mason was acquainted with, or initiated into, the speculative science. Even now, there are thousands of skilful artisans who know as little of that as they do of the Hebrew language which was spoken by its founder. But operative Masonry was, in the inception of our history, and is, in some measure, even now, the skeleton upon which was strung the living muscles, and tendons, and nerves of the speculative system. It was the block of marble—rude and unpolished it may have been—from which was sculptured the life-breathing statue.*

Speculative Masonry (which is but another name for Freemasonary in its modern acceptation) may be briefly defined as the scientific application and the religious consecration of the rules and principles, the language, the implements and materials of operative Masonry to the veneration of God, the purification of the heart, and the inculcation of the dogmas of a religious philosophy.

* "Thus did our wise Grand Master contrive a plan, by mechanical and practical allusions, to instruct the craftsmen in principles of the most sublime speculative philosophy, tending to the glory of God, and to secure to them temporal blessings here and eternal life hereafter, as well as to unite the speculative and operative Masons, thereby forming a twofold advantage, from the principles of geometry and architecture on the one part, and the precepts of wisdom and ethics on the other."—CALCOTT, *Candid Disquisition,* p. 31, ed. 1769.

XII.

THE SYMBOLISM OF SOLOMON'S TEMPLE.

I HAVE said that the operative art is symbolized — that is to say, used as a symbol—in the speculative science. Let us now inquire, as the subject of the present essay, how this is done in reference to a system of symbolism dependent for its construction on types and figures derived from the temple of Solomon, and which we hence call the "Temple Symbolism of Freemasonry."

Bearing in mind that speculative Masonry dates its origin from the building of King Solomon's temple by Jewish and Tyrian artisans,* the first important fact that attracts the attention is, that the operative masons at Jerusalem were engaged in the construction of an earthly and material temple, to be dedicated to the service and worship of God—a house in which Jehovah was to dwell visibly by his Shekinah, and whence he was, by the

---

* This proposition I ask to be conceded; the evidences of its truth are, however, abundant, were it necessary to produce them. The craft, generally, will, I presume, assent to it.

Urim and Thummim, to send forth his oracles for the government and direction of his chosen people.

Now, the operative art having, *for us,* ceased, we, as speculative Masons, symbolize the labors of our predecessors by engaging in the construction of a spiritual temple in our hearts, pure and spotless, fit for the dwelling-place of Him who is the author of purity—where God is to be worshipped in spirit and in truth, and whence every evil thought and unruly passion is to be banished, as the sinner and the Gentile were excluded from the sanctuary of the Jewish temple.

This spiritualizing of the temple of Solomon is the first, the most prominent and most pervading of all the symbolic instructions of Freemasonry. It is the link that binds the operative and speculative divisions of the order. It is this which gives it its religious character. Take from Freemasonry its dependence on the temple, leave out of its ritual all reference to that sacred edifice, and to the legends connected with it, and the system itself must at once decay and die, or at best remain only as some fossilized bone, imperfectly to show the nature of the living body to which it once belonged.

Temple worship is in itself an ancient type of the religious sentiment in its progress towards spiritual elevation. As soon as a nation emerged, in the world's progress, out of Fetichism, or the worship of visible objects,—the most degraded form of idolatry,—its people began to establish a priesthood and to erect temples.*

* "The groves were God's first temples. Ere man learned
    To hew the shaft, and lay the architrave,
    And spread the roof above them—ere he framed
    The lofty vault, to gather and roll back

The Scandinavians, the Celts, the Egyptians, and the Greeks, however much they may have differed in the ritual and the objects of their polytheistic worship, all were possessed of priests and temples. The Jews first constructed their tabernacle, or portable temple, and then, when time and opportunity permitted, transferred their monotheistic worship to that more permanent edifice which is now the subject of our contemplation. The mosque of the Mohammedan and the church or the chapel of the Christian are but embodiments of the same idea of temple worship in a simpler form.

The adaptation, therefore, of the material temple to a science of symbolism would be an easy, and by no means a novel task, to both the Jewish and the Tyrian mind. Doubtless, at its original conception, the idea was rude and unembellished, to be perfected and polished only by future aggregations of succeeding intellects. And yet no biblical scholar will venture to deny that there was, in the mode of building, and in all the circumstances connected with the construction of King Solomon's temple, an apparent design to establish a foundation for symbolism.*

> The sound of anthems—in the darkling wood,
> Amid the cool and silence, he knelt down,
> And offered to the Mightiest solemn thanks
> And supplication."—BRYANT.

* Theologians have always given a spiritual application to the temple of Solomon, referring it to the mysteries of the Christian dispensation. For this, consult all the biblical commentators. But I may particularly mention, on this subject, Bunyan's "Solomon's Temple Spiritualized," and a rare work in folio, by Samuel Lee, Fellow of Wadham College, Oxford, published at London in 1659, and entitled "Orbis Miraculum, or the Temple of Solomon portrayed by Scripture Light." A copy of this scarce work, which treats very learnedly of "the spiritual mysteries of the gospel veiled under the temple," I have lately been, by good fortune, enabled to add to my library.

I propose now to illustrate, by a few examples, the method in which the speculative Masons have appropriated this design of King Solomon to their own use.

To construct his earthly temple, the operative mason followed the architectural designs laid down on the *trestleboard,* or tracing-board, or book of plans of the architect. By these he hewed and squared his materials; by these he raised his walls; by these he constructed his arches; and by these strength and durability, combined with grace and beauty, were bestowed upon the edifice which he was constructing.

The trestle-board becomes, therefore, one of our elementary symbols. For in the masonic ritual the speculative Mason is reminded that, as the operative artist erects his temporal building, in accordance with the rules and designs laid down on the trestle-board of the masterworkman, so should he erect that spiritual building, of which the material is a type, in obedience to the rules and designs, the precepts and commands, laid down by the grand Architect of the universe, in those great books of nature and revelation, which constitute the spiritual trestle-board of every Freemason.

The trestle-board is, then, the symbol of the natural and moral law. Like every other symbol of the order, it is universal and tolerant in its application; and while, as Christian Masons, we cling with unfaltering integrity to that explanation which makes the Scriptures of both dispensations our trestle-board, we permit our Jewish and Mohammedan brethren to content themselves with the books of the Old Testament, or the Koran. Masonry does not interfere with the peculiar form or development of any one's religious faith. All that it asks is, that the interpretation of the symbol shall be according to what each one supposes to be the revealed will of his Creator. But so rigidly exacting is it that the symbol shall be preserved, and, in some rational way, interpreted, that it peremptorily excludes the Atheist from its communion, because, believing in no Supreme Being, no divine Architect, he must necessarily be without a spiritual trestle-board on which the designs of that Being may be inscribed for his direction.

But the operative mason required materials wherewith to construct his temple. There was, for instance, the *rough ashlar*—the stone in its rude and natural state—unformed and unpolished, as it had been lying in the quarries of Tyre from the foundation of the earth. This stone was to be hewed and squared, to be fitted and adjusted, by simple, but appropriate implements, until it became a *perfect ashlar,* or well-finished stone, ready to take its destined place in the building.

Here, then, again, in these materials do we find other elementary symbols. The rough and unpolished stone is a symbol of man's natural state—ignorant, uncultivated, and, as the Roman historian expresses it, "grovelling to the earth, like the beasts of the field, and obedient to every sordid appetite;"* but when education has exerted its salutary influences in expanding his intellect, in restraining his hitherto unruly passions, and purifying his life, he is then represented by the perfect ashlar, or finished stone, which, under the skilful hands of the workman, has been smoothed, and squared, and fitted for its appropriate place in the building.

* Veluti pecora, quæ natura finxit prona et obedientia ventri.— SALLUST, *Bell. Catil.* i.

Here an interesting circumstance in the history of the preparation of these materials has been seized and beautifully appropriated by our symbolic science. We learn from the account of the temple, contained in the First Book of Kings, that "The house, when it was in building, was built of stone, made ready before it was brought thither, so that there was neither hammer nor axe, nor any tool of iron, heard in the house while it was in building."*

Now, this mode of construction, undoubtedly adopted to avoid confusion and discord among so many thousand workmen,† has been selected as an elementary symbol of concord and harmony—virtues which are not more essential to the preservation and perpetuity of our own society than they are to that of every human association.

The perfect ashlar, therefore,—the stone thus fitted for its appropriate position in the temple,—becomes not only a symbol of human perfection (in itself, of course, only a comparative term), but also, when we refer to the mode in which it was prepared, of that species of perfection which results from the concord and union of men in society. It is, in fact, a symbol of the social character of the institution.

There are other elementary symbols, to which I may hereafter have occasion to revert; the three, however, already described,—the rough ashlar, the perfect ashlar, and the trestle-board,—and which, from their importance,

---

* I Kings 7:7.

† In further illustration of the wisdom of these temple contrivances, it may be mentioned that, by marks placed upon the materials which had been thus prepared at a distance, the individual production of every craftsman was easily ascertained, and the means were provided of rewarding merit and punishing indolence.

have received the name of "jewels," will be sufficient to give some idea of the nature of what may be called the "symbolic alphabet" of Masonry. Let us now proceed to a brief consideration of the method in which this alphabet of the science is applied to the more elevated and abstruser portions of the system, and which, as the temple constitutes its most important type, I have chosen to call the "Temple Symbolism of Masonry."

Both Scripture and tradition inform us that, at the building of King Solomon's temple, the masons were divided into different classes, each engaged in different tasks. We learn, from the Second Book of Chronicles, that these classes were the bearers of burdens, the hewers of stones, and the overseers, called by the old masonic writers the *Ish sabal,* the *Ish chotzeb,* and the *Menatzchim.* Now, without pretending to say that the modern institution has preserved precisely the same system of regulations as that which was observed at the temple, we shall certainly find a similarity in these divisions to the Apprentices, Fellow Crafts and Master Masons of our own day. At all events, the three divisions made by King Solomon, in the workmen at Jerusalem, have been adopted as the types of the three degrees now practised in speculative Masonry; and as such we are, therefore, to consider them. The mode in which these three divisions of workmen labored in constructing the temple, has been beautifully symbolized in speculative Masonry, and constitutes an important and interesting part of temple symbolism.

Thus we know, from our own experience among modern workmen, who still pursue the same method, as well as from the traditions of the order, that the implements used in the quarries were few and simple, the work there requiring necessarily, indeed, but two tools, namely, the *twenty-four inch gauge,* or two foot rule, and the *common gavel,* or stone-cutter's hammer. With the former implement, the operative mason took the necessary dimensions of the stone he was about to prepare, and with the latter, by repeated blows, skilfully applied, he broke off every unnecessary protuberance, and rendered it smooth and square, and fit to take its place in the building.

And thus, in the first degree of speculative Masonry, the Entered Apprentice receives these simple implements, as the emblematic working tools of his profession, with their appropriate symbolical instruction. To the operative mason their mechanical and practical use alone is signified, and nothing more of value does their presence convey to his mind. To the speculative Mason the sight of them is suggestive of far nobler and sublimer thoughts; they teach him to measure, not stones, but time; not to smooth and polish the marble for the builder's use, but to purify and cleanse his heart from every vice and imperfection that would render it unfit for a place in the spiritual temple of his body.

In the symbolic alphabet of Freemasonry, therefore, the twenty-four inch gauge is a symbol of time well employed; the common gavel, of the purification of the heart.

Here we may pause for a moment to refer to one of the coincidences between Freemasonry and those *Mysteries** which formed so important a part of the ancient religions,

---

* "Each of the pagan gods had (besides the *public* and *open)* a *secret worship* paid unto him; to which none were admitted but those who had been selected by preparatory ceremonies, called Initiation. This *secret worship* was termed the Mysteries."— WARBURTON, *Div. Leg. I. i. p.* 189.

and which coincidences have led the writers on this subject to the formation of a well-supported theory that there was a common connection between them. The coincidence to which I at present allude is this: in all these Mysteries—the incipient ceremony of initiation—the first step taken by the candidate was a lustration or purification. The aspirant was not permitted to enter the sacred vestibule, or take any part in the secret formula of initiation, until, by water or by fire, he was emblematically purified from the corruptions of the world which he was about to leave behind. I need not, after this, do more than suggest the similarity of this formula, in principle, to a corresponding one in Freemasonry, where the first symbols presented to the apprentice are those which inculcate a purification of the heart, of which the purification of the body in the ancient Mysteries was symbolic.

We no longer use the bath or the fountain, because in our philosophical system the symbolization is more abstract, if I may use the term; but we present the aspirant with the *lamb-skin apron,* the *gauge,* and the *gavel,* as symbols of a spiritual purification. The design is the same, but the mode in which it is accomplished is different.

Let us now resume the connected series of temple symbolism.

At the building of the temple, the stones having been thus prepared by the workmen of the lowest degree (the Apprentices, as we now call them, the aspirants of the ancient Mysteries), we are informed that they were transported to the site of the edifice on Mount Moriah, and were there placed in the hands of another class of workmen, who are now technically called the Fellow Crafts, and who correspond to the Mystes, or those who had received the second degree of the ancient Mysteries. At this stage of the operative work more extensive and important labors were to be performed, and accordingly a greater amount of skill and knowledge was required of those to whom these labors were intrusted. The stones, having been prepared by the Apprentices* (for hereafter, in speaking of the workmen of the temple, I shall use the equivalent appellations of the more modern Masons), were now to be deposited in their destined places in the building, and the massive walls were to be erected. For these purposes implements of a higher and more complicated character than the gauge and gavel were necessary. The *square* was required to fit the joints with sufficient accuracy, the *level* to run the courses in a horizontal line, and the *plumb* to erect the whole with due regard to perfect perpendicularity. This portion of the labor finds its symbolism in the second degree of the speculative science, and in applying this symbolism we still continue to refer to the idea of erecting a spiritual temple in the heart.

The necessary preparations, then, having been made in the first degree, the lessons having been received by which the aspirant is taught to commence the labor of life with the purification of the heart, as a Fellow Craft he continues the task by cultivating those virtues which give form

---

* It must be remarked, however, that many of the Fellow Crafts were also stone-cutters in the mountains, *chotzeb bahor,* and, with their nicer implements, more accurately adjusted the stones which had been imperfectly prepared by the apprentices. This fact does not at all affect the character of the symbolism we are describing. The due preparation of the materials, the symbol of purification, was necessarily continued in all the degrees. The task of purification never ceases.

and impression to the character, as well adapted stones give shape and stability to the building. And hence the "working tools" of the Fellow Craft are referred, in their symbolic application, to those virtues. In the alphabet of symbolism, we find the square, the level, and the plumb appropriated to this second degree. The square is a symbol denoting morality. It teaches us to apply the unerring principles of moral science to every action of our lives, to see that all the motives and results of our conduct shall coincide with the dictates of divine justice, and that all our thoughts, words, and deeds shall harmoniously conspire, like the well-adjusted and rightlysquared joints of an edifice, to produce a smooth, unbroken life of virtue.

The plumb is a symbol of rectitude of conduct, and inculcates that integrity of life and undeviating course of moral uprightness which can alone distinguish the good and just man. As the operative workman erects his temporal building with strict observance of that plumb-line, which will not permit him to deviate a hair's breadth to the right or to the left, so the speculative Mason, guided by the unerring principles of right and truth inculcated in the symbolic teachings of the same implement, is steadfast in the pursuit of truth, neither bending beneath the frowns of adversity nor yielding to the seductions of prosperity.*

The level, the last of the three working tools of the operative craftsman, is a symbol of equality of station. Not that equality of civil or social position which is to be

---

* The classical reader will here be reminded of that beautiful passage of Horace, commencing with "Justum et tenacem propositi virum."—Lib. iii. od. 3.

found only in the vain dreams of the anarchist or the Utopian, but that great moral and physical equality which affects the whole human race as the children of one common Father, who causes his sun to shine and his rain to fall on all alike, and who has so appointed the universal lot of humanity, that death, the leveller of all human greatness, is made to visit with equal pace the prince's palace and the peasant's hut.*

Here, then, we have three more signs or hieroglyphics added to our alphabet of symbolism. Others there are in this degree, but they belong to a higher grade of interpretation, and cannot be appropriately discussed in an essay on temple symbolism only.

We now reach the third degree, the Master Masons of the modern science, and the Epopts, or beholders of the sacred things in the ancient Mysteries.

In the third degree the symbolic allusions to the temple of Solomon, and the implements of Masonry employed in its construction, are extended and fully completed. At the building of that edifice, we have already seen that one class of the workmen was employed in the preparation of the materials, while another was engaged in placing those materials in their proper position. But there was a third and higher class,—the master workmen,—whose duty it was to superintend the two other classes, and to see that the stones were not only duly prepared, but that the most exact accuracy had been observed in giving to them their true juxtaposition in the edifice. It was then only that the last and finishing labor † was performed, and

---

* "Pallida mors æquo pulsat pede pauperum tabernas Regumque turres."—Hor. lib. i. od. 4.

† It is worth noticing that the verb *natzach,* from which the title

the cement was applied by these skilful workmen, to secure the materials in their appropriate places, and to unite the building in one enduring and connected mass. Hence the *trowel,* we are informed, was the most important, though of course not the only, implement in use among the master builders. They did not permit this last, indelible operation to be performed by any hands less skilful than their own. They required that the craftsmen should prove the correctness of their work by the square, level, and plumb, and test, by these unerring instruments, the accuracy of their joints; and, when satisfied of the just arrangement of every part, the cement, which was to give an unchangeable union to the whole, was then applied by themselves.

Hence, in speculative Masonry, the trowel has been assigned to the third degree as its proper implement, and the symbolic meaning which accompanies it has a strict and beautiful reference to the purposes for which it was used in the ancient temple; for as it was there employed "to spread the cement which united the building in one common mass," so is it selected as the symbol of brotherly love—that cement whose object is to unite our mystic association in one sacred and harmonious band of brethren.

of the *menatzchim* (the oyerseers or Master Masons in the ancient temple), is derived, signifies also in Hebrew *to be perfected, to be completed.* The third degree is the perfection of the symbolism of the temple, and its lessons lead us to the completion of life. In like manner the Mysteries, says Christie, "were termed τελεται, *perfections,* because they were supposed to induce a perfectness of life. Those who were purified by them were styled τελουμένοι, and τετελεσμένοι, that is, brought to perfection." — *Observations on Ouvaroff's Essay on the Eleusinian Mysteries, p.* 183.

Here, then, we perceive the first, or, as I have already called it, the elementary form of our symbolism—the adaptation of the terms, and implements, and processes of an operative art to a speculative science. The temple is now completed. The stones having been hewed, squared, and numbered in the quarries by the apprentices, — having been properly adjusted by the craftsmen, and finally secured in their appropriate places, with the strongest and purest cement, by the master builders,— the temple of King Solomon presented, in its finished condition, so noble an appearance of sublimity and grandeur as to well deserve to be selected, as it has been, for the type or symbol of that immortal temple of the body, to which Christ significantly and symbolically alluded when he said, "Destroy this temple, and in three days I will raise it up."

This idea of representing the interior and spiritual man by a material temple is so apposite in all its parts as to have occurred on more than one occasion to the first teachers of Christianity. Christ himself repeatedly alludes to it in other passages, and the eloquent and figurative St. Paul beautifully extends the idea in one of his Epistles to the Corinthians, in the following language: "Know ye not that ye are the temple of God, and that the spirit of God dwelleth in you?" And again, in a subsequent passage of the same Epistle, he reiterates the idea in a more positive form: "What, know ye not that your body is the temple of the Holy Ghost which is in you, which ye have of God, and ye are not your own?" And Dr. Adam Clarke, while commenting on this latter passage, makes the very allusions which have been the topic of discussion in the present essay. "As truly," says he, "as the living God dwelt in the Mosaic tabernacle and in the temple of Solomon, so truly does the Holy Ghost dwell in the souls of genuine Christians; and as the temple and all its *utensils* were holy, separated from all common and profane uses, and dedicated alone to the service of God, so the bodies of genuine Christians are holy, and should be employed in the service of God alone."

The idea, therefore, of making the temple a symbol of the body, is not exclusively masonic; but the mode of treating the symbolism by a reference to the particular temple of Solomon, and to the operative art engaged in its construction, is peculiar to Freemasonry. It is this which isolates it from all other similar associations. Having many things in common with the secret societies and religious Mysteries of antiquity, in this "temple symbolism" it differs from them all.

XIII.

THE FORM OF THE LODGE.

IN the last essay, I treated of that symbolism of the masonic system which makes the temple of Jerusalem the archetype of a lodge, and in which, in consequence, all the symbols are referred to the connection of a speculative science with an operative art. I propose in the present to discourse of a higher and abstruser mode of symbolism; and it may be observed that, in coming to this topic, we arrive, for the first time, at that chain of resemblances which unites Freemasonry with the ancient systems of religion, and which has given rise, among masonic writers, to the names of Pure and Spurious Freemasonry —the pure Freemasonry being that system of philosophical religion which, coming through the line of the patriarchs, was eventually modified by influences exerted at the building of King Solomon's temple, and the spurious being the same system as it was altered and corrupted by the polytheism of the nations of heathendom.*

* Dr. Oliver, in the first or preliminary lecture of his "Historical Landmarks," very accurately describes the difference between

As this abstruser mode of symbolism, if less peculiar to the masonic system, is, however, far more interesting than the one which was treated in the previous essay, — because it is more philosophical, — I propose to give an extended investigation of its character. And, in the first place, there is what may be called an elementary view of this abstruser symbolism, which seems almost to be a corollary from what has already been described in the preceding article.

As each individual mason has been supposed to be the symbol of a spiritual temple, — "a temple not made with hands, eternal in the heavens," — the lodge or collected assemblage of these masons, is adopted as a symbol of the world.*

the pure or primitive Freemasonry of the Noachites, and the spurious Freemasonry of the heathens.

* The idea of the world, as symbolically representing God's temple, has been thus beautifully developed in a hymn by N. P. Willis, written for the dedication of a church: —

> "The perfect world by Adam trod
>   Was the first temple built by God;
>   His fiat laid the corner stone,
>   And heaved its pillars, one by one.
>
> "He hung its starry roof on high —
>   The broad, illimitable sky;
>   He spread its pavement, green and bright,
>   And curtained it with morning light.
>
> "The mountains in their places stood,
>   The sea, the sky, and 'all was good;'
>   And when its first pure praises rang,
>   The 'morning stars together sang.'
>
> "Lord, 'tis not ours to make the sea,
>   And earth, and sky, a house for thee;
>   But in thy sight our offering stands,
>   A humbler temple, made with hands."

It is in the first degree of Masonry, more particularly, that this species of symbolism is developed. In its details it derives the characteristics of resemblance upon which it is founded, from the form, the supports, the ornaments, and general construction and internal organization of a lodge, in all of which the symbolic reference to the world is beautifully and consistently sustained.

The form of a masonic lodge is said to be a parallelogram, or oblong square; its greatest length being from east to west, its breadth from north to south. A square, a circle, a triangle, or any other form but that of an *oblong square,* would be eminently incorrect and unmasonic, because such a figure would not be an expression of the symbolic idea which is intended to be conveyed.

Now, as the world is a globe, or, to speak more accurately, an oblate spheroid, the attempt to make an oblong square its symbol would seem, at first view, to present insuperable difficulties. But the system of masonic symbolism has stood the test of too long an experience to be easily found at fault; and therefore this very symbol furnishes a striking evidence of the antiquity of the order. At the Solomonic era — the era of the building of the temple at Jerusalem — the world, it must be remembered, was supposed to have that very oblong form,* which has been here symbolized. If, for instance, on a map of the world we should inscribe an oblong figure whose boundary lines would circumscribe and include

* "The idea," says Dudley, "that the earth is a level surface, and of a square form, is so likely to have been entertained by persons of little experience and limited observation, that it may be justly supposed to have prevailed generally in the early ages of the world." — *Naology,* p. 7.

just that portion which was known to be inhabited in the days of Solomon, these lines, running a short distance north and south of the Mediterranean Sea, and extending from Spain in the west to Asia Minor in the east, would form an oblong square, including the southern shore of Europe, the northern shore of Africa, and the western district of Asia, the length of the parallelogram being about sixty degrees from east to west, and its breadth being about twenty degrees from north to south. This oblong square, thus enclosing the whole of what was then supposed to be the habitable globe,* would precisely represent what is symbolically said to be *the form of the lodge,* while the Pillars of Hercules in the west, on each side of the straits of Gades or Gibraltar, might appropriately be referred to the two pillars that stood at the porch of the temple.

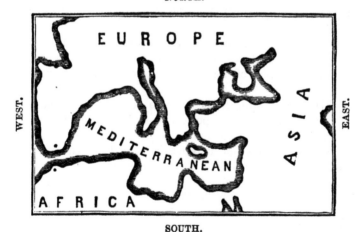

* The quadrangular form of the earth is preserved in almost all the scriptural allusions that are made to it. Thus Isaiah (11:12)

A Masonic lodge is, therefore, a symbol of the world.

This symbol is sometimes, by a very usual figure of speech, extended, in its application, and the world and the universe are made synonymous, when the lodge becomes, of course, a symbol of the universe. But in this case the definition of the symbol is extended, and to the ideas of length and breadth are added those of height and depth, and the lodge is said to assume the form of a double cube.* The solid contents of the earth below and the expanse of the heavens above will then give the outlines of the cube, and the whole created universe† will be included within the symbolic limits of a mason's lodge.

By always remembering that the lodge is the symbol, in its form and extent, of the world, we are enabled, readily and rationally, to explain many other symbols, attached principally to the first degree; and we are enabled to collate and compare them with similar symbols of other kindred institutions of antiquity, for it should be

says, "The Lord shall gather together the dispersed of Judah from the *four corners* of the earth;" and we find in the Apocalypse (xx. 9) the prophetic version of "four angels standing on the *four corners* of the earth."

* "The form of the lodge ought to be a double cube, as an expressive emblem of the powers of darkness and light in the creation." — OLIVER, *Landmarks,* i. p. 135, note 37.

† Not that whole visible universe, in its modern signification, as including solar systems upon solar systems, rolling in illimitable space, but in the more contracted view of the ancients, where the earth formed the floor, and the sky the ceiling. "To the vulgar and untaught eye," says Dudley, "the heaven or sky above the earth appears to be co-extensive with the earth, and to take the same form, enclosing a cubical space, of which the earth was the base, the heaven or sky the upper surface." — *Naology,* 7.—And it is to this notion of the universe that the masonic symbol of the lodge refers.

observed that this symbolism of the world, represented by a place of initiation, widely pervaded all the ancient rites and mysteries.

It will, no doubt, be interesting to extend our investigations on this subject, with a particular view to the method in which this symbolism of the world or the universe was developed, in some of its most prominent details; and for this purpose I shall select the mystical explanation of the *officers* of a lodge, its *covering,* and a portion of its *ornaments.*

XIV.

THE OFFICERS OF A LODGE.

THE Three Principal Officers of a lodge are, it is needless to say, situated in the east, the west, and the south. Now, bearing in mind that the lodge is a symbol of the world, or the universe, the reference of these three officers to the sun at its rising, its setting, and its meridian height, must at once suggest itself.

This is the first development of the symbol, and a very brief inquiry will furnish ample evidence of its antiquity and its universality.

In the Brahminical initiations of Hindostan, which are among the earliest that have been transmitted to us, and may almost be considered as the cradle of all the others of subsequent ages and various countries, the ceremonies were performed in vast caverns, the remains of some of which, at Salsette, Elephanta, and a few other places, will give the spectator but a very inadequate idea of the extent and splendor of these ancient Indian lodges.*

* "These rocky shrines, the formation of which Mr. Grose supposes to have been a labor equal to that of erecting the Pyramids

More imperfect remains than these are still to be found in great numbers throughout Hindostan and Cashmere. Their form was sometimes that of a cross, emblematic of the four elements of which the earth is composed, — fire, water, air, and earth, — but more generally an oval, as a representation of the mundane egg, which, in the ancient systems, was a symbol of the world.*

The interior of the cavern of initiation was lighted by innumerable lamps, and there sat in the east, the west, and the south the principal Hierophants, or explainers of the Mysteries, as the representatives of Brahma, Vishnu, and Siva. Now, Brahma was the supreme deity of the

of Egypt, are of various height, extent, and depth. They are partitioned out, by the labor of the hammer and the chisel, into many separate chambers, and the roof, which in the pagoda of Elephanta is flat, but in that of Salsette is arched, is supported by rows of pillars of great thickness, and arranged with much regularity. The walls are crowded with gigantic figures of men and women, engaged in various actions, and portrayed in various whimsical attitudes; and they are adorned with several evident symbols of the religion now prevailing in India. Above, as in a sky, once probably adorned with gold and azure, in the same manner as Mr. Savary lately observed in the ruinous remains of some ancient Egyptian temples, are seen floating the children of imagination, genii and dewtahs, in multitudes, and along the cornice, in high relief, are the figures of elephants, horses, and lions, executed with great accuracy. Two of the principal figures at Salsette are twenty-seven feet in height, and of proportionate magnitude; the very bust only of the triple-headed deity in the grand pagoda of Elephanta measures fifteen feet from the base to the top of the cap, while the face of another, if Mr. Grose, who measured it, may be credited, is above five feet in length, and of corresponding breadth." — MAURICE, *Ind. Ant.* vol. ii. p. 135.

* According to Faber, the egg was a symbol of the world or megacosm, and also of the ark, or microcosm, as the lunette or crescent was a symbol of the Great Father, the egg and lunette— which was the hieroglyphic of the god Lunus, at Heliopolis— was a symbol of the world proceeding from the Great Father.—*Pagan Idolatry,* vol. i. b. i. ch. iv.

Hindoos, borrowed or derived from the Sun-god of their Sabean ancestors, and Vishnu and Siva were but manifestations of his attributes. We learn from the Indian Pantheon that "when the sun rises in the east, he is Brahma; when he gains his meridian in the south, he is Siva; and when he sets in the west, he is Vishnu."

Again, in the Zoroasteric mysteries of Persia, the temple of initiation was circular, being made so to represent the universe; and the sun in the east, with the surrounding zodiac, formed an indispensable part of the ceremony of reception.*

In the Egyptian mysteries of Osiris, the same reference to the sun is contained, and Herodotus, who was himself an initiate, intimates that the ceremonies consisted in the representation of a Sun-god, who had been incarnate, that is, had appeared upon earth, or rose, and who was at length put to death by Typhon, the symbol of darkness, typical of the sun's setting.

---

* Zoroaster taught that the sun was the most perfect fire of God, the throne of his glory, and the residence of his divine presence, and he therefore instructed his disciples "to direct all their worship to God first towards the sun (which they called Mithras), and next towards their sacred fires, as being the things in which God chiefly dwelt; and their ordinary way of worship was to do so towards both. For when they came before these fires to worship, *they always approached them on the west side,* that, having their faces towards them and also towards the rising sun at the same time, they might direct their worship to both. And in this posture they always performed every act of their worship." — PRIDEAUX, *Connection,* i. 216.

† "The mysteries of Ceres (or Eleusis) are principally distinguished from all others as having been the depositories of certain traditions coeval with the world." — OUVAROFF, *Essay on the Mysteries of Eleusis,* p. 6.

In the great mysteries of Eleusis,† which were celebrated at Athens, we learn from St. Chrysostom, as well as other authorities, that the temple of initiation was symbolic of the universe, and we know that one of the officers represented the sun.*

In the Celtic mysteries of the Druids, the temple of initiation was either oval, to represent the mundane egg — a symbol, as has already been said, of the world; or circular, because the circle was a symbol of the universe; or cruciform, in allusion to the four elements, or constituents of the universe. In the Island of Lewis, in Scotland, there is one combining the cruciform and circular form. There is a circle, consisting of twelve stones, while three more are placed in the east, and as many in the west and south, and thirty-eight, in two parallel lines, in the north, forming an avenue to the circular temple. In the centre of the circle is the image of the god. In the initiations into these rites, the solar deity performed an important part, and the celebrations commenced at daybreak, when the sun was hailed on his appearance above the horizon as "the god of victory, the king who rises in light and ascends the sky."

But I need not multiply these instances of sun-worship. Every country and religion of the ancient world would afford one.† Sufficient has been cited to show the complete

---

* The dadouchus, or torch-bearer, carried a symbol of the sun.

† "Indeed, the most ancient superstition of all nations," says Maurice, "has been the worship of the sun, as the lord of heaven and the governor of the world; and in particular it prevailed in Phœnicia, Chaldæa, Egypt, and from later information we may add, Peru and Mexico, represented in a variety of ways, and concealed under a multitude of fanciful names. Through all the revolutions of time the great luminary of heaven hath exacted from the generations of men the tribute of devotion." — *Indian Antiquities,* vol. ii. p. 91.

coincidence, in reference to the sun, between the symbolism of Freemasonry and that of the ancient rites and Mysteries, and to suggest for them a common origin, the sun being always in the former system, from the earliest times of the primitive or patriarchal Masonry, considered simply as a manifestation of the Wisdom, Strength, and Beauty of the Divine Architect, visibly represented by the position of the three principal officers of a lodge, while by the latter, in their degeneration from, and corruption of the true Noachic faith, it was adopted as the special object of adoration.

XV.

THE POINT WITHIN A CIRCLE.

THE Point within a Circle is another symbol of great importance in Freemasonry, and commands peculiar attention in this connection with the ancient symbolism of the universe and the solar orb. Everybody who has read a masonic "Monitor" is well acquainted with the usual explanation of this symbol. We are told that the point represents an individual brother, the circle the boundary line of his duty to God and man, and the two perpendicular parallel lines the patron saints of the order —St. John the Baptist and St. John the Evangelist.

Now, this explanation, trite and meagre as it is, may do very well for the exoteric teaching of the order; but the question at this time is, not how it has been explained by modern lecturers and masonic system-makers, but what was the ancient interpretation of the symbol, and how should it be read as a sacred hieroglyphic in reference to the true philosophic system which constitutes the real essence and character of Freemasonry?

Perfectly to understand this symbol, I must refer, as a preliminary matter, to the worship of the *Phallus,* a peculiar modification of sun-worship, which prevailed to a great extent among the nations of antiquity.

The Phallus was a sculptured representation of the *membrum virile,* or male organ of generation,* and the worship of it is said to have originated in Egypt, where, after the murder of Osiris by Typhon, which is symbolically to be explained as the destruction or deprivation of the sun's light by night, Isis, his wife, or the symbol of nature, in the search for his mutilated body, is said to have found all the parts except the organs of generation, which myth is simply symbolic of the fact, that the sun having set, its fecundating and invigorating power had ceased. The Phallus, therefore, as the symbol of the male generative principle, was very universally venerated among the ancients,† and that too as a religious rite, without the slightest reference to any impure or lascivious

---

* Facciolatus thus defines the Phallus: "penis ligneus, vel vitreus, vel coriaceus, and quem in Bacchi festis plaustro impositum per rura et urbes magno honore circumferebant." — *Lex. in voc.*

† The exhibition of these images in a colossal form, before the gates of ancient temples, was common. Lucian tells us of two colossal Phalli, each one hundred and eighty feet high, which stood in the fore court of the temple at Hierapolis. Müller, in his "Ancient Art and its Remains," mentions, on the authority of Leake, the fact that a colossal Phallus, which once stood on the top of the tomb of the Lydian king Halyattes, is now lying near the same spot; it is not an entire Phallus, but only the head of one; it is twelve feet in diameter below and nine feet over the glands. The Phallus has even been found, so universal was this worship, among the savages of America. Dr. Arthaut discovered, in the year 1790, a marble Phallic image in a cave of the island of St. Domingo.— CLAVEL, *Hist. Pittoresq. des Religions,* p. 9.

application.* He is supposed, by some commentators, to be the god mentioned under the name of Baal-peor, in the Book of Numbers,† as having been worshipped by the idolatrous Moabites. Among the eastern nations of India the same symbol was prevalent, under the name of "Lingam." But the Phallus or Lingam was a representation of the male principle only. To perfect the circle of generation it is necessary to advance one step farther. Accordingly we find in the *Cteis* of the Greeks, and the *Roni* of the Indians, a symbol of the female generative principle, of co-extensive prevalence with the Phallus. The *Cteis* was a circular and concave pedestal, or receptacle, on which the Phallus or column rested, and from the centre of which it sprang.

The union of the Phallus and Cteis, or the Lingam and Yoni, in one compound figure, as an object of adoration, was the most usual mode of representation. This was in

* Sonnerat (Voyage aux Indes Orient. i. p. 118) observes, that the professors of this worship were of the purest principles and most unblemished conduct, and it seems never to have entered into the heads of the Indian legislator and people that anything natural could be grossly obscene. — Sir William Jones remarks (Asiatic Researches, i. 254), that from the earliest periods the women of Asia, Greece, and Italy wore this symbol as a jewel, and Clavel tells us that a similar usage prevails at this day among the women in some of the villages of Brittany. Seely tells us that the Lingam, or Indian Phallus, is an emblem as frequently met with in Hindostan as the cross is in Catholic countries.— *Wonders of Elora,* p. 278.

† Num. 25:1-3. See also Psalm 106:28: "They joined themselves also unto Baal-peor, and ate the sacrifices of the dead." This last expression, according to Russel, has a distinct reference to the physical qualities of matter, and to the time when death, by the winter absence of the solar heat, gets, as it were, possession of the earth. Baal-peor was, he says, the sun exercising his powers of fecundity. — *Connection of Sacred and Profane History.*

strict accordance with the whole system of ancient mythology, which was founded upon a worship of the prolific powers of nature. All the deities of pagan antiquity, however numerous they may be, can always be reduced to the two different forms of the generative principle— the active, or male, and the passive, or female. Hence the gods were always arranged in pairs, as Jupiter and Juno, Bacchus and Venus, Osiris and Isis. But the ancients went farther. Believing that the procreative and productive powers of nature might be conceived to exist in the same individual, they made the older of their deities hermaphrodite, and used the term ἀρρενοθέλυς, or *manvirgin,* to denote the union of the two sexes in the same divine person.*

Thus, in one of the Orphic Hymns, we find this line: —

"Ζεὺς ἄρσην γένετο, Ζεὺς ἄμβροτος ἔπλετο νύμψη."
Jove was created a male and an unspotted virgin.

And Plutarch, in his tract "On Isis and Osiris," says, "God, who is a male and female intelligence, being both life and light, brought forth another intelligence, the Creator of the World."

Now, this hermaphrodism of the Supreme Divinity was again supposed to be represented by the sun, which was the male generative energy, and by nature, or the universe, which was the female prolific principle.† And

* Is there not a seeming reference to this thought of divine hermaphrodism in the well-known passage of Genesis? "So God created man in his own image, in the image of God created he him: *male and female* created he them." And so being created "male and female," they were "in the image of God."

† The world being animated by man, says Creuzer, in his learned work on Symbolism, received from him the two sexes,

this union was symbolized in different ways, but principally by *the point within the circle,* the point indicating the sun, and the circle the universe, invigorated and fertilized by his generative rays. And in some of the Indian cave-temples, this allusion was made more manifest by the inscription of the signs of the zodiac on the circle.

So far, then, we arrive at the true interpretation of the masonic symbolism of the point within the circle. It is the same thing, but under a different form, as the Master and Wardens of a lodge. The Master and Wardens are symbols of the sun, the lodge of the universe, or world, just as the point is the symbol of the same sun, and the surrounding circle of the universe.

But the two perpendicular parallel lines remain to be explained. Every one is familiar with the very recent interpretation, that they represent the two Saints John, the Baptist and the Evangelist. But this modern exposition must be abandoned, if we desire to obtain the true ancient signification.

In the first place, we must call to mind the fact that, at two particular points of his course, the sun is found in the zodiacal signs of Cancer and Capricorn. These points are astronomically distinguished as the summer and winter solstice. When the sun is in these points, he

represented by heaven and the earth. Heaven, as the fecundating principle, was male, and the source of fire; the earth, as the fecundated, was female, and the source of humidity. All things issued from the alliance of these two principles. The vivifying powers of the heavens are concentrated in the sun, and the earth, eternally fixed in the place which it occupies, receives the emanations from the sun, through the medium of the moon, which sheds upon the earth the germs which the sun had deposited in its fertile bosom. The Lingam is at once the symbol and the mystery of this religious idea.

has reached his greatest northern and southern declination, and produces the most evident effects on the temperature of the seasons, and on the length of the days and nights. These points, if we suppose the circle to represent the sun's apparent course, will be indicated by the points where the parallel lines touch the circle, or, in other words, the parallels will indicate the limits of the sun's extreme northern and southern declination, when he arrives at the solstitial points of Cancer and Capricorn.

But the days when the sun reaches these points are, respectively, the 21st of June and the 22d of December, and this will account for their subsequent application to the two Saints John, whose anniversaries have been placed by the church near those days.

XVI.

THE COVERING OF THE LODGE.

THE Covering of the lodge is another, and must be our last reference to this symbolism of the world or the universe. The mere mention of the fact that this covering is figuratively supposed to be "a clouded canopy," or the firmament, on which the host of stars is represented, will be enough to indicate the continued allusion to the symbolism of the world. The lodge, as a representative of the world, is of course supposed to have no other roof than the heavens;* and it would scarcely be necessary to enter into any discussion on the subject, were it not that another symbol —the theological ladder —is so intimately connected with it, that the one naturally suggests the other. Now, this mystic ladder, which connects the ground floor of the

---

* Such was the opinion of some of the ancient sun-worshippers, whose adorations were always performed in the open air, because they thought no temple was spacious enough to contain the sun; and hence the saying, "Mundus universus est templum solis" — the universe is the temple of the sun. Like our ancient brethren, they worshipped only on *the highest hills.* Another analogy.

lodge with its roof or covering, is another important and interesting link, which binds, with one common chain, the symbolism and ceremonies of Freemasonry, and the symbolism and rites of the ancient initiations.

This mystical ladder, which in Masonry is referred to "the theological ladder, which Jacob in his vision saw, reaching from earth to heaven," was widely dispersed among the religions of antiquity, where it was always supposed to consist of seven rounds or steps.

For instance, in the Mysteries of Mithras, in Persia, where there were seven stages or degrees of initiation, there was erected in the temples, or rather caves, — for it was in them that the initiation was conducted, — a high ladder, of seven steps or gates, each of which was dedicated to one of the planets, which was typified by one of the metals, the topmost step representing the sun, so that, beginning at the bottom, we have Saturn represented by lead, Venus by tin, Jupiter by brass, Mercury by iron, Mars by a mixed metal, the Moon by silver, and the Sun by gold, the whole being a symbol of the sidereal progress of the solar orb through the universe.

In the Mysteries of Brahma we find the same reference to the ladder of seven steps; but here the names were different, although there was the same allusion to the symbol of the universe. The seven steps were emblematical of the seven worlds which constituted the Indian universe. The lowest was the Earth; the second, the World of Reëxistence; the third, Heaven; the fourth, the Middle World, or intermediate region between the lower and upper worlds; the fifth, the World of Births, in which souls are again born; the sixth, the Mansion of the Blessed; and the seventh, or topmost round, the

Sphere of Truth, the abode of Brahma, he himself being but a symbol of the sun, and hence we arrive once more at the masonic symbolism of the universe and the solar orb.

Dr. Oliver thinks that in the Scandinavian Mysteries he has found the mystic ladder in the sacred tree *Rdrasil;* * but here the reference to the septenary division is so imperfect, or at least abstruse, that I am unwilling to press it into our catalogue of coincidences, although there is no doubt that we shall find in this sacred tree the same allusion as in the ladder of Jacob, to an ascent from earth, where its roots were planted, to heaven, where its branches expanded, which ascent being but a change from mortality to immortality, from time to eternity, was the doctrine taught in all the initiations. The ascent of the ladder or of the tree was the ascent from life here to life hereafter — from earth to heaven.

It is unnecessary to carry these parallelisms any farther. Any one can, however, see in them an undoubted reference to that septenary division which so universally prevailed throughout the ancient world, and the influence of which is still felt even in the common day life and observances of our time. Seven was, among the Hebrews, their perfect number; and hence we see it continually recurring in all their sacred rites. The creation was perfected

---

* *Asgard,* the abode of the gods, is shaded by the ash tree, *Rdrasil,* where the gods assemble every day to do justice. The branches of this tree extend themselves over the whole world, and reach above the heavens. It hath three roots, extremely distant from each other: one of them is among the gods; the second is among the giants, where the abyss formerly was; the third covers *Niflheim,* or hell, and under this root is the fountain *Vergelmer,* whence flow the infernal rivers. — *Edda, Fab.* 8.

in seven days; seven priests, with seven trumpets, encompassed the walls of Jericho for seven days; Noah received seven days' notice of the commencement of the deluge, and seven persons accompanied him into the ark, which rested on Mount Ararat on the seventh month; Solomon was seven years in building the temple: and there are hundreds of other instances of the prominence of this talismanic number, if there were either time or necessity to cite them.

Among the Gentiles the same number was equally sacred. Pythagoras called it a "venerable number." The septenary division of time into weeks of seven days, although not universal, as has been generally supposed, was sufficiently so to indicate the influence of the number. And it is remarkable, as perhaps in some way referring to the seven-stepped ladder which we have been considering, that in the ancient Mysteries, as Apuleius informs us, the candidate was seven times washed in the consecrated waters of ablution.

There is, then, an anomaly in giving to the mystical ladder of Masonry only *three* rounds. It is an anomaly, however, with which Masonry has had nothing to do. The error arose from the ignorance of those inventors who first engraved the masonic symbols for our monitors. The ladder of Masonry, like the equipollent ladders of its kindred institutions, always had seven steps, although in modern times the three principal or upper ones are alone alluded to. These rounds, beginning at the lowest, are *Temperance, Fortitude, Prudence, Fustice, Faith, Hope,* and *Charity.* Charity, therefore, takes the same place in the ladder of masonic virtues as the sun does in the ladder of planets. In the ladder of metals we find gold, and in that of colors yellow, occupying the same elevated position. Now, St. Paul explains Charity as signifying, not alms-giving, which is the modern popular meaning, but love — that love which "suffereth long and is kind;" and when, in our lectures on this subject, we speak of it as the greatest of virtues, because, when Faith is lost and Hope has ceased, it extends "beyond the grave to realms of endless bliss," we there refer it to the Divine Love of our Creator. But Portal, in his Essay on Symbolic Colors, informs us that the sun represents Divine Love, and gold indicates the goodness of God.

So that if Charity is equivalent to Divine Love, and Divine Love is represented by the sun, and lastly, if Charity be the topmost round of the masonic ladder, then again we arrive, as the result of our researches, at the symbol so often already repeated of the solar orb. The natural sun or the spiritual sun — the sun, either as the vivifying principle of animated nature, and therefore the special object of adoration, or as the most prominent instrument of the Creator's benevolence — was ever a leading idea in the symbolism of antiquity.

Its prevalence, therefore, in the masonic institution, is a pregnant evidence of the close analogy existing between it and all these systems. How that analogy was first introduced, and how it is to be explained, without detriment to the purity and truthfulness of our own religious character, would involve a long inquiry into the origin of Freemasonry, and the history of its connection with the ancient systems.

These researches might have been extended still farther;

enough, however, has been said to establish the following leading principles: —

1. That Freemasonry is, strictly speaking, a science of symbolism.

2. That in this symbolism it bears a striking analogy to the same science, as seen in the mystic rites of the ancient religions.

3. That as in these ancient religions the universe was symbolized to the candidate, and the sun, as its vivifying principle, made the object of his adoration, or at least of his veneration, so, in Masonry, the lodge is made the representative of the world or the universe, and the sun is presented as its most prominent symbol.

4. That this identity of symbolism proves an identity of origin, which identity of origin can be shown to be strictly compatible with the true religious sentiment of Masonry.

5. And fifthly and lastly, that the whole symbolism of Freemasonry has an exclusive reference to what the Kabalists have called the ALGABIL — the *Master Builder* — him whom Freemasons have designated as the Grand Architect of the Universe.

XVII.

RITUALISTIC SYMBOLISM.

WE have hitherto been engaged in the consideration of these simple symbols, which appear to express one single and independent idea. They have sometimes been called the "alphabet of Freemasonry," but improperly, I think, since the letters of the alphabet have, in themselves, unlike these masonic symbols, no significance, but are simply the component parts of words, themselves the representatives of ideas.

These masonic symbols rather may be compared to the elementary characters of the Chinese language, each of which denotes an idea; or, still better, to the hieroglyphics of the ancient Egyptians, in which one object was represented in full by another which bore some subjective relation to it, as the wind was represented by the wings of a bird, or courage by the head and shoulders of a lion.

It is in the same way that in Masonry the plumb represents rectitude, the level, human equality, and the trowel, concord or harmony. Each is, in itself, independent, each expresses a single elementary idea.

But we now arrive at a higher division of masonic symbolism, which, passing beyond these tangible symbols, brings us to those which are of a more abstruse nature, and which, as being developed in a ceremonial form, controlled and directed by the ritual of the order, may be designated as the *ritualistic symbolism* of Freemasonry.

It is to this higher division that I now invite attention; and for the purpose of exemplifying the definition that I have given, I shall select a few of the most prominent and interesting ceremonies of the ritual.

Our first researches were into the symbolism of objects; our next will be into the symbolism of ceremonies.

In the explanations which I shall venture to give of this ritualistic symbolism, or the symbolism of ceremonies, a reference will constantly be made to what has so often already been alluded to, namely, to the analogy existing between the system of Freemasonry and the ancient rites and Mysteries, and hence we will again develop the identity of their origin.

Each of the degrees of Ancient Craft Masonry contains some of these ritualistic symbols: the lessons of the whole order are, indeed, veiled in their allegoric clothing; but it is only to the most important that I can find opportunity to refer. Such, among others, are the rites of discalceation, of investiture, of circumambulation, and of intrusting. Each of these will furnish an appropriate subject for consideration.

XVIII.

THE RITE OF DISCALCEATION.

THE *rite of discalceation,* or uncovering the feet on approaching holy ground, is derived from the Latin word *discalceare,* to pluck off one's shoes. The usage has the prestige of antiquity and universality in its favor.

That it not only very generally prevailed, but that its symbolic signification was well understood in the days of Moses, we learn from that passage of Exodus where the angel of the Lord, at the burning bush, exclaims to the patriarch, "Draw not nigh hither; put off thy shoes from off thy feet, for the place whereon thou standest is holy ground."* Clarke † thinks it is from this command that the Eastern nations have derived the custom of performing all their acts of religious worship with bare feet. But it is much more probable that the ceremony was in use long anterior to the circumstance of the burning bush, and that the Jewish lawgiver at once recognized it as a well-known sign of reverence.

---

* Exod. 3:5.   † Commentaries *in loco.*

Bishop Patrick* entertains this opinion, and thinks that the custom was derived from the ancient patriarchs, and was transmitted by a general tradition to succeeding times.

Abundant evidence might be furnished from ancient authors of the existence of the custom among all nations, both Jewish and Gentile. A few of them, principally collected by Dr. Mede, must be curious and interesting.

The direction of Pythagoras to his disciples was in these words: "Ανυπόδητος θύε χαὶ πρόσχυνει;" that is, Offer sacrifice and worship with thy shoes off. †

Justin Martyr says that those who came to worship in the sanctuaries and temples of the Gentiles were commanded by their priests to put off their shoes.

Drusius, in his Notes on the Book of Joshua, says that among most of the Eastern nations it was a pious duty to tread the pavement of the temple with unshod feet. ‡

Maimonides, the great expounder of the Jewish law, asserts that "it was not lawful for a man to come into the mountain of God's house with his shoes on his feet, or with his staff, or in his working garments, or with dust on his feet." §

Rabbi Solomon, commenting on the command in Leviticus xix. 30, "Ye shall reverence my sanctuary," makes the same remark in relation to this custom. On this subject Dr. Oliver observes, "Now, the act of going

* Commentary on Exod. 3:5.

† Iamblichi Vita Pythag. c. 105. In another place he says, "Θύειν χρὴ ἀνυπόδετον, χαὶ πρὸς τα ἱερὰ προστιέναι"— We must sacrifice and enter temples with the shoes off. Ibid. c. 85.

‡ "Quod etiam nunc apud plerasque Orientis nationes piaculum sit, calceato pede templorum pavimenta calcasse."

§ Beth Habbechirah, cap. vii.

with naked feet was always considered a token of humility and reverence; and the priests, in the temple worship, always officiated with feet uncovered, although it was frequently injurious to their health."*

Mede quotes Zago Zaba, an Ethiopian bishop, who was ambassador from David, King of Abyssinia, to John III., of Portugal, as saying, "We are not permitted to enter the church, except barefooted." †

The Mohammedans, when about to perform their devotions, always leave their slippers at the door of the mosque. The Druids practised the same custom whenever they celebrated their sacred rites; and the ancient Peruvians are said always to have left their shoes at the porch when they entered the magnificent temple consecrated to the worship of the sun.

Adam Clarke thinks that the custom of worshipping the Deity barefooted was so general among all nations of antiquity, that he assigns it as one of his thirteen proofs that the whole human race have been derived from one family.‡

A theory might be advanced as follows: The shoes, or sandals, were worn on ordinary occasions as a protection from the defilement of the ground. To continue to wear them, then, in a consecrated place, would be a tacit insinuation that the ground there was equally polluted and capable of producing defilement. But, as the very character of a holy and consecrated spot precludes the idea of any sort of defilement or impurity, the acknowledgment

---

* Histor. Landm. vol. ii. p. 481.

† "Non datur nobis potestas adeundi templum nisi nudibus pedibus."

‡ Commentaries, *ut supra.*

that such was the case was conveyed, symbolically, by divesting the feet of all that protection from pollution and uncleanness which would be necessary in unconsecrated places.

So, in modern times, we uncover the head to express the sentiment of esteem and respect. Now, in former days, when there was more violence to be apprehended than now, the casque, or helmet, afforded an ample protection from any sudden blow of an unexpected adversary. But we can fear no violence from one whom we esteem and respect; and, therefore, to deprive the head of its accustomed protection, is to give an evidence of our unlimited confidence in the person to whom the gesture is made.

The rite of discalceation is, therefore, a symbol of reverence. It signifies, in the language of symbolism, that the spot which is about to be approached in this humble and reverential manner is consecrated to some holy purpose.

Now, as to all that has been said, the intelligent mason will at once see its application to the third degree. Of all the degrees of Masonry, this is by far the most important and sublime. The solemn lessons which it teaches, the sacred scene which it represents, and the impressive ceremonies with which it is conducted, are all calculated to inspire the mind with feelings of awe and reverence. Into the holy of holies of the temple, when the ark of the covenant had been deposited in its appropriate place, and the Shekinah was hovering over it, the high priest alone, and on one day only in the whole year, was permitted, after the most careful purification, to enter with bare feet, and to pronounce, with fearful veneration, the tetragrammaton or omnific word.

And into the Master Mason's lodge — this holy of holies of the masonic temple, where the solemn truths of death and immortality are inculcated — the aspirant, on entering, should purify his heart from every contamination, and remember, with a due sense of their symbolic application, those words that once broke upon the astonished ears of the old patriarch, "Put off thy shoes from off thy feet, for the place whereon thou standest is holy ground."

XIX.

THE RITE OF INVESTITURE.

ANOTHER ritualistic symbolism, of still more importance and interest, is the *rite of investiture.*
The rite of investiture, called, in the colloquially technical language of the order, the *ceremony of clothing,* brings us at once to the consideration of that well-known symbol of Freemasonry, the LAMB-SKIN APRON.

This rite of investiture, or the placing upon the aspirant some garment, as an indication of his appropriate preparation for the ceremonies in which he was about to engage, prevailed in all the ancient initiations. A few of them only it will be requisite to consider.

Thus in the Levitical economy of the Israelites the priests always wore the abnet, or linen apron, or girdle, as a part of the investiture of the priesthood. This, with the other garments, was to be worn, as the text expresses it, "for glory and for beauty," or, as it has been explained by a learned commentator, "as emblematical of that holiness and purity which ever characterize the divine nature, and the worship which is worthy of him."

In the Persian Mysteries of Mithras, the candidate, having first received light, was invested with a girdle, a crown or mitre, a purple tunic, and, lastly, a white apron.

In the initiations practised in Hindostan, in the ceremony of investiture was substituted the sash, or sacred zennaar, consisting of a cord, composed of nine threads twisted into a knot at the end, and hanging from the left shoulder to the right hip. This was, perhaps, the type of the masonic scarf, which is, or ought to be, always worn in the same position.

The Jewish sect of the Essenes, who approached nearer than any other secret institution of antiquity to Freemasonry in their organization, always invested their novices with a white robe.

And, lastly, in the Scandinavian rites, where the military genius of the people had introduced a warlike species of initiation, instead of the apron we find the candidate receiving a white shield, which was, however, always presented with the accompaniment of some symbolic instruction, not very dissimilar to that which is connected with the masonic apron.

In all these modes of investiture, no matter what was the material or the form, the symbolic signification intended to be conveyed was that of purity.

And hence, in Freemasonry, the same symbolism is communicated by the apron, which, because it is the first gift which the aspirant receives, — the first symbol in which he is instructed, — has been called the "badge of a mason." And most appropriately has it been so called;

for, whatever may be the future advancement of the candidate in the "Royal Art," into whatever deeper arcana his devotion to the mystic institution or his thirst for knowledge may carry him, with the apron — his first investiture — he never parts. Changing, perhaps, its form and its decorations, and conveying at each step some new and beautiful allusion, its substance is still there, and it continues to claim the honorable title by which it was first made known to him on the night of his initiation.

The apron derives its significance, as the symbol of purity, from two sources — from its color and from its material. In each of these points of view it is, then, to be considered, before its symbolism can be properly appreciated.

And, first, the color of the apron must be an unspotted white. This color has, in all ages, been esteemed an emblem of innocence and purity. It was with reference to this symbolism that a portion of the vestments of the Jewish priesthood was directed to be made white. And hence Aaron was commanded, when he entered into the holy of holies to make an expiation for the sins of the people, to appear clothed in white linen, with his linen apron, or girdle, about his loins. It is worthy of remark that the Hebrew word LABAN, which signifies *to make white*, denotes also *to purify*; and hence we find, throughout the Scriptures, many allusions to that color as an emblem of purity. "Though thy sins be as scarlet," says Isaiah, "they shall be *white* as snow;" and Jeremiah, in describing the once innocent condition of Zion, says, "Her Nazarites were purer than snow; they were *whiter* than milk."

In the Apocalypse a *white stone* was the reward promised by the Spirit to those who overcame; and in the same mystical book the apostle is instructed to say, that fine linen, clean and *white* is the righteousness of the saints.

In the early ages of the Christian church a *white garment* was always placed upon the catechumen who had been recently baptized, to denote that he had been cleansed from his former sins, and was thenceforth to lead a life of innocence and purity. Hence it was presented to him with this appropriate charge: "Receive the white and undefiled garment, and produce it unspotted before the tribunal of our Lord Jesus Christ, that you may obtain immortal life."

The *white alb* still constitutes a part of the vestments of the Roman church, and its color is said by Bishop England "to excite to piety by teaching us the purity of heart and body which we should possess in being present at the holy mysteries."

The heathens paid the same attention to the symbolic signification of this color. The Egyptians, for instance, decorated the head of their principal deity, Osiris, with a white tiara, and the priests wore robes of the whitest linen.

In the school of Pythagoras, the sacred hymns were chanted by the disciples clothed in garments of white. The Druids gave white vestments to those of their initiates who had arrived at the ultimate degree, or that of perfection. And this was intended, according to their ritual, to teach the aspirant that none were admitted to that honor but such as were cleansed from all impurities, both of body and mind.

In all the Mysteries and religious rites of the other

nations of antiquity the same use of white garments was observed.

Portal, in his "Treatise on Symbolic Colors," says that "white, the symbol of the divinity and of the priesthood, represents divine wisdom; applied to a young girl, it denotes virginity; to an accused person, innocence; to a judge, justice;" and he adds — what in reference to its use in Masonry will be peculiarly appropriate — that, "as a characteristic sign of purity, it exhibits a promise of hope after death." We see, therefore, the propriety of adopting this color in the masonic system as a symbol of purity. This symbolism pervades the whole of the ritual, from the lowest to the highest degree, wherever white vestments or white decorations are used.

As to the material of the apron, this is imperatively required to be of lamb-skin. No other substance, such as linen, silk, or satin, could be substituted without entirely destroying the symbolism of the vestment. Now, the lamb has, as the ritual expresses it, "been, in all ages, deemed an emblem of innocence;" but more particularly in the Jewish and Christian churches has this symbolism been observed. Instances of this need hardly be cited. They abound throughout the Old Testament, where we learn that a lamb was selected by the Israelites for their sin and burnt offerings, and in the New, where the word *lamb* is almost constantly employed as synonymous with innocence. "The paschal lamb," says Didron, "which was eaten by the Israelites on the night preceding their departure, is the type of that other divine Lamb, of whom Christians are to partake at Easter, in order thereby to free themselves from the bondage in which they are held by vice." The paschal lamb, a lamb bearing a cross,was, therefore, from an early period, depicted by the Christians as referring to Christ crucified, "that spotless Lamb of God, who was slain from the foundation of the world."

The material, then, of the apron, unites with its color to give to the investiture of a mason the symbolic signification of purity. This, then, together with the fact which I have already shown, that the ceremony of investiture was common to all the ancient religious rites, will form another proof of the identity of origin between these and the masonic institution.

This symbolism also indicates the sacred and religious character which its founders sought to impose upon Freemasonry, and to which both the moral and physical qualifications of our candidates undoubtedly have a reference, since it is with the masonic lodge as it was with the Jewish church, where it was declared that "no man that had a blemish should come nigh unto the altar;" and with the heathen priesthood, among whom we are told that it was thought to be a dishonor to the gods to be served by any one that was maimed, lame, or in any other way imperfect; and with both, also, in requiring that no one should approach the sacred things who was not pure and uncorrupt.

The pure, unspotted lamb-skin apron is, then, in Masonry, symbolic of that perfection of body and purity of mind which are essential qualifications in all who would participate in its sacred mysteries.

XX.

THE SYMBOLISM OF THE GLOVES.

THE investiture with the gloves is very closely connected with the investiture with the apron, and the consideration of the symbolism of the one naturally follows the consideration of the symbolism of the other.

In the continental rites of Masonry, as practised in France, in Germany, and in other countries of Europe, it is an invariable custom to present the newly-initiated candidate not only, as we do, with a white leather apron, but also with two pairs of white kid gloves, one a man's pair for himself, and the other a woman's, to be presented by him in turn to his wife or his betrothed, according to the custom of the German masons, or, according to the French, to the female whom he most esteems, which, indeed, amounts, or should amount, to the same thing.

There is in this, of course, as there is in everything else which pertains to Freemasonry, a symbolism. The gloves given to the candidate for himself are intended to

136

teach him that the acts of a mason should be as pure and spotless as the gloves now given to him. In the German lodges, the word used for *acts* is of course *handlungen,* or *handlings,* "the works of his hands," which makes the symbolic idea more impressive.

Dr. Robert Plott — no friend of Masonry, but still an historian of much research — says, in his "Natural History of Staffordshire," that the Society of Freemasons, in his time (and he wrote in 1660), presented their candidates with gloves for themselves and their wives. This shows that the custom still preserved on the continent of Europe was formerly practised in England, although there as well as in America, it is discontinued, which is, perhaps, to be regretted.

But although the presentation of the gloves to the candidate is no longer practised as a ceremony in England or America, yet the use of them as a part of the proper professional clothing of a mason in the duties of the lodge, or in processions, is still retained, and in many well-regulated lodges the members are almost as regularly clothed in their white gloves as in their white aprons.

The symbolism of the gloves, it will be admitted, is, in fact, but a modification of that of the apron. They both signify the same thing; both are allusive to a purification of life. "Who shall ascend," says the Psalmist, "into the hill of the Lord? or who shall stand in his holy place? He that hath clean hands and a pure heart." The apron may be said to refer to the "pure heart," the gloves to the "clean hands." Both are significant of purification —of that purification which was always symbolized by the ablution which preceded the ancient initiations into the sacred Mysteries. But while our American and English masons have adhered only to the apron, and rejected the gloves as a Masonic symbol, the latter appear to be far more important in symbolic science, because the allusions to pure or clean hands are abundant in all the ancient writers.

"Hands," says Wemyss, in his "Clavis Symbolica," are the symbols of human actions; pure hands are pure actions; unjust hands are deeds of injustice." There are numerous references in sacred and profane writers to this symbolism. The washing of the hands has the outward sign of an internal purification. Hence the Psalmist says, "I will wash my hands in innocence, and I will encompass thine altar, Jehovah."

In the ancient Mysteries the washing of the hands was always an introductory ceremony to the initiation, and, of course, it was used symbolically to indicate the necessity of purity from crime as a qualification of those who sought admission into the sacred rites; and hence on a temple in the Island of Crete this inscription was placed: "Cleanse your feet, wash your hands, and then enter."

Indeed, the washing of hands, as symbolic of purity, was among the ancients a peculiarly religious rite. No one dared to pray to the gods until he had cleansed his hands. Thus Homer makes Hector say, —

"Χεροὶ δ' ἀνίπτοισιν Διὶ λείβειν αἴθοπα οἶνον
Ἅζομαι"— *Iliad.* vi. 266.

"I dread with unwashed hands to bring
My incensed wine to Jove an offering."

In a similar spirit of religion, Æneas, when leaving burning Troy, refuses to enter the temple of Ceres until his hands, polluted by recent strife, had been washed in the living stream.

"Me bello e tanto digressum et cæde recenti,
Attrectare nefas, donec me flumine vivo
Abluero." — *Æn.* ii. 718.

"In me, now fresh from war and recent strife,
'Tis impious the sacred things to touch
Till in the living stream myself I bathe."

The same practice prevailed among the Jews, and a striking instance of the symbolism is exhibited in that well-known action of Pilate, who, when the Jews clamored for Jesus, that they might crucify him, appeared before the people, and, having taken water, washed his hands, saying at the same time, "I am innocent of the blood of this just man. See ye to it." In the Christian church of the middle ages, gloves were always worn by bishops or priests when in the performance of ecclesiastical functions. They were made of linen, and were white; and Durandus, a celebrated ritualist, says that "by the white gloves were denoted chastity and purity, because the hands were thus kept clean and free from all impurity."

There is no necessity to extend examples any further. There is no doubt that the use of the gloves in Masonry is a symbolic idea borrowed from the ancient and universal language of symbolism, and was intended, like the apron, to denote the necessity of purity of life.

We have thus traced the gloves and the apron to the same symbolic source. Let us see if we cannot also derive them from the same historic origin.

The apron evidently owes its adoption in Freemasonry to the use of that necessary garment by the operative masons of the middle ages. It is one of the most positive evidences — indeed we may say, absolutely, the most tangible evidence — of the derivation of our speculative science from an operative art. The builders, who associated in companies, who traversed Europe, and were engaged in the construction of palaces and cathedrals, have left to us, as their descendants, their name, their technical language, and that distinctive piece of clothing by which they protected their garments from the pollutions of their laborious employment. Did they also bequeath to us their gloves? This is a question which some modern discoveries will at last enable us to solve.

M. Didron, in his "Annales Archeologiques," presents us with an engraving, copied from the painted glass of a window in the cathedral of Chartres, in France. The painting was executed in the thirteenth century, and represents a number of operative masons at work. *Three* of them are adorned with laurel crowns. May not these be intended to represent the three officers of a lodge? All of the Masons wear gloves. M. Didron remarks that in the old documents which he has examined, mention is often made of gloves which are intended to be presented to masons and stone-cutters. In a subsequent number of the "Annales," he gives the following three examples of this fact: —

In the year 1331, the Chatelan of Villaines, in Duemois, bought a considerable quantity of gloves, to be given to the workmen, in order, as it is said, "to shield their hands from the stone and lime."

In October, 1383, as he learns from a document of that period, three dozen pairs of gloves were bought and distributed to the masons when they commenced the buildings at the Chartreuse of Dijon.

And, lastly, in 1486 or 1487, twenty-two pair of gloves were given to the masons and stone-cutters who were engaged in work at the city of Amiens.

It is thus evident that the builders—the operative masons—of the middle ages wore gloves to protect their hands from the effects of their work. It is equally evident that the speculative masons have received from their operative predecessors the gloves as well as the apron, both of which, being used by the latter for practical uses, have been, in the spirit of symbolism, appropriated by the former to "a more noble and glorious purpose."

XXI.

THE RITE OF CIRCUMAMBULATION.

HE *rite of circumambulation* will supply us with another ritualistic symbol, in which we may again trace the identity of the origin of Freemasonry with that of the religious and mystical ceremonies of the ancients.

"Circumambulation" is the name given by sacred archæologists to that religious rite in the ancient initiations which consisted in a formal procession around the altar, or other holy and consecrated object.

The prevalence of this rite among the ancients appears to have been universal, and it originally (as I shall have occasion to show) alluded to the apparent course of the sun in the firmament, which is from east to west by the way of the south.

In ancient Greece, when the priests were engaged in the rites of sacrifice, they and the people always walked three times around the altar while chanting a sacred hymn or ode. Sometimes, while the people stood around the altar, the rite of circumambulation was performed by the priest alone, who, turning towards the right hand, went around it, and sprinkled it with meal and holy water. In making this circumambulation, it was considered absolutely necessary that the right side should always be next to the altar, and consequently, that the procession should move from the east to the south, then to the west, next to the north, and afterwards to the east again. It was in this way that the apparent revolution was represented.

This ceremony the Greeks called moving εχ δεξια εν δεξια, *from the right to the right,* which was the direction of the motion, and the Romans applied to it the term *dextrovorsum,* or *dextrorsum,* which signifies the same thing. Thus Plautus makes Palinurus, a character in his comedy of "Curculio," say, "If you would do reverence to the gods, you must turn to the right hand." Gronovius, in commenting on this passage of Plautus, says, "In worshipping and praying to the gods they were accustomed to *turn to the right hand."*

A hymn of Callimachus has been preserved, which is said to have been chanted by the priests of Apollo at Delos, while performing this ceremony of circumambulation, the substance of which is, "We imitate the example of the sun, and follow his benevolent course."

It will be observed that this circumambulation around the altar was accompanied by the singing or chanting of a sacred ode. Of the three parts of the ode, the *strophe,* the *antistrophe,* and the *epode,* each was to be sung at a particular part of the procession. The analogy between this chanting of an ode by the ancients and the recitation of a passage of Scripture in the masonic circumambulation, will be at once apparent.

Among the Romans, the ceremony of circumambulation was always used in the rites of sacrifice, of expiation or purification. Thus Virgil describes Corynæus as purifying his companions, at the funeral of Misenus, by passing three times around them while aspersing them with the lustral waters; and to do so conveniently, it was necessary that he should have moved with his right hand towards them.

> "Idem ter socios pura circumtulit unda,
> Spargens rore levi et ramo felicis olivæ."
>
> *Æn.* vi. 229.

> "Thrice with pure water compassed he the crew,
> Sprinkling, with olive branch, the gentle dew."

In fact, so common was it to unite the ceremony of circumambulation with that of expiation or purification, or, in other words, to make a circuitous procession in performing the latter rite, that the term *lustrare,* whose primitive meaning is "to purify," came at last to be synonymous with *circuire,* to walk round anything; and hence a purification and a circumambulation were often expressed by the same word.

Among the Hindoos, the same rite of circumambulation has always been practised. As an instance, we may cite the ceremonies which are to be performed by a Brahmin upon first rising from bed in the morning, an accurate account of which has been given by Mr. Colebrooke in the "Asiatic Researches." The priest, having first adored the sun while directing his face to the east, then walks towards the west by the way of the south, saying, at the same time, "I follow the course of the sun," which he thus explains: "As the sun in his course moves round the world by the way of the south, so do I follow that luminary, to obtain the benefit arising from a journey round the earth by the way of the south."*

Lastly, I may refer to the preservation of this rite among the Druids, whose "mystical dance" around the *cairn,* or sacred stones, was nothing more or less than the rite of circumambulation. On these occasions the priest always made three circuits, from east to west, by the right hand, around the altar or cairn, accompanied by all the worshippers. And so sacred was the rite once considered, that we learn from Toland † that in the Scottish Isles, once a principal seat of the Druidical religion, the people "never come to the ancient sacrificing and firehallowing *cairns,* but they walk three times around them, from east to west, according to the course of the sun." This sanctified tour, or round by the south, he observes, is called *Deiseal,* as the contrary, or unhallowed one by the north, is called *Tuapholl.* And he further remarks, that this word *Deiscal* was derived "from *Deas,* the *right* (understanding *hand*) and *soil,* one of the ancient names of the sun, the right hand in this round being ever next the heap."

I might pursue these researches still further, and trace this rite of circumambulation to other nations of antiquity; but I conceive that enough has been said to show its universality, as well as the tenacity with which the essential ceremony of performing the motion a mystical number of times, and always by the right hand, from the east, through the south, to the west, was preserved. And I

---

* See a paper "on the religious ceremonies of the Hindus," by H. T. Colebrooke, Esq., in the Asiatic Researches, vol. vi. p. 357.

† A Specimen of the Critical History of the Celtic Religion and Learning, Letter ii. § xvii.

think that this singular analogy to the same rite in Freemasonry must lead us to the legitimate conclusion, that the common source of all these rites is to be found in the identical origin of the Spurious Freemasonry or pagan mysteries, and the pure, Primitive Freemasonry, from which the former seceded only to be deteriorated.

In reviewing what has been said on this subject, it will at once be perceived that the essence of the ancient rite consisted in making the circumambulation around the altar, from the east to the south, from the south to the west, thence to the north, and to the east again.

Now, in this the masonic rite of circumambulation strictly agrees with the ancient one.

But this circuit by the right hand, it is admitted, was done as a representation of the sun's motion. It was a symbol of the sun's apparent course around the earth.

And so, then, here again we have in Masonry that old and often-repeated allusion to sun-worship, which has already been seen in the officers of a lodge, and in the point within a circle. And as the circumambulation is made around the lodge, just as the sun was supposed to move around the earth, we are brought back to the original symbolism with which we commenced—that the lodge is a symbol of the world.

XXII.

THE RITE OF INTRUSTING, AND THE SYMBOLISM OF LIGHT.

D HE *rite of intrusting,* to which we are now to direct our attention, will supply us with many important and interesting symbols.

There is an important period in the ceremony of masonic initiation, when the candidate is about to receive a full communication of the mysteries through which he has passed, and to which the trials and labors which he has undergone can only entitle him. This ceremony is technically called the *"rite of intrusting"* because it is then that the aspirant begins to be intrusted with that for the possession of which he was seeking.* It is equivalent to what, in the ancient Mysteries, was called the "autopsy,"† or the seeing of what only the initiated were permitted to behold.

---

* Dr. Oliver, referring to the "twelve grand points in Masonry," which formed a part of the old English lectures, says, "When the candidate was *intrusted,* he represented Asher, for he was then presented with the glorious fruit of masonic knowledge, as Asher was represented by fatness and royal dainties." —*Hist. Landm.,* vol. i. lect. xi. p. 313.

† From the Greek αὐτοψία, signifying *a seeing with one's own eyes.* The candidate, who had previously been called a *mystes,* or a

This *rite of intrusting* is, of course, divided into several parts or periods; for the *aporreta,* or secret things of Masonry, are not to be given at once, but in gradual progression. It begins, however, with the communication of LIGHT, which, although but a preparation for the development of the mysteries which are to follow, must be considered as one of the most important symbols in the whole science of masonic symbolism. So important, indeed, is it, and so much does it pervade with its influence and its relations the whole masonic system, that Freemasonry itself anciently received, among other appellations, that of Lux, or Light, to signify that it is to be regarded as that sublime doctrine of Divine Truth by which the path of him who has attained it is to be illuminated in his pilgrimage of life.

The Hebrew cosmogonist commences his description of the creation by the declaration that "God said, Let there be light, and there was light"—a phrase which, in the more emphatic form that it has received in the original language of "Be light, and light was,"* is said to have won the praise, for its sublimity, of the greatest of Grecian critics. "The singularly emphatic summons," says a profound modern writer,† "by which light is called into existence, is probably owing to the preëminent utility and glory of that element, together with its mysterious nature, which made it seem as

'The God of this new world,'

and won for it the earliest adoration of mankind."

---

blind man, from μύω, *to shut the eyes,* began at this point to change his title to that of an *epopt,* or an *eye-witness.*

*יחי אור ויחי אור   *Yehi aur va yehi aur.*

† Robert William Mackay, Progress of the Intellect, vol. i. p. 93.

Light was, in accordance with this old religious sentiment, the great object of attainment in all the ancient religious Mysteries. It was there, as it is now, in Masonry, made the symbol of *truth* and *knowledge.* This was always its ancient symbolism, and we must never lose sight of this emblematic meaning, when we are considering the nature and signification of masonic light. When the candidate makes a demand for light, it is not merely for that material light which is to remove a physical darkness; that is only the outward form, which conceals the inward symbolism. He craves an intellectual illumination which will dispel the darkness of mental and moral ignorance, and bring to his view, as an eyewitness, the sublime truths of religion, philosophy, and science, which it is the great design of Freemasonry to teach.

In all the ancient systems this reverence for light, as the symbol of truth, was predominant. In the Mysteries of every nation, the candidate was made to pass, during his initiation, through scenes of utter darkness, and at length terminated his trials by an admission to the splendidly-illuminated sacellum, or sanctuary, where he was said to have attained pure and perfect light, and where he received the necessary instructions which were to invest him with that knowledge of the divine truth which it had been the object of all his labors to gain, and the design of the institution, into which he had been initiated, to bestow.

Light, therefore, became synonymous with truth and knowledge, and *darkness* with falsehood and ignorance. We shall find this symbolism pervading not only the institutions, but the very languages, of antiquity.

Thus, among the Hebrews, the word AUR, in the singular, signified *light,* but in the plural, AURIM, it denoted the revelation of the divine will; and the *aurim* and *thummim,* literally the *lights* and *truths,* constituted a part of the breastplate whence the high priest obtained oracular responses to the questions which he proposed.*

There is a peculiarity about the word "light," in the old Egyptian language, which is well worth consideration in this connection. Among the Egyptians, the *hare* was the hieroglyphic of *eyes that are open;* and it was adopted because that timid animal was supposed never to close his organs of vision, being always on the watch for his enemies. The hare was afterwards adopted by the priests as a symbol of the mental illumination or mystic light which was revealed to the neophytes, in the contemplation of divine truth, during the progress of their initiation; and hence, according to Champollion, the hare was also the symbol of Osiris, their chief god; thus showing the intimate connection which they believed to exist between the process of initiation into their sacred rites and the contemplation of the divine nature. But the Hebrew word for hare is ARNaBeT. Now, this is compounded of the two words AUR, *light,* and NaBaT, *to behold,* and therefore the word which in the Egyptian denoted *initiation,* in the Hebrew signified *to behold the*

---

* "And thou shalt put in the breastplate of judgment the Urim and the Thummim." — *Exod.* 28:30. — The Egyptian judges also wore breastplates, on which was represented the figure of *Ra,* the sun, and *Thme,* the goddess of Truth, representing, says Gliddon, "*Ra,* or the sun, in a double capacity — physical and intellectual light; and *Thme,* in a double capacity — justice and truth." — *Ancient Egypt,* p. 33.

light. In two nations so intimately connected in history as the Hebrew and the Egyptian, such a coincidence could not have been accidental. It shows the prevalence of the sentiment, at that period, that the communication of light was the prominent design of the Mysteries — so prominent that the one was made the synonyme of the other.*

The worship of light, either in its pure essence or in the forms of sun-worship and fire-worship, because the sun and the fire were causes of light, was among the earliest and most universal superstitions of the world. Light was considered as the primordial source of all that was holy and intelligent; and darkness, as its opposite, was viewed as but another name for evil and ignorance. Dr. Beard, in an article on this subject, in Kitto's Cyclopædia of Biblical Literature, attributes this view of the divine nature of light, which was entertained by the nations of the East, to the fact that, in that part of the world, light "has a clearness and brilliancy, is accompanied by an intensity of heat, and is followed in its influence by a largeness of good, of which the inhabitants of less genial climates have no conception. Light easily and naturally became, in consequence, with Orientals, a representative of the highest human good. All the more joyous emotions of the mind, all the pleasing sensations of the frame, all the happy hours of domestic intercourse,

---

* We owe this interesting discovery to F. Portal, who has given it in his elaborate work on Egyptian symbols as compared with those of the Hebrews. To those who cannot consult the original work in French, I can safely recommend the excellent translation by my esteemed friend, Bro. John W. Simons, of New York, and which will be found in the thirtieth volume of the "Universal Masonic Library."

were described under imagery derived from light. The transition was natural — from earthly to heavenly, from corporeal to spiritual things; and so light came to typify true religion and the felicity which it imparts. But as light not only came from God, but also makes man's way clear before him, so it was employed to signify moral truth, and preëminently that divine system of truth which is set forth in the Bible, from its earliest gleamings onward to the perfect day of the Great Sun of Righteousness."

I am inclined to believe that in this passage the learned author has erred, not in the definition of the symbol, but in his deduction of its origin. Light became the object of religious veneration, not because of the brilliancy and clearness of a particular sky, nor the warmth and genial influence of a particular climate, — for the worship was universal, in Scandinavia as in India, — but because it was the natural and inevitable result of the worship of the sun, the chief deity of Sabianism — a faith which pervaded to an extraordinary extent the whole religious sentiment of antiquity.*

Light was venerated because it was an emanation from the sun, and, in the materialism of the ancient faith, *light* and *darkness* were both personified as positive existences, the one being the enemy of the other. Two principles were thus supposed to reign over the world, antagonistic to each other, and each alternately presiding over the destinies of mankind.†

---

* "The earliest defection to Idolatry," says Bryant, "consisted in the adoration of the sun and the worship of demons, styled Baalim." —*Analysis of Anc. Mythol.* vol. iii. p. 431.

† The remarks of Mr. Duncan on this subject are well worth perusal. "Light has always formed one of the primary objects

The contests between the good and evil principle, symbolized by light and darkness, composed a very large part of the ancient mythology in all countries.

Among the Egyptians, Osiris was light, or the sun; and his arch-enemy, Typhon, who ultimately destroyed him, was the representative of darkness.

Zoroaster, the father of the ancient Persian religion, taught the same doctrine, and called the principle of light, or good, Ormuzd, and the principle of darkness, or evil,

of heathen adoration. The glorious spectacle of animated nature would lose all its interest if man were deprived of vision, and light extinguished; for that which is unseen and unknown becomes, for all practical purposes, as valueless as if it were non-existent. Light is a source of positive happiness; without it, man could barely exist; and since all religious opinion is based on the ideas of pleasure and pain, and the corresponding sensations of hope and fear, it is not to be wondered if the heathen reverenced light. Darkness, on the contrary, by replunging nature, as it were, into a state of nothingness, and depriving man of the pleasurable emotions conveyed through the organ of sight, was ever held in abhorrence, as a source of misery and fear. The two opposite conditions in which man thus found himself placed, occasioned by the enjoyment or the banishment of light, and induced him to imagine the existence of two antagonist principles in nature, to whose dominion he was alternately subject. Light multiplied his enjoyments, and darkness diminished them. The former, accordingly, became his friend, and the latter his enemy. The words 'light' and 'good,' and 'darkness' and 'evil,' conveyed similar ideas, and became, in sacred language, synonymous terms. But as good and evil were not supposed to flow from one and the same source, no more than light and darkness were supposed to have a common origin, two distinct and independent principles were established, totally different in their nature, of opposite characters, pursuing a conflicting line of action, and creating antagonistic effects. Such was the origin of this famous dogma, recognized by all the heathens, and incorporated with all the sacred fables, cosmogonies, and mysteries of antiquity." — *The Religions of Profane Antiquity,* p. 186.

Ahriman. The former, born of the purest light, and the latter, sprung from utter darkness, are, in this mythology, continually making war on each other.

Manes, or Manichæus, the founder of the sect of Manichees, in the third century, taught that there are two principles from which all things proceed; the one is a pure and subtile matter, called Light, and the other a gross and corrupt substance, called Darkness. Each of these is subject to the dominion of a superintending being, whose existence is from all eternity. The being who presides over the light is called *God;* he that rules over the darkness is called *Hyle,* or *Demon.* The ruler of the light is supremely happy, good, and benevolent, while the ruler over darkness is unhappy, evil, and malignant.

Pythagoras also maintained this doctrine of two antagonistic principles. He called the one, unity, *light,* the right hand, equality, stability, and a straight line; the other he named binary, *darkness,* the left hand, inequality, instability, and a curved line. Of the colors, he attributed white to the good principle, and black to the evil one.

The Cabalists gave a prominent place to light in their system of cosmogony. They taught that, before the creation of the world, all space was filled with what they called *Aur en soph,* or the *Eternal Light,* and that when the Divine Mind determined or willed the production of Nature, the Eternal Light withdrew to a central point, leaving around it an empty space, in which the process of creation went on by means of emanations from the central mass of light. It is unnecessary to enter into the Cabalistic account of creation; it is sufficient here to remark that all was done through the mediate influence of the *Aur en soph,* or eternal light, which produces coarse matter, but one degree above nonentity, only when it becomes so attenuated as to be lost in darkness.

The Brahminical doctrine was, that "light and darkness are esteemed the world's eternal ways; he who walketh in the former returneth not; that is to say, he goeth to eternal bliss; whilst he who walketh in the latter cometh back again upon earth," and is thus destined to pass through further transmigrations, until his soul is perfectly purified by light.*

In all the ancient systems of initiation the candidate was shrouded in darkness, as a preparation for the reception of light. The duration varied in the different rites. In the Celtic Mysteries of Druidism, the period in which the aspirant was immersed in darkness was nine days and nights; among the Greeks, at Eleusis, it was three times as long; and in the still severer rites of Mithras, in Persia, fifty days of darkness, solitude, and fasting were imposed upon the adventurous neophyte, who, by these excessive trials, was at length entitled to the full communication of the light of knowledge.

Thus it will be perceived that the religious sentiment of a good and an evil principle gave to darkness, in the

---

* See the "Bhagvat Geeta," one of the religious books of Brahminism. A writer in Blackwood, in an article on the "Castes and Creeds of India," vol. lxxxi. p. 316, thus accounts for the adoration of light by the early nations of the world: "Can we wonder at the worship of light by those early nations? Carry our thoughts back to their remote times, and our only wonder would be if they did not so adore it. The sun is life as well as light to all that is on the earth — as we of the present day know even better than they of old. Moving in dazzling radiance or brillianthued pageantry through the sky, scanning in calm royalty all that passes below, it seems the very god of this fair world, which lives and blooms but in his smile."

ancient symbolism, a place equally as prominent as that of light.

The same religious sentiment of the ancients, modified, however, in its details, by our better knowledge of divine things, has supplied Freemasonry with a double symbolism — that of *Light* and *Darkness.*

Darkness is the symbol of initiation. It is intended to remind the candidate of his ignorance, which Masonry is to enlighten; of his evil nature, which Masonry is to purify; of the world, in whose obscurity he has been wandering, and from which Masonry is to rescue him.

Light, on the other hand, is the symbol of the autopsy, the sight of the mysteries, the intrusting, the full fruition of masonic truth and knowledge.

Initiation precedes the communication of knowledge in Masonry, as darkness preceded light in the old cosmogonies. Thus, in Genesis, we see that in the beginning "the world was without form, and void, and darkness was on the face of the deep." The Chaldean cosmogony taught that in the beginning "all was darkness and water." The Phœnicians supposed that "the beginning of all things was a wind of black air, and a chaos dark as Erebus."*

* The *Institutes of Menu,* which are the acknowledged code of the Brahmins, inform us that "the world was all darkness, undiscernible, undistinguishable altogether, as in a profound sleep, till the self-existent, invisible God, making it manifest with five elements and other glorious forms, perfectly dispelled the gloom." — Sir WILLIAM JONES, *On the Gods of Greece. Asiatic Researches,* i. 244.

Among the Rosicrucians, who have, by some, been improperly confounded with the Freemasons, the word *lux* was used to signify a knowledge of the philosopher's stone, or the great desideratum of a universal elixir and a universal menstruum. This was their *truth*

But out of all this darkness sprang forth light, at the divine command, and the sublime phrase, "Let there be light," is repeated, in some substantially identical form, in all the ancient histories of creation.

So, too, out of the mysterious darkness of Masonry comes the full blaze of masonic light. One must precede the other, as the evening preceded the morning. "So the evening and the morning were the first day."

This thought is preserved in the great motto of the Order, "*Lux e tenebris*" — Light out of darkness. It is equivalent to this other sentence: Truth out of initiation. *Lux,* or light, is truth; *tenebræ,* or darkness, is initiation.

It is a beautiful and instructive portion of our symbolism, this connection of darkness and light, and well deserves a further investigation.

"Genesis and the cosmogonies," says Portal, "mention the antagonism of light and darkness. The form of this fable varies according to each nation, but the foundation is everywhere the same. Under the symbol of the creation of the world it presents the picture of regeneration and initiation."*

Plutarch says that to die is to be initiated into the greater Mysteries; and the Greek word τελευτᾳν, which signifies *to die,* means also *to be initiated.* But black, which is the symbolic color of darkness, is also the symbol of death. And hence, again, darkness, like death, is the symbol of initiation. It was for this reason that all the ancient initiations were performed at night. The celebration of the Mysteries was always nocturnal. The same custom prevails in Freemasonry, and the explanation is the same. Death and the resurrection were taught

* On Symbolic Colors, p. 23, Inman's translation.

in the Mysteries, as they are in Freemasonry. The
initiation was the lesson of death. The full fruition or
autopsy, the reception of light, was the lesson of
regeneration or resurrection.

Light is, therefore, a fundamental symbol in
Freemasonry. It is, in fact, the first important symbol
that is presented to the neophyte in his instructions, and
contains within itself the very essence of Speculative
Masonry, which is nothing more than the contemplation
of intellectual light or truth.*

* Freemasonry having received the name of *lux,* or light, its disciples
have, very appropriately, been called "the Sons of Light." Thus Burns,
in his celebrated Farewell: —

> "Oft have I met your social band,
>   And spent the cheerful, festive night;
> Oft, honored with supreme command,
>   Presided o'er the *sons of light."*

XXIII.

SYMBOLISM OF THE CORNER-STONE.

W E come next, in a due order of precedence, to the consideration of the symbolism connected with an important ceremony in the ritual of the first degree of Masonry, which refers to the northeast corner of the lodge. In this ceremony the candidate becomes the representative of a spiritual corner-stone. And hence, to thoroughly comprehend the true meaning of the emblematic ceremony, it is essential that we should investigate the symbolism of the *corner-stone.*

The corner-stone,* as the foundation on which the entire building is supposed to rest, is, of course, the most important stone in the whole edifice. It is, at least, so considered by operative masons. It is laid with impressive ceremonies; the assistance of speculative masons is often, and always ought to be, invited, to give dignity to

---

* Thus defined: "The stone which lies at the corner of two walls, and unites them; the principal stone, and especially the stone which forms the corner of the foundation of an edifice."—WEBSTER.

the occasion; and the event is viewed by the workmen as an important era in the construction of the edifice.*

In the rich imagery of Orientalism, the corner-stone is frequently referred to as the appropriate symbol of a chief or prince who is the defence and bulwark of his people, and more particularly in Scripture, as denoting that promised Messiah who was to be the sure prop and support of all who should put their trust in his divine mission.†

To the various properties that are necessary to constitute a true corner-stone, — its firmness and durability, its

* Among the ancients the corner-stone of important edifices was laid with impressive ceremonies. These are well described by Tacitus, in his history of the rebuilding of the Capitol. After detailing the preliminary ceremonies which consisted in a procession of vestals, who with chaplets of flowers encompassed the ground and consecrated it by libations of living water, he adds that, after solemn prayer, Helvidius, to whom the care of rebuilding the Capitol had been committed, "laid his hand upon the fillets that adorned the foundation stone, and also the cords by which it was to be drawn to its place. In that instant the magistrates, the priests, the senators, the Roman knights, and a number of citizens, all acting with one effort and general demonstrations of joy, laid hold of the ropes and dragged the ponderous load to its destined spot. They then threw in ingots of gold and silver, and other metals, which had never been melted in the furnace, but still retained, untouched by human art, their first formation in the bowels of the earth." — *Tac. Hist.*, l. iv. c. 53, Murphy's transl.

† As, for instance, in Psalm 118:22, "The stone which the builders refused is become the head-stone of the corner," which, Clarke says, "seems to have been originally spoken of David, who was at first rejected by the Jewish rulers, but was afterwards chosen by the Lord to be the great ruler of his people in Israel;" and in Isaiah 28:16, "Behold, I lay in Zion, for a foundation, a stone, a tried stone, a precious corner-stone, a sure foundation," which clearly refers to the promised Messiah.

perfect form, and its peculiar position as the connecting link between the walls, —we must attribute the important character that it has assumed in the language of symbolism. Freemasonry, which alone, of all existing institutions, has preserved this ancient and universal language, could not, as it may well be supposed, have neglected to adopt the corner-stone among its most cherished and impressive symbols; and hence it has referred to it many of its most significant lessons of morality and truth.

I have already alluded to that peculiar mode of masonic symbolism by which the speculative mason is supposed to be engaged in the construction of a spiritual temple, in imitation of, or, rather, in reference to, that material one which was erected by his operative predecessors at Jerusalem. Let us again, for a few moments, direct our attention to this important fact, and revert to the connection which originally existed between the operative and speculative divisions of Freemasonry. This is an essential introduction to any inquiry into the symbolism of the corner-stone.

The difference between operative and speculative Masonry is simply this—that while the former was engaged in the construction of a material temple, formed, it is true, of the most magnificent materials which the quarries of Palestine, the mountains of Lebanon, and the golden shores of Ophir could contribute, the latter occupies itself in the erection of a spiritual house,—a house not made with hands,—in which, for stones and cedar, and gold and precious stones, are substituted the virtues of the heart, the pure emotions of the soul, the warm affections gushing forth from the hidden fountains of the spirit, so that the very presence of Jehovah, our Father and our God, shall be enshrined within us as his Shekinah was in the holy of holies of the material temple at Jerusalem.

The Speculative Mason, then, if he rightly comprehends the scope and design of his profession, is occupied, from his very first admission into the order until the close of his labors and his life,—and the true mason's labor ends only with his life,—in the construction, the adornment, and the completion of this spiritual temple of his body. He lays its foundation in a firm belief and an unshaken confidence in the wisdom, power, and goodness of God. This is his first step. Unless his trust is in God, and in him only, he can advance no further than the threshold of initiation. And then he prepares his materials with the gauge and gavel of Truth, raises the walls by the plumbline of Rectitude, squares his work with the square of Virtue, connects the whole with the cement of Brotherly Love, and thus skilfully erects the living edifice of thoughts, and words, and deeds, in accordance with the designs laid down by the Master Architect of the universe in the great Book of Revelation.

The aspirant for masonic light—the Neophyte—on his first entrance within our sacred porch, prepares himself for this consecrated labor of erecting within his own bosom a fit dwelling-place for the Divine Spirit, and thus commences the noble work by becoming himself the corner-stone on which this spiritual edifice is to be erected.

Here, then, is the beginning of the symbolism of the corner-stone; and it is singularly curious to observe how every portion of the archetype has been made to perform its appropriate duty in thoroughly carrying out the emblematic allusions.

As, for example, this symbolic reference of the cornerstone of a material edifice to a mason, when, at his first initiation, he commences the intellectual task of erecting a spiritual temple in his heart, is beautifully sustained in the allusions to all the various parts and qualities which are to be found in a "well-formed, true and trusty" cornerstone.* Its form and substance are both seized by the comprehensive grasp of the symbolic science.

Let us trace this symbolism in its minute details. And, first, as to the form of the corner-stone.

The corner-stone of an edifice must be perfectly square on its surfaces, lest, by a violation of this true geometric figure, the walls to be erected upon it should deviate from the required line of perpendicularity which can alone give strength and proportion to the building.

Perfectly square on its surfaces, it is, in its form and solid contents, a cube. Now, the square and the cube are both important and significant symbols.

The square is an emblem of morality, or the strict performance of every duty.† Among the Greeks, who were a highly poetical and imaginative people, the square was

---

* In the ritual "observed at laying the foundation-stone of public structures," it is said, "The principal architect then presents the working tools to the Grand Master, who applies the plumb, square, and level to the stone, in their proper positions, and pronounces it to be *well-formed, true, and trusty.*"—WEBB'S *Monitor,* p. 120.

† "The square teaches us to regulate our conduct by the principles of morality and virtue."—*Ritual of the E. A. Degree.*— The old York lectures define the square thus: "The square is the theory of universal duty, and consisteth in two right lines, forming an angle of perfect sincerity, or ninety degrees; the longest side is the sum of the lengths of the several duties which we owe to all men. And every man should be agreeable to this square, when perfectly finished."

deemed a figure of perfection, and the ἀνὴρ τετράγωνος – "the square or cubical man," as the words may be translated —was a term used to designate a man of unsullied integrity. Hence one of their most eminent metaphysicians* has said that "he who valiantly sustains the shocks of adverse fortune, demeaning himself uprightly, is truly good and of a square posture, without reproof; and he who would assume such a square posture should often subject himself to the perfectly square test of justice and integrity."

The cube, in the language of symbolism, denotes truth.† Among the pagan mythologists, Mercury, or Hermes, was always represented by a cubical stone, because he was the type of truth,‡ and the same form was adopted by the Israelites in the construction of the tabernacle, which was to be the dwelling-place of divine truth.

And, then, as to its material: This, too, is an essential element of all symbolism. Constructed of a material finer and more polished than that which constitutes the remainder of the edifice, often carved with appropriate devices and fitted for its distinguished purpose by the utmost skill of the sculptor's art, it becomes the symbol of that

---

* Aristotle.

† "The cube is a symbol of truth, of wisdom, and moral perfection. The new Jerusalem, promised in the Apocalypse, is equal in length, breadth, and height. The Mystical city ought to be considered as a new church, where divine wisdom will reign."— OLIVER'S *Landmarks,* ii. p. 357.—And he might have added, where eternal truth will be present.

‡ In the most primitive times, all the gods appear to have been represented by cubical blocks of stone; and Pausanias says that he saw thirty of these stones in the city of Pharæ, which represented as many deities. The first of the kind, it is probable, were dedicated to Hermes, whence they derived their name of "Hermæ."

beauty of holiness with which the Hebrew Psalmist has said that we are to worship Jehovah.*

The ceremony, then, of the north-east corner of the lodge, since it derives all its typical value from this symbolism of the corner-stone, was undoubtedly intended to portray, in this consecrated language, the necessity of integrity and stability of conduct, of truthfulness and uprightness of character, and of purity and holiness of life, which, just at that time and in that place, the candidate is most impressively charged to maintain.

But there is also a symbolism about the position of the corner-stone, which is well worthy of attention. It is familiar to every one,—even to those who are without the pale of initiation,—that the custom of laying the corner-stones of public buildings has always been performed by the masonic order with peculiar and impressive ceremonies, and that this stone is invariably deposited in the north-east corner of the foundation of the intended structure. Now, the question naturally suggests itself, Whence does this ancient and invariable usage derive its origin? Why may not the stone be deposited in any other corner or portion of the edifice, as convenience or necessity may dictate? The custom of placing the foundation-stone in the north-east corner must have been originally adopted for some good and sufficient reason; for we have a right to suppose that it was not an arbitrary selection.† Was it in reference to the ceremony which

---

* "Give unto Jehovah the glory due unto His name; worship Jehovah in the beauty of holiness."—*Psalm* xxix. 2.

† It is at least a singular coincidence that in the Brahminical religion great respect was paid to the north-east point of the heavens. Thus it is said in the Institutes of Menu, "If he has any incurable disease, let him advance in a straight path towards

takes place in the lodge? Or is that in reference to the position of the material stone? No matter which has the precedence in point of time, the principle is the same. The position of the stone in the north-east corner of the building is altogether symbolic, and the symbolism exclusively alludes to certain doctrines which are taught in the speculative science of Masonry.

The interpretation, I conceive, is briefly this: Every Speculative Mason is familiar with the fact that the east, as the source of material light, is a symbol of his own order, which professes to contain within its bosom the pure light of truth. As, in the physical world, the morning of each day is ushered into existence by the reddening dawn of the eastern sky, whence the rising sun dispenses his illuminating and prolific rays to every portion of the visible horizon, warming the whole earth with his embrace of light, and giving new-born life and energy to flower and tree, and beast and man, who, at the magic touch, awake from the sleep of darkness, so in the moral world, when intellectual night was, in the earliest days, brooding over the world, it was from the ancient priesthood living in the east that those lessons of God, of nature, and of humanity first emanated, which, travelling westward, revealed to man his future destiny, and his dependence on a superior power. Thus every new and true doctrine, coming from these "wise men of the east," was, as it were, a new day arising, and dissipating the clouds of intellectual darkness and error. It was a universal opinion among the ancients that the first learning came

the invincible north-east point, feeding on water and air till his mortal frame totally decay, and his soul become united with the Supreme."

from the east; and the often-quoted line of Bishop
Berkeley, that—

"Westward the course of empire takes its way"—

is but the modern utterance of an ancient thought, for it
was always believed that the empire of truth and
knowledge was advancing from the east to the west.

Again: the north, as the point in the horizon which is
most remote from the vivifying rays of the sun when at
his meridian height, has, with equal metaphorical
propriety, been called the place of darkness, and is,
therefore, symbolic of the profane world, which has not
yet been penetrated and illumined by the intellectual
rays of masonic light. All history concurs in recording
the fact that, in the early ages of the world, its northern
portion was enveloped in the most profound moral and
mental darkness. It was from the remotest regions of
Northern Europe that those barbarian hordes "came
down like the wolf on the fold," and devastated the fair
plains of the south, bringing with them a dark curtain of
ignorance, beneath whose heavy folds the nations of the
world lay for centuries overwhelmed. The extreme north
has ever been, physically and intellectually, cold, and
dark, and dreary. Hence, in Masonry, the north has ever
been esteemed the place of darkness; and, in obedience
to this principle, no symbolic light is allowed to illumine
the northern part of the lodge.

The east, then, is, in Masonry, the symbol of the order,
and the north the symbol of the profane world.

Now, the spiritual corner-stone is deposited in the
north-east corner of the lodge, because it is symbolic of
the position of the neophyte, or candidate, who represents

it in his relation to the order and to the world. From the profane world he has just emerged. Some of its imperfections are still upon him; some of its darkness is still about him; he as yet belongs in part to the north. But he is striving for light and truth; the pathway upon which he has entered is directed towards the east. His allegiance, if I may use the word, is divided. He is not altogether a profane, or altogether a mason. If he were wholly in the world, the north would be the place to find him—the north, which is the reign of darkness. If he were wholly in the order,—a Master Mason,—the east would have received him—the east, which is the place of light. But he is neither; he is an Apprentice, with some of the ignorance of the world cleaving to him, and some of the light of the order beaming upon him. And hence this divided allegiance—this double character—this mingling of the departing darkness of the north with the approaching brightness of the east—is well expressed, in our symbolism, by the appropriate position of the spiritual corner-stone in the north-east corner of the lodge. One surface of the stone faces the north, and the other surface faces the east. It is neither wholly in the one part nor wholly in the other, and in so far it is a symbol of initiation not fully developed—that which is incomplete and imperfect, and is, therefore, fitly represented by the recipient of the first degree, at the very moment of his initiation.*

* This symbolism of the double position of the corner-stone has not escaped the attention of the religious symbologists. Etsius, an early commentator, in 1682, referring to the passage in Ephesians 2:20, says, "That is called the corner-stone, or chief corner-stone, which is placed in the extreme angle of a foundation, conjoining and holding together two walls of the pile, meeting

But the strength and durability of the corner-stone are also eminently suggestive of symbolic ideas. To fulfil its design as the foundation and support of the massive building whose erection it precedes, it should be constructed of a material which may outlast all other parts of the edifice, so that when that "eternal ocean whose waves are years" shall have ingulfed all who were present at the construction of the building in the vast vortex of its ever-flowing current; and when generation after generation shall have passed away, and the crumbling stones of the ruined edifice shall begin to attest the power of time and the evanescent nature of all human undertakings, the corner-stone will still remain to tell, by its inscriptions, and its form, and its beauty, to every passer-by, that there once existed in that, perhaps then desolate, spot, a building consecrated to some noble or some sacred purpose by the zeal and liberality of men who now no longer live.

So, too, do this permanence and durability of the corner-stone, in contrast with the decay and ruin of the building in whose foundations it was placed, remind the

from different quarters. And the apostle not only would be understood by this metaphor that Christ is the principal foundation of the whole church, but also that in him, as in a cornerstone, the two peoples, Jews and Gentiles, are conjoined, and so conjoined as to rise together into one edifice, and become one church." And Julius Firmicius, who wrote in the sixteenth century, says that Christ is called the corner-stone, because, being placed in the angle of the two walls, which are the Old and the New Testament, he collects the nations into one fold. "Lapis sanctus, i. e. Christus, aut fidei fundamenta sustentat aut in angulo positus duorum parietum membra æquata moderatione conjungit, i. e., Veteris et Novi Testamenti in unum colligit gentes."—*De Errore profan. Religionum,* chap. xxi.

mason that when this earthly house of his tabernacle shall have passed away, he has within him a sure foundation of eternal life—a corner-stone of immortality—an emanation from that Divine Spirit which pervades all nature and which, therefore, must survive the tomb, and rise, triumphant and eternal, above the decaying dust of death and the grave.*

It is in this way that the student of masonic symbolism is reminded by the corner-stone—by its form, its position, and its permanence—of significant doctrines of duty, and virtue, and religious truth, which it is the great object of Masonry to teach.

But I have said that the material corner-stone is deposited in its appropriate place with solemn rites and ceremonies, for which the order has established a peculiar ritual. These, too, have a beautiful and significant symbolism, the investigation of which will next attract our attention.

And here it may be observed, in passing, that the accompaniment of such an act of consecration to a particular purpose, with solemn rites and ceremonies, claims our respect, from the prestige that it has of all antiquity.

---

* This permanence of position was also attributed to those cubical stones among the Romans which represented the statues of the god Terminus. They could never lawfully be removed from the spot which they occupied. Hence, when Tarquin was about to build the temple of Jupiter, on the Capitoline Hill, all the shrines and statues of the other gods were removed from the eminence to make way for the new edifice, except that of Terminus, represented by a stone. This remained untouched, and was enclosed within the temple, to show, says Dudley, "that the stone, having been a personification of the God Supreme, could not be reasonably required to yield to Jupiter himself in dignity and power."— DUDLEY'S *Naology*, p. 145.

A learned writer on symbolism makes, on this subject, the following judicious remarks, which may be quoted as a sufficient defence of our masonic ceremonies:—

"It has been an opinion, entertained in all past ages, that by the performance of certain acts, things, places, and persons acquire a character which they would not have had without such performances. The reason is plain: certain acts signify firmness of purpose, which, by consigning the object to the intended use, gives it, in the public opinion, an accordant character. This is most especially true of things, places, and persons connected with religion and religious worship. After the performance of certain acts or rites, they are held to be altogether different from what they were before; they acquire a sacred character, and in some instances a character absolutely divine. Such are the effects imagined to be produced by religious dedication."*

The stone, therefore, thus properly constructed, is, when it is to be deposited by the constituted authorities of our order, carefully examined with the necessary implements of operative masonry,—the square, the level, and the plumb,—and declared to be "well-formed, true, and trusty." This is not a vain or unmeaning ceremony. It teaches the mason that his virtues are to be tested by temptation and trial, by suffering and adversity, before they can be pronounced by the Master Builder of souls to be materials worthy of the spiritual building of eternal life, fitted "as living stones, for that house not made with hands, eternal in the heavens." But if he be faithful, and withstand these trials,—if he shall come forth from these

* Dudley's Naology, p. 476.

temptations and sufferings like pure gold from the refiner's fire,—then, indeed, shall he be deemed "well-formed, true, and trusty," and worthy to offer "unto the Lord an offering in righteousness."

In the ceremony of depositing the corner-stone, the sacred elements of masonic consecration are then produced, and the stone is solemnly set apart by pouring corn, wine, and oil upon its surface. Each of these elements has a beautiful significance in our symbolism.

Collectively, they allude to the Corn of Nourishment, the Wine of Refreshment, and the Oil of Joy, which are the promised rewards of a faithful and diligent performance of duty, and often specifically refer to the anticipated success of the undertaking whose incipiency they have consecrated. They are, in fact, types and symbols of all those abundant gifts of Divine Providence for which we are daily called upon to make an offering of our thanks, and which are enumerated by King David, in his catalogue of blessings, as "wine that maketh glad the heart of man, and oil to make his face to shine, and bread which strengtheneth man's heart."

"Wherefore, my brethren," says Harris, "do you carry *corn, wine, and oil* in your processions, but to remind you that in the pilgrimage of human life you are to impart a portion of your bread to feed the hungry, to send a cup of your wine to cheer the sorrowful, and to pour the healing oil of your consolation into the wounds which sickness hath made in the bodies, or affliction rent in the hearts, of your fellow-travellers?"*

But, individually, each of these elements of consecration has also an appropriate significance, which is well worth investigation.

* Masonic Discourses, Dis. iv. p. 81.

Corn, in the language of Scripture, is an emblem of the resurrection, and St. Paul, in that eloquent discourse which is so familiar to all, as a beautiful argument for the great Christian doctrine of a future life, adduces the seed of grain, which, being sown, first dieth, and then quickeneth, as the appropriate type of that corruptible which must put on incorruption, and of that mortal which must assume immortality. But, in Masonry, the sprig of acacia, for reasons purely masonic, has been always adopted as the symbol of immortality, and the ear of corn is appropriated as the symbol of plenty. This is in accordance with the Hebrew derivation of the word, as well as with the usage of all ancient nations. The word *dagan*, דגן, which signifies *corn,* is derived from the verb *dagah,* דגה, *to increase, to multiply,* and in all the ancient religions the horn or vase, filled with fruits and with grain, was the recognized symbol of plenty. Hence, as an element of consecration, corn is intended to remind us of those temporal blessings of life and health, and comfortable support, which we derive from the Giver of all good, and to merit which we should strive, with "clean hands and a pure heart," to erect on the corner-stone of our initiation a spiritual temple, which shall be adorned with the "beauty of holiness."

Wine is a symbol of that inward and abiding comfort with which the heart of the man who faithfully performs his part on the great stage of life is to be refreshed; and as, in the figurative language of the East, Jacob prophetically promises to Judah, as his reward, that he shall wash his garments in wine, and his clothes in the blood of the grape, it seems intended, morally, to remind us of those immortal refreshments which, when the labors of this earthly lodge are forever closed, we shall receive in the celestial lodge above, where the G. A. O. T. U. forever presides.

Oil is a symbol of prosperity, and happiness, and joy. The custom of anointing every thing or person destined for a sacred purpose is of venerable antiquity.* The statues of the heathen deities, as well as the altars on which the sacrifices were offered to them, and the priests who presided over the sacred rites, were always anointed with perfumed ointment, as a consecration of them to the objects of religious worship.

When Jacob set up the stone on which he had slept in his journey to Padan-aram, and where he was blessed with the vision of ascending and descending angels, he anointed it with oil, and thus consecrated it as an altar to God. Such an inunction was, in ancient times, as it still continues to be in many modern countries and contemporary religions, a symbol of the setting apart of the thing or person so anointed and consecrated to a holy purpose.

* "The act of consecration chiefly consisted in the unction, which was a ceremony derived from the most primitive antiquity. The sacred tabernacle, with all the vessels and utensils, as also the altar and the priests themselves, were consecrated in this manner by Moses, at the divine command. It is well known that the Jewish kings and prophets were admitted to their several offices by unction. The patriarch Jacob, by the same right, consecrated the altars which he made use of; in doing which it is more probable that he followed the tradition of his forefathers, than that he was the author of this custom. The same, or something like it, was also continued down to the times of Christianity."—POTTER'S *Archæologia Græca,* b. ii. p. 176.

Hence, then, we are reminded by this last impressive ceremony, that the cultivation of virtue, the practice of duty, the resistance of temptation, the submission to suffering, the devotion to truth, the maintenance of integrity, and all those other graces by which we strive to fit our bodies, as living stones, for the spiritual building of eternal life, must, after all, to make the object effectual and the labor successful, be consecrated by a holy obedience to God's will and a firm reliance on God's providence, which alone constitute the chief corner-stone and sure foundation, on which any man can build with the reasonable hope of a prosperous issue to his work.

It may be noticed, in concluding this topic, that the corner-stone seems to be peculiarly a Jewish symbol. I can find no reference to it in any of the ancient pagan rites, and the EBEN PINAH, the *corner-stone,* which is so frequently mentioned in Scripture as the emblem of an important personage, and most usually, in the Old Testament, of the expected Messiah, appears, in its use in Masonry, to have had, unlike almost every other symbol of the order, an exclusively temple origin.

XXIV.

THE INEFFABLE NAME.

ANOTHER important symbol is the Ineffable Name, with which the series of ritualistic symbols will be concluded.

The Tetragrammaton,* or Ineffable Word,—the Incommunicable Name,—is a symbol—for rightly considered it is nothing more than a symbol—that has more than any other (except, perhaps, the symbols connected with sun-worship), pervaded the rites of antiquity. I know, indeed, of no system of ancient initiation in which it has not some prominent form and place.

But as it was, perhaps, the earliest symbol which was

---

* From the Greek τετρὰς, four, and γράμμα, letter, because it is composed of four Hebrew letters. Brande thus defines it: "Among several ancient nations, the name of the mystic number *four,* which was often symbolized to represent the Deity, whose name was expressed by four letters." But this definition is incorrect. The tetragrammaton is not the name of the number *four,* but the word which expresses the name of God in four letters, and is always applied to the Hebrew word only.

corrupted by the spurious Freemasonry of the pagans, in their secession from the primitive system of the patriarchs and ancient priesthood, it will be most expedient for the thorough discussion of the subject which is proposed in the present paper, that we should begin the investigation with an inquiry into the nature of the symbol among the Israelites.

That name of God, which we, at a venture, pronounce Jehovah,—although whether this is, or is not, the true pronunciation ‚can now never be authoritatively settled,— was ever held by the Jews in the most profound veneration. They derived its origin from the immediate inspiration of the Almighty, who communicated it to Moses as his especial appellation, to be used only by his chosen people; and this communication was made at the Burning Bush, when he said to him, "Thus shalt thou say unto the children of Israel: Jehovah, the God of your fathers, the God of Abraham, the God of Isaac, and the God of Jacob, hath sent me unto you: this [Jehovah] is my name forever, and this is my memorial unto all generations."* And at a subsequent period he still more emphatically declared this to be his peculiar name: "I am *Fehovah;* and I appeared unto Abraham, unto Isaac, and unto Jacob, by the name of *El Shaddai;* but by my name *Fehovah* was I not known unto them."†

It will be perceived that I have not here followed precisely the somewhat unsatisfactory version of King James's Bible, which, by translating or anglicizing one name, and not the other, leaves the whole passage less intelligible

---

* Exod. 3:15. In our common version of the Bible, the word "Lord" is substituted for "Jehovah," whence the true import of the original is lost.

† Exod. 6:2-3.

and impressive than it should be. I have retained the original Hebrew for both names. El Shaddai, "the Almighty One," was the name by which he had been heretofore known to the preceding patriarchs; in its meaning it was analogous to Elohim, who is described in the first chapter of Genesis as creating the world. But his name of Jehovah was now for the first time to be communicated to his people.

Ushered to their notice with all the solemnity and religious consecration of these scenes and events, this name of God became invested among the Israelites with the profoundest veneration and awe. To add to this mysticism, the Cabalists, by the change of a single letter, read the passage, "This is my name forever," or, as it is in the original, *Zeh shemi l'olam,* זה שמי לעלם, as if written *Zeh shemi l'alam,* זה שמי לעלם, that is to say, "This is my name to be concealed."

This interpretation, although founded on a blunder, and in all probability an intentional one, soon became a precept, and has been strictly obeyed to this day.* The

* "The Jews have many superstitious stories and opinions relative to this name, which, because they were forbidden to mention *in vain,* they would not mention *at all.* They substituted *Adonai,* &c., in its room, whenever it occurred to them in reading or speaking, or else simply and emphatically styled it השם, *the Name.* Some of them attributed to a certain repetition of this name the virtue of a charm, and others have had the boldness to assert that our blessed Savior wrought all his miracles (for they do not deny them to be such) by that mystical use of this venerable name. See the *Toldoth Feschu,* an infamously scurrilous life of Jesus, written by a Jew not later than the thirteenth century. On p. 7, edition of Wagenseilius, 1681, is a succinct detail of the manner in which our Savior is said to have entered the temple and obtained possession of the Holy Name. Leusden says that he had offered to give a sum of money to a very poor Jew at Amsterdam, if he would

word *Fehovah* is never pronounced by a pious Jew, who, whenever he meets with it in Scripture, substitutes for it the word *Adonai* or *Lord*—a practice which has been followed by the translators of the common English version of the Bible with almost Jewish scrupulosity, the word "Jehovah" in the original being invariably translated by the word "Lord."* The pronunciation of the word, being thus abandoned, became ultimately lost, as, by the peculiar construction of the Hebrew language, which is entirely without vowels, the letters, being all consonants, can give no possible indication, to one who has not heard it before, of the true pronunciation of any given word.

To make this subject plainer to the reader who is unacquainted with the Hebrew, I will venture to furnish an explanation which will, perhaps, be intelligible.

The Hebrew alphabet consists entirely of consonants, the vowel sounds having always been inserted orally, and never marked in writing until the "vowel points," as they are called, were invented by the Masorites, some six centuries after the Christian era. As the vowel sounds were originally supplied by the reader, while reading, from a

only once deliberately pronounce the name *Fehovah;* but he refused it by saying that he did not dare."—*Horæ Solitariæ,* vol. i. p. 3.— "A Brahmin will not pronounce the name of the Almighty, without drawing down his sleeve and placing it on his mouth with fear and trembling."—MURRAY, *Truth of Revelation,* p. 321.

* The same scrupulous avoidance of a strict translation has been pursued in other versions. For Jehovah, the Septuagint substitutes "Κύριος," the Vulgate "Dominus," and the German "der Herr," all equivalent to "the Lord." The French version uses the title "l'Eternel." But, with a better comprehension of the value of the word, Lowth in his "Isaiah," the Swedenborgian version of the Psalms, and some other recent versions, have restored the original name.

knowledge which he had previously received, by means of oral instruction, of the proper pronunciation of the word, he was necessarily unable to pronounce any word which had never before been uttered in his presence. As we know that *Dr.* is to be pronounced *Doctor,* and *Mr. Mister,* because we have always heard those peculiar combinations of letters thus enunciated, and not because the letters themselves give any such sound; so the Jew knew from instruction and constant practice, and not from the power of the letters, how the consonants in the different words in daily use were to be vocalized. But as the four letters which compose the word *Fehovah,* as we now call it, were never pronounced in his presence, but were made to represent another word, *Adonai,* which was substituted for it, and as the combination of these four consonants would give no more indication for any sort of enunciation than the combinations *Dr.* or *Mr.* give in our language, the Jew, being ignorant of what vocal sounds were to be supplied, was unable to pronounce the word, so that its true pronunciation was in time lost to the masses of the people.

There was one person, however, who, it is said, was in possession of the proper sound of the letters and the true pronunciation of the word. This was the high priest, who, receiving it from his predecessor, preserved the recollection of the sound by pronouncing it three times, once a year, on the day of the atonement, when he entered the holy of holies of the tabernacle or the temple. If the traditions of Masonry on this subject are correct, the kings, after the establishment of the monarchy, must have participated in this privilege; for Solomon is said to have been in possession of the word, and to have communicated it to his two colleagues at the building of the temple.

This is the word which, from the number of its letters, was called the "tetragrammaton," or four-lettered name, and, from its sacred inviolability, the "ineffable" or unutterable name.

The Cabalists and Talmudists have enveloped it in a host of mystical superstitions, most of which are as absurd as they are incredible, but all of them tending to show the great veneration that has always been paid to it.* Thus they say that it is possessed of unlimited powers, and that he who pronounces it shakes heaven and earth, and inspires the very angels with terror and astonishment.

The Rabbins called it "shem hamphorash," that is to say, "the name that is declaratory," and they say that David found it engraved on a stone while digging into the earth.

From the sacredness with which the name was venerated, it was seldom, if ever, written in full, and, consequently, a great many symbols, or hieroglyphics, were invented to express it. One of these was the letter ׳, or Yod, equivalent nearly to the English I, or J, or Y, which was the initial of the word, and it was often inscribed within an equilateral triangle, thus: the triangle itself being a symbol of Deity.

---

* In the Talmudical treatise, *Majan Hachochima,* quoted by Stephelin (Rabbinical Literature, i. p. 131), we are informed that rightly to understand the shem hamphorash is a key to the unlocking of all mysteries. "There," says the treatise, "shalt thou understand the words of men, the words of cattle, the singing of birds, the language of beasts, the barking of dogs, the language of devils, the language of ministering angels, the language of datetrees, the motion of the sea, the unity of hearts, and the murmuring of the tongue—nay, even the thoughts of the reins."

This symbol of the name of God is peculiarly worthy of our attention, since not only is the triangle to be found in many of the ancient religions occupying the same position, but the whole symbol itself is undoubtedly the origin of that hieroglyphic exhibited in the second degree of Masonry, where, the explanation of the symbolism being the same, the form of it, as far as it respects the letter, has only been anglicized by modern innovators. In my own opinion, the letter *G,* which is used in the Fellow Craft's degree, should never have been permitted to intrude into Masonry; it presents an instance of absurd anachronism, which would never have occurred if the original Hebrew symbol had been retained. But being there now, without the possibility of removal, we have only to remember that it is in fact but the symbol of a symbol.*

Widely spread, as I have already said, was this reverence for the name of God; and, consequently, its symbolism, in some peculiar form, is to be found in all the ancient rites.

Thus the Ineffable Name itself, of which we have been discoursing, is said to have been preserved in its true pronunciation by the Essenes, who, in their secret rites, communicated it to each other only in a whisper, and in such form, that while its component parts were known, they were so separated as to make the whole word a mystery.

Among the Egyptians, whose connection with the Hebrews was more immediate than that of any other people, and where, consequently, there was a greater similarity of rites, the same sacred name is said to have been used

---

* The gamma, Γ, or Greek letter G, is said to have been sacred among the Pythagoreans as the initial of Γεωμετρία or Geometry.

as a password, for the purpose of gaining admission to their Mysteries.

In the Brahminic Mysteries of Hindostan the ceremony of initiation was terminated by intrusting the aspirant with the sacred, triliteral name, which was AUM, the three letters of which were symbolic of the creative, preservative, and destructive principles of the Supreme Deity, personified in the three manifestations of Bramah, Siva, and Vishnu. This word was forbidden to be pronounced aloud. It was to be the subject of silent meditation to the pious Hindoo.

In the rites of Persia an ineffable name was also communicated to the candidate after his initiation.* Mithras, the principal divinity in these rites, who took the place of the Hebrew Jehovah, and represented the sun, had this peculiarity in his name—that the numeral value of the letters of which it was composed amounted to precisely 365, the number of days which constitute a revolution of the earth around the sun, or, as they then supposed, of the sun around the earth.

In the Mysteries introduced by Pythagoras into Greece we again find the ineffable name of the Hebrews, obtained doubtless by the Samian Sage during his visit to Babylon.† The symbol adopted by him to express it was,

---

* Vide Oliver, *Hist. Init.* p. 68, note.

† Jamblichus says that Pythagoras passed over from Miletus to Sidon, thinking that he could thence go more easily into Egypt, and that while there he caused himself to be initiated into all the mysteries of Byblos and Tyre, and those which were practised in many parts of Syria, not because he was under the influence of any superstitious motives, but from the fear that if he were not to avail himself of these opportunities, he might neglect to acquire some knowledge in those rites which was worthy of observation. But

however, somewhat different, being ten points distributed in the form of a triangle, each side containing four points, as in the annexed figure.

The apex of the triangle was consequently a single point then followed below two others, then three; and lastly, the base consisted of four. These points were, by the number in each rank, intended, according to the Pythagorean system, to denote respectively the *monad*, or active principle of nature; the *duad*, or passive principle; the *triad*, or world emanating from their union; and the *quaterniad*, or intellectual science; the whole number of points amounting to ten, the symbol of perfection and consummation. This figure was called by Pythagoras the *tetractys*—a word equivalent in signification to the *tetragrammaton;* and it was deemed so sacred that on it the oath of secrecy and fidelity was administered to the aspirants in the Pythagorean rites.*

Among the Scandinavians, as among the Jewish Cabalists, the Supreme God who was made known in their mysteries had twelve names, of which the principal and most sacred one was *Alfader,* the Universal Father.

as these mysteries were originally received by the Phœnicians from Egypt, he passed over into that country, where he remained twenty-two years, occupying himself in the study of geometry, astronomy, and all the initiations of the gods (πάσας θεῶν τελετάς), until he was carried a captive into Babylon by the soldiers of Cambyses, and that twelve years afterwards he returned to Samos at the age of sixty years.—*Vit. Pythag.* cap. iii., iv.

* "The sacred words were intrusted to him, of which the Ineffable Tetractys, or name of God, was the chief."—OLIVER, *Hist. Init.* p. 109.

Among the Druids, the sacred name of God was *Hu**—a name which, although it is supposed, by Bryant, to have been intended by them for Noah, will be recognized as one of the modifications of the Hebrew tetragrammaton. It is, in fact, the masculine pronoun in Hebrew, and may be considered as the symbolization of the male or generative principle in nature—a sort of modification of the system of Phallic worship.

This sacred name among the Druids reminds me of what is the latest, and undoubtedly the most philosophical, speculation on the true meaning, as well as pronunciation, of the ineffable tetragrammaton. It is from the ingenious mind of the celebrated Lanci; and I have already, in another work, given it to the public as I received it from his pupil, and my friend, Mr. Gliddon, the distinguished archæologist. But the results are too curious to be omitted whenever the tetragrammaton is discussed.

Elsewhere I have very fully alluded to the prevailing sentiment among the ancients, that the Supreme Deity was bisexual, or hermaphrodite, including in the essence of his being the male and female principles, the generative and prolific powers of nature. This was the universal doctrine in all the ancient religions, and was very naturally developed in the symbol of the *phallus* and *cteis* among the Greeks, and in the corresponding one of the *lingam*

---

* "Hu, the mighty, whose history as a patriarch is precisely that of Noah, was promoted to the rank of the principal demongod among the Britons; and, as his chariot was composed of rays of the sun, it may be presumed that he was worshipped in conjunction with that luminary, and to the same superstition we may refer what is said of his light and swift course."—DAVIES, *Mythol. and Rites of the Brit. Druids,* p. 110.

and *yoni* among the Orientalists; from which symbols the masonic *point within a circle* is a legitimate derivation. They all taught that God, the Creator, was both male and female.

Now, this theory is undoubtedly unobjectionable on the score of orthodoxy, if we view it in the spiritual sense, in which its first propounders must necessarily have intended it to be presented to the mind, and not in the gross, sensual meaning in which it was subsequently received. For, taking the word *sex,* not in its ordinary and colloquial signification, as denoting the indication of a particular physical organization, but in that purely philosophical one which alone can be used in such a connection, and which simply signifies the mere manifestation of a power, it is not to be denied that the Supreme Being must possess in himself, and in himself alone, both a generative and a prolific power. This idea, which was so extensively prevalent among all the nations of antiquity,* has also been traced in the tetragrammaton, or name of Jehovah, with singular ingenuity, by Lanci; and, what is almost equally as interesting, he has, by this discovery, been enabled to demonstrate what was, in all probability, the true pronunciation of the word.

In giving the details of this philological discovery, I will endeavor to make it as comprehensible as it can be

---

* "All the male gods (of the ancients) may be reduced to one, the generative energy; and all the female to one, the prolific principle. In fact, they may all be included in the one great Hermaphrodite, the ἀρρενοθηλυς, who combines irr his nature all the elements of production, and who continues to support the vast creation which originally proceeded from his will." RUSSELL'S *Connection,* i. p.402.

made to those who are not critically acquainted with the construction of the Hebrew language; those who are will at once appreciate its peculiar character, and will excuse the explanatory details, of course unnecessary to them.

The ineffable name, the tetragrammaton, the shem hamphorash,—for it is known by all these appellations,—consists of four letters, *yod, heh, vau,* and *heh,* forming the word יהוה. This word, of course, in accordance with the genius of the Hebrew language, is read, as we would say, backward, or from right to left, beginning with *yod* [י], and ending with *heh* [ה].

Of these letters, the first, *yod* [י], is equivalent to the English *i* pronounced as *e* in the word *machine.*

The second and fourth letter, *heh* [ה], is an aspirate, and has here the sound of the English *h.*

And the third letter, *vau* [ו], has the sound of open *o.*

Now, reading these four letters, י, or I, ה, or H, ו, or O, and ה, or H, as the Hebrew requires, from right to left, we have the word יהוה, equivalent in English to IH-OH, which is really as near to the pronunciation as we can well come, notwithstanding it forms neither of the seven ways in which the word is said to have been pronounced, at different times, by the patriarchs.*

But, thus pronounced, the word gives us no meaning, for there is no such word in Hebrew as *ihoh;* and, as all the Hebrew names were significative of something, it is but fair to conclude that this was not the original pronunciation,

---

* It is a tradition that it was pronounced in the following seven different ways by the patriarchs, from Methuselah to David, viz.: *Fuha, Feva, Fova, Fevo, Feveh, Fohe,* and *Fehovah.* In all these words the *j* is to be pronounced as *y,* the *a* as *ah,* the *e* as *a,* and the *v* as *w.*

and that we must look for another which will give a meaning to the word. Now, Lanci proceeds to the discovery of this true pronunciation, as follows:—

In the Cabala, a hidden meaning is often deduced from a word by transposing or reversing its letters, and it was in this way that the Cabalists concealed many of their mysteries.

Now, to reverse a word in English is to read its letters from *right to left,* because our normal mode of reading is from *left to right.* But in Hebrew the contrary rule takes place, for there the normal mode of reading is from *right to left;* and therefore, to reverse the reading of a word, is to read it from *left to right.*

Lanci applied this cabalistic mode to the tetragrammaton, when he found that IH-OH, being read reversely, makes the word HO-HI.*

But in Hebrew, *ho* is the masculine pronoun, equivalent to the English *he;* and *hi* is the feminine pronoun, equivalent to *she;* and therefore the word HO-HI, literally translated, is equivalent to the English compound HESHE; that is to say, the Ineffable Name of God in Hebrew, being read cabalistically, includes within itself the male and female principle, the generative and prolific energy of creation; and here we have, again, the widelyspread symbolism of the phallus and the cteis, the lingam and the yoni, or their equivalent, the point within a circle, and another pregnant proof of the connection between Freemasonry and the ancient Mysteries.

And here, perhaps, we may begin to find some meaning

---

* The *i* is to be pronounced as *e,* and the whole word as if spelled in English *ho-he.*

for the hitherto incomprehensible passage in Genesis (1:27): "So God created man *in his own image; in the image of God* created he him; *male and female* created he them." They could not have been "in the image" of IHOH, if they had not been "male and female."

The Cabalists have exhausted their ingenuity and imagination in speculations on this sacred name, and some of their fancies are really sufficiently interesting to repay an investigation. Sufficient, however, has been here said to account for the important position that it occupies in the masonic system, and to enable us to appreciate the symbols by which it has been represented.

The great reverence, or indeed the superstitious veneration, entertained by the ancients for the name of the Supreme Being, led them to express it rather in symbols or hieroglyphics than in any word at length.

We know, for instance, from the recent researches of the archæologists, that in all the documents of the ancient Egyptians, written in the demotic or common character of the country, the names of the gods were invariably denoted by symbols; and I have already alluded to the different modes by which the Jews expressed the tetragrammaton. A similar practice prevailed among the other nations of antiquity. Freemasonry has adopted the same expedient, and the Grand Architect of the Universe, whom it is the usage, even in ordinary writing, to designate by the initials G∴A∴O∴T∴U∴, is accordingly presented to us in a variety of symbols, three of which particularly require attention. These are the letter *G,* the equilateral triangle, and the All-Seeing Eye.

Of the letter *G* I have already spoken. A letter of the

English alphabet can scarcely be considered an
appropriate symbol of an institution which dates its
organization and refers its primitive history to a period
long anterior to the origin of that language. Such a
symbol is deficient in the two elements of antiquity and
universality which should characterize every masonic
symbol. There can, therefore, be no doubt that, in its
present form, it is a corruption of the old Hebrew
symbol, the letter *yod,* by which the sacred name was
often expressed. This letter is the initial of the word
Fehovah, or *Ihoh,* as I have already stated, and is
constantly to be met with in Hebrew writings as the
symbol or abbreviature of *Fehovah,* which word, it will
be remembered, is never written at length. But because
G is, in like manner, the initial of *God,* the equivalent of
Fehovah, this letter has been incorrectly, and, I cannot
refrain from again saying, most injudiciously, selected to
supply, in modern lodges, the place of the Hebrew
symbol.

Having, then, the same meaning and force as the
Hebrew *yod,* the letter *G* must be considered, like its
prototype, as the symbol of the life-giving and life-
sustaining power of God, as manifested in the meaning
of the word Jehovah, or Ihoh, the generative and prolific
energy of the Creator.

The *All-Seeing Eye* is another, and a still more
important, symbol of the same great Being. Both the
Hebrews and the Egyptians appear to have derived its
use from that natural inclination of figurative minds to
select an organ as the symbol of the function which it is
intended peculiarly to discharge. Thus the foot was
often adopted as the symbol of swiftness, the arm of
strength, and the hand of fidelity. On the same principle,

the open eye was selected as the symbol of watchfulness, and the eye of God as the symbol of divine watchfulness and care of the universe. The use of the symbol in this sense is repeatedly to be found in the Hebrew writers. Thus the Psalmist says (Ps. 34:15), "The eyes of the Lord are upon the righteous, and his ears are open to their cry," which explains a subsequent passage (Ps. 121:4), in which it is said, "Behold, he that keepeth Israel shall neither slumber nor sleep." *

On the same principle, the Egyptians represented Osiris, their chief deity, by the symbol of an open eye, and placed this hieroglyphic of him in all their temples. His symbolic name, on the monuments, was represented by the eye accompanying a throne, to which was sometimes added an abbreviated figure of the god, and sometimes what has been called a hatchet, but which, I consider, may as correctly be supposed to be a representation of a square.

The All-Seeing Eye may, then, be considered as a

---

* In the apocryphal "Book of the Conversation of God with Moses on Mount Sinai," translated by the Rev. W. Cureton from an Arabic MS. of the fifteenth century, and published by the Philobiblon Society of London, the idea of the eternal watchfulness of God is thus beautifully allegorized:—

"Then Moses said to the Lord, O Lord, dost thou sleep or not? The Lord said unto Moses, I never sleep: but take a cup and fill it with water. Then Moses took a cup and filled it with water, as the Lord commanded him. Then the Lord cast into'the heart of Moses the breath of slumber; so he slept, and the cup fell from his hand, and the water which was therein was spilled. Then Moses awoke from his sleep. Then said God to Moses, I declare by my power, and by my glory, that if I were to withdraw my providence from the heavens and the earth for no longer a space of time than thou hast slept, they would at once fall to ruin and confusion, like as the cup fell from thy hand."

symbol of God manifested in his omnipresence—his guardian and preserving character—to which Solomon alludes in the Book of Proverbs (15:3), when he says, "The eyes of Jehovah are in every place, beholding (or as it might be more faithfully translated, watching) the evil and the good." It is a symbol of the Omnipresent Deity.

The *triangle* is another symbol which is entitled to our consideration. There is, in fact, no other symbol which is more various in its application or more generally diffused throughout the whole system of both the Spurious and the Pure Freemasonry.

The equilateral triangle appears to have been adopted by nearly all the nations of antiquity as a symbol of the Deity.

Among the Hebrews, it has already been stated that this figure, with a *yod* in the centre, was used to represent the tetragrammaton, or ineffable name of God.

The Egyptians considered the equilateral triangle as the most perfect of figures, and a representative of the great principle of animated existence, each of its sides referring to one of the three departments of creation— the animal, the vegetable, and the mineral.

The symbol of universal nature among the Egyptians was the right-angled triangle, of which the perpendicular side represented Osiris, or the male principle; the base, Isis, or the female principle; and the hypothenuse, their offspring, Horus, or the world emanating from the union of both principles.

All this, of course, is nothing more nor less than the phallus and cteis, or lingam and yoni, under a different form.

The symbol of the right-angled triangle was afterwards adopted by Pythagoras when he visited the banks of the Nile; and the discovery which he is said to have made in relation to the properties of this figure, but which he really learned from the Egyptian priests, is commemorated in Masonry by the introduction of the forty-seventh problem of Euclid's First Book among the symbols of the third degree. Here the same mystical application is supplied as in the Egyptian figure, namely, that the union of the male and female, or active and passive principles of nature, has produced the world. For the geometrical proposition being that the squares of the perpendicular and base are equal to the square of the hypothenuse, they may be said to produce it in the same way as Osiris and Isis are equal to, or produce, the world.

Thus the perpendicular—Osiris, or the active, male principle—being represented by a line whose measurement is 3; and the base—Isis, or the passive, female principle—by a line whose measurement is 4; then their union, or the addition of the squares of these numbers, will produce a square whose root will be the hypothenuse, or a line whose measurement must be 5. For the square of 3 is 9, and the square of 4 is 16, and the square of 5 is 25; but 9 added to 16 is equal to 25; and thus, out of the addition, or coming together, of the squares of the perpendicular and base, arises the square of the hypothenuse, just as, out of the coming together, in the Egyptian system, of the active and passive principles, arises, or is generated, the world.

In the mediæval history of the Christian church, the

great ignorance of the people, and their inclination to a sort of materialism, led them to abandon the symbolic representations of the Deity, and to depict the Father with the form and lineaments of an aged man, many of which irreverent paintings, as far back as the twelfth century, are to be found in the religious books and edifices of Europe.* But, after the period of the renaissance, a better spirit and a purer taste began to pervade the artists of the church, and thenceforth the Supreme Being was represented only by his name—the tetragrammaton— inscribed within an equilateral triangle, and placed within a circle of rays. Didron, in his invaluable work on Christian Iconography, gives one of these symbols, which was carved on wood in the seventeenth century, of which I annex a copy.

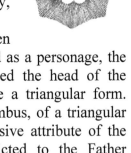

But even in the earliest ages, when the Deity was painted or sculptured as a personage, the nimbus, or glory, which surrounded the head of the Father, was often made to assume a triangular form. Didron says on this subject, "A nimbus, of a triangular form, is thus seen to be the exclusive attribute of the Deity, and most frequently restricted to the Father Eternal. The other persons of the trinity sometimes wear the triangle, but only in representations of the trinity, and because the Father is with them. Still, even then, beside the Father,

---

* I have in my possession a rare copy of the Vulgate Bible, in black letter, printed at Lyons, in 1522. The frontispiece is a coarsely executed wood cut, divided into six compartments, and representing the six days of the creation. The Father is, in each compartment, pictured as an aged man engaged in his creative task.

who has a triangle, the Son and the Holy Ghost are often drawn with a circular nimbus only."*

The triangle has, in all ages and in all religions, been deemed a symbol of Deity.

The Egyptians, the Greeks, and the other nations of antiquity, considered this figure, with its three sides, as a symbol of the creative energy displayed in the active and passive, or male and female, principles, and their product, the world; the Christians referred it to their dogma of the trinity as a manifestation of the Supreme God; and the Jews and the primitive masons to the three periods of existence included in the signification of the tetragrammaton—the past, the present, and the future.

In the higher degrees of Masonry, the triangle is the most important of all symbols, and most generally assumes the name of the *Delta,* in allusion to the fourth letter of the Greek alphabet, which is of the same form and bears that appellation.

The Delta, or mystical triangle, is generally surrounded by a circle of rays, called a "glory." When this glory is distinct from the figure, and surrounds it in the form of a circle (as in the example just given from Didron), it is then an emblem of God's eternal glory. When, as is most usual in the masonic symbol, the rays emanate from the centre of the triangle, and, as it were, enshroud it in their brilliancy, it is symbolic of the Divine Light. The perverted ideas of the pagans referred these rays of light to their Sun-god and their Sabian worship.

But the true masonic idea of this glory is, that it symbolizes that Eternal Light of Wisdom which surrounds the

* Christian Iconography, Millington's trans., vol. i. p. 59.

Supreme Architect as with a sea of glory, and from him, as a common centre, emanates to the universe of his creation, and to which the prophet Ezekiel alludes in his eloquent description of Jehovah: "And I saw as the color of amber, as the appearance of fire round about within it, from the appearance of his loins even upward, and from his loins even downward, I saw, as it were, the appearance of fire, and it had brightness round about." (Chap. 1, ver. 27.)

Dante has also beautifully described this circumfused light of Deity:—

> "There is in heaven a light whose goodly shine
> Makes the Creator visible to all
> Created, that in seeing him, alone
> Have peace; and in a circle spreads so far,
> That the circumference were too loose a zone
> To girdle in the sun."

On a recapitulation, then, of the views that have been advanced in relation to these three symbols of the Deity which are to be found in the masonic system, we may say that each one expresses a different attribute.

The letter *G* is the symbol of the self-existent Jehovah.

The *All-Seeing Eye* is the symbol of the omnipresent God.

The *triangle** is the symbol of the Supreme Architect

---

* The triangle, or delta, is the symbol of Deity for this reason. In geometry a single line cannot represent a perfect figure; neither can two lines; three lines, however, constitute the triangle or first perfect and demonstrable figure. Hence this figure symbolizes the Eternal God, infinitely perfect in his nature. But the triangle properly refers to God only in his quality as an Eternal Being, its three sides representing the Past, the Present, and the Future. Some Christian symbologists have made the three sides represent the Father, Son, and Holy Ghost; but they evidently thereby the Universe—the Creator; and when surrounded by rays of glory, it becomes a symbol of the Architect and Bestower of Light.

And now, after all, is there not in this whole prevalence of the name of God, in so many different symbols, throughout the masonic system, something more than a mere evidence of the religious proclivities of the institution? Is there not behind this a more profound symbolism, which constitutes, in fact, the very essence of Freemasonry? "The names of God," said a learned theologian at the beginning of this century, "were intended to communicate the knowledge of God himself. By these, men were enabled to receive some scanty ideas of his essential majesty, goodness, and power, and to know both whom we are to believe, and what we are to believe of him."

And this train of thought is eminently applicable to the admission of the name into the system of Masonry. With us, the name of God, however expressed, is a symbol of DIVINE TRUTH, which it should be the incessant labor of a Mason to seek.

destroy the divine unity, making a trinity of Gods in the unity of a Godhead. The Gnostic trinity of Manes consisted of one God and two principles, one of good and the other of evil. The Indian trinity, symbolized also by the triangle, consisted of Brahma, Siva, and Vishnu, the Creator, Preserver, and Destroyer, represented by Earth, Water, and Air. This symbolism of the Eternal God by the triangle is the reason why a trinitarian scheme has been so prevalent in all religions—the three sides naturally suggesting the three divisions of the Godhead. But in the Pagan and Oriental religions this trinity was nothing else but a tritheism.

XXV.

THE LEGENDS OF FREEMASONRY.

THE compound character of a speculative science and an operative art, which the masonic institution assumed at the building of King Solomon's temple, in consequence of the union, at that era, of the Pure Freemasonry of the Noachidæ* with the Spurious Freemasonry of the Tyrian workmen, has supplied it with two distinct kinds of symbols—the *mythical,* or *legendary,* and the *material;* but these are so thoroughly

---

* Noachidæ, or Noachites, the descendants of Noah. This patriarch having alone preserved the true name and worship of God amid a race of impious idolaters, the Freemasons claim to be his descendants, because they preserve that pure religion which distinguished this second father of the human race from the rest of the world. (See the author's *Lexicon of Freemasonry.)* The Tyrian workmen at the temple of Solomon were the descendants of that other division of the race who fell off, at Shinar, from the true worship, and repudiated the principles of Noah. The Tyrians, however, like many other ancient mystics, had recovered some portion of the lost light, and the complete repossession was finally achieved by their union with the Jewish masons, who were Noachidæ.

united in object and design, that it is impossible to appreciate the one without an investigation of the other.

Thus, by way of illustration, it may be observed, that the temple itself has been adopted as a material symbol of the world (as I have already shown in former articles), while the legendary history of the fate of its builder is a mythical symbol of man's destiny in the world. Whatever is visible or tangible to the senses in our types and emblems—such as the implements of operative masonry, the furniture and ornaments of a lodge, or the ladder of seven steps—is a *material symbol;* while whatever derives its existence from tradition, and presents itself in the form of an allegory or legend, is a *mythical symbol.* Hiram the Builder, therefore, and all that refers to the legend of his connection with the temple, and his fate,—such as the sprig of acacia, the hill near Mount Moriah, and the lost word,—are to be considered as belonging to the class of mythical or legendary symbols.

And this division is not arbitrary, but depends on the nature of the types and the aspect in which they present themselves to our view.

Thus the sprig of acacia, although it is material, visible, and tangible, is, nevertheless, not to be treated as a material symbol; for, as it derives all its significance from its intimate connection with the legend of Hiram Abif, which is a mythical symbol, it cannot, without a violent and inexpedient disruption, be separated from the same class. For the same reason, the small hill near Mount Moriah, the search of the twelve Fellow Crafts, and the whole train of circumstances connected with the lost word, are to be viewed simply as mythical or legendary, and not as material symbols.

These legends of Freemasonry constitute a considerable and a very important part of its ritual. Without them, the most valuable portions of the masonic as a scientific system would cease to exist. It is, in fact, in the traditions and legends of Freemasonry, more, even, than in its material symbols, that we are to find the deep religious instruction which the institution is intended to inculcate. It must be remembered that Freemasonry has been defined to be "a system of morality, veiled in allegory and illustrated by symbols." Symbols, then, alone, do not constitute the whole of the system: allegory comes in for its share; and this allegory, which veils the divine truths of masonry, is presented to the neophyte in the various legends which have been traditionally preserved in the order.

The close connection, at least in design and method of execution, between the institution of Freemasonry and the ancient Mysteries, which were largely imbued with the mythical character of the ancient religions, led, undoubtedly, to the introduction of the same mythical character into the masonic system.

So general, indeed, was the diffusion of the myth or legend among the philosophical, historical, and religious systems of antiquity, that Heyne remarks, on this subject, that all the history and philosophy of the ancients proceeded from myths.*

The word *myth,* from the Greek μῦθος, *a story,* in its

---

* "A mythis omnis priscorum hominum tum historia tum philosophia procedit."—*Ad Apollod. Athen. Biblioth. not.* f. p. 3.— And Faber says, "Allegory and personification were peculiarly agreeable to the genius of antiquity; and the simplicity of truth was continually sacrificed at the shrine of poetical decoration."— *On the Cabiri.*

original acceptation, signified simply a statement or narrative of an event, without any necessary implication of truth or falsehood; but, as the word is now used, it conveys the idea of a personal narrative of remote date, which, although not necessarily untrue, is certified only by the internal evidence of the tradition itself.*

Creuzer, in his "Symbolik," says that myths and symbols were derived, on the one hand, from the helpless condition and the poor and scanty beginnings of religious knowledge among the ancient peoples, and on the other, from the benevolent designs of the priests educated in the East, or of Eastern origin, to form them to a purer and higher knowledge.

But the observations of that profoundly philosophical historian, Mr. Grote, give so correct a view of the probable origin of this universality of the mythical element in all the ancient religions, and are, withal, so appropriate to the subject of masonic legends which I am now about to discuss, that I cannot justly refrain from a liberal quotation of his remarks.

"The allegorical interpretation of the myths," he says, "has been, by several learned investigators, especially by Creuzer, connected with the hypothesis of an ancient and highly-instructed body of priests, having their origin either in Egypt or the East, and communicating to the rude and barbarous Greeks religious, physical, and historical knowledge, under the veil of symbols. At a time (we are told) when language was yet in its infancy, visible

* See Grote, History of Greece, vol. i. ch. xvi. p. 479, whence this definition has been substantially derived. The definitions of Creuzer, Hermann, Buttmann, Heyne, Welcker, Voss, and Müller are none of them better, and some of them not as good.

symbols were the most vivid means of acting upon the minds of ignorant hearers. The next step was to pass to symbolical language and expressions; for a plain and literal exposition, even if understood at all, would at least have been listened to with indifference, as not corresponding with any mental demand. In such allegorizing way, then, the early priests set forth their doctrines respecting God, nature, and humanity, — a refined monotheism and theological philosophy, — and to this purpose the earliest myths were turned. But another class of myths, more popular and more captivating, grew up under the hands of the poets — myths purely epical, and descriptive of real or supposed past events. The allegorical myths, being taken up by the poets, insensibly became confounded in the same category with the purely narrative myths; the matter symbolized was no longer thought of, while the symbolizing words came to be construed in their own literal meaning, and the basis of the early allegory, thus lost among the general public, was only preserved as a secret among various religious fraternities, composed of members allied together by initiation in certain mystical ceremonies, and administered by hereditary families of presiding priests.

"In the Orphic and Bacchic sects, in the Eleusinian and Samothracian Mysteries, was thus treasured up the secret doctrine of the old theological and philosophical myths, which had once constituted the primitive legendary stock of Greece in the hands of the original priesthood and in the ages anterior to Homer. Persons who had gone through the preliminary ceremonies of initiation were permitted at length to hear, though under strict obligation of secrecy, this ancient religion and cosmogonic doctrine, revealing the destination of man and the certainty of posthumous rewards and punishments, all disengaged from the corruptions of poets, as well as from the symbols and allegories under which they still remained buried in the eyes of the vulgar. The Mysteries of Greece were thus traced up to the earliest ages, and represented as the only faithful depositaries of that purer theology and physics which had been originally comm-unicated, though under the unavoidable inconvenience of a symbolical expression, by an enlightened priesthood, coming from abroad, to the then rude barbarians of the country."*

* Hist. of Greece, vol. i. ch. xvi. p. 579. The idea of the existence of an enlightened people, who lived at a remote era, and came from the East, was a very prevalent notion among the ancient traditions. It is corroborative of this that the Hebrew word קֶדֶם, *kedem,* signifies, in respect to place, *the east,* and, in respect to time, *olden time, ancient days.* The phrase in Isaiah xix. II, which reads, "I am the son of the wise, the son of ancient kings," might just as well have been translated "the son of kings of the East." In a note to the passage Ezek. 43:2, "the glory of the God of Israel came from the way of the East," Adam Clarke says, "All knowledge, all religion, and all arts and sciences, have travelled, according to the *course of the sun,* FROM EAST TO WEST!" Bazot tells us (in his Manuel du Franc-maçon, p. 154) that "the veneration which masons entertain for the east confirms an opinion previously announced, that the religious system of Masonry came from the east, and has reference to the *primitive religion,* whose first corruption was the worship of the sun." And lastly, the masonic reader will recollect the answer given in the Leland MS. to the question respecting the origin of Masonry, namely, "It did begin" (I modernize the orthography) "with the first men in the east, which were before the first men of the west; and coming westerly, it hath brought herewith all comforts to the wild and comfortless." Locke's commentary on this answer may conclude this note: "It should seem, by this, that masons believe there were men in the east before Adam, who is called the 'first man of the west,' and that arts and sciences began in the east. Some

In this long but interesting extract we find not only a philosophical account of the origin and design of the ancient myths, but a fair synopsis of all that can be taught in relation to the symbolical construction of Freemasonry, as one of the depositaries of a mythical theology.

The myths of Masonry, at first perhaps nothing more than the simple traditions of the Pure Freemasonry of the antediluvian system, having been corrupted and misunderstood in the separation of the races, were again purified, and adapted to the inculcation of truth, at first by the disciples of the Spurious Freemasonry, and then, more fully and perfectly, in the development of that system which we now practise. And if there be any leaven of error still remaining in the interpretation of our masonic myths, we must seek to disengage them from the corruptions with which they have been invested by ignorance and by misinterpretation. We must give to them their true significance, and trace them back to those ancient doctrines and faith whence the ideas which they are intended to embody were derived.

The myths or legends which present themselves to our attention in the course of a complete study of the symbolic system of Freemasonry may be considered as divided into three classes:—

authors, of great note for learning, have been of the same opinion; and it is certain that Europe and Africa (which, in respect to Asia, may be called western countries) were wild and savage long after arts and politeness of manners were in great perfection in China and the Indies." The Talmudists make the same allusions to the superiority of the east. Thus, Rabbi Bechai says, "Adam was created with his face towards the east that he might behold the light and the rising sun, whence the east was to him the anterior part of the world."

1. The historical myth.
2. The philosophical myth.
3. The mythical history.

And these three classes may be defined as follows:—

1. The myth may be engaged in the transmission of a narrative of early deeds and events, having a foundation in truth, which truth, however, has been greatly distorted and perverted by the omission or introduction of circumstances and personages, and then it constitutes the *historical myth.*

2. Or it may have been invented and adopted as the medium of enunciating a particular thought, or of inculcating a certain doctrine, when it becomes a *philosophical myth.*

3. Or, lastly, the truthful elements of actual history may greatly predominate over the fictitious and invented materials of the myth, and the narrative may be, in the main, made up of facts, with a slight coloring of imagination, when it forms a *mythical history.* *

These form the three divisions of the legend or myth (for I am not disposed, on the present occasion, like some of the German mythological writers, to make a distinction between the two words†); and to one of these three

* Strauss makes a division of myths into historical, philosophical, and poetical.—*Leben Fesu.*—His poetical myth agrees with my first division, his philosophical with my second, and his historical with my third. But I object to the word *poetical,* as a distinctive term, because all myths have their foundation in the poetic idea.

† Ulmann, for instance, distinguishes between a myth and a legend—the former containing, to a great degree, fiction combined with history, and the latter having but a few faint echoes of mythical history.

divisions we must appropriate every legend which belongs to the mythical symbolism of Freemasonry.

These masonic myths partake, in their general character, of the nature of the myths which constituted the foundation of the ancient religions, as they have just been described in the language of Mr. Grote. Of these latter myths, Müller* says that "their source is to be found, for the most part, in oral tradition," and that the real and the ideal—that is to say, the facts of history and the inventions of imagination—concurred, by their union and reciprocal fusion, in producing the myth.

Those are the very principles that govern the construction of the masonic myths or legends. These, too, owe their existence entirely to oral tradition, and are made up, as I have just observed, of a due admixture of the real and the ideal—the true and the false—the facts of history and the inventions of allegory.

Dr. Oliver remarks that "the first series of historical facts, after the fall of man, must necessarily have been traditional, and transmitted from father to son by oral communication."† The same system, adopted in all the Mysteries, has been continued in the masonic institution; and all the esoteric instructions contained in the legends of Freemasonry are forbidden to be written, and can be communicated only in the oral intercourse of Freemasons with each other.‡

* In his "Prolegomena zu einer wissenshaftlichen Mythologie," cap. iv. This valuable work was translated in 1844, by Mr. John Leitch.

† Historical Landmarks, i. 53.

‡ See an article, by the author, on "The Unwritten Landmarks of Freemasonry," in the first volume of the Masonic Miscellany, in which this subject is treated at considerable length.

De Wette, in his Criticism on the Mosaic History, lays down the test by which a myth is to be distinguished from a strictly historical narrative, as follows, namely: that the myth must owe its origin to the intention of the inventor not to satisfy the natural thirst for historical truth by a simple narration of facts, but rather to delight or touch the feelings, or to illustrate some philosophical or religious truth.

This definition precisely fits the character of the myths of Masonry. Take, for instance, the legend of the master's degree, or the myth of Hiram Abif. As "a simple narration of facts," it is of no great value—certainly not of value commensurate with the labor that has been engaged in its transmission. Its invention—by which is meant, not the invention or imagination of all the incidents of which it is composed, for there are abundant materials of the true and real in its details, but its invention or composition in the form of a myth by the addition of some features, the suppression of others, and the general arrangement of the whole—was not intended to add a single item to the great mass of history, but altogether, as De Wette says, "to illustrate a philosophical or religious truth," which truth, it is hardly necessary for me to say, is the doctrine of the immortality of the soul.

It must be evident, from all that has been said respecting the analogy in origin and design between the masonic and the ancient religious myths, that no one acquainted with the true science of this subject can, for a moment, contend that all the legends and traditions of the order are, to the very letter, historical facts. All that can be claimed for them is, that in some there is simply a substratum of history, the edifice constructed on this foundation being purely inventive, to serve as a medium for inculcating some religious truth; in others, nothing more than an idea to which the legend or myth is indebted for its existence, and of which it is, as a symbol, the exponent; and in others, again, a great deal of truthful narrative, more or less intermixed with fiction, but the historical always predominating.

Thus there is a legend, contained in some of our old records, which states that Euclid was a distinguished Mason, and that he introduced Masonry among the Egyptians.* Now, it is not at all necessary to the

* As a matter of some interest to the curious reader, I insert the legend as published in the Gentleman's Magazine of June, 1815, from, it is said, a parchment roll supposed to have been written early in the seventeenth century, and which, if so, was in all probability copied from one of an older date:—

"Moreover, when Abraham and Sara his wife went into Egipt, there he taught the Seaven Scyences to the Egiptians; and he had a worthy Scoller that height Ewclyde, and he learned right well, and was a master of all the vij Sciences liberall. And in his dayes it befell that the lord and the estates of the realme had soe many sonns that they had gotten some by their wifes and some by other ladyes of the realme; for that land is a hott land and a plentious of generacion. And they had not competent livehode to find with their children; wherefor they made much care. And then the King of the land made a great counsell and a parliament, to witt, how they might find their children honestly as gentlemen. And they could find no manner of good way. And then they did crye through all the realme, if there were any man that could enforme them, that he should come to them, and he should be soe rewarded for his travail, that he should hold him pleased.

"After that this cry was made, then came this worthy Clarke Ewclyde, and said to the King and to all his great lords: 'If yee will, take me your children to govern, and to teach them one of the Seaven Scyences, wherewith they may live honestly as gentlemen should, under a condition that yee will grant me and them a commission that I may have power to rule them after the manner that the science ought to be ruled.' And that the Kings and orthodoxy of a Mason's creed that he should literally believe that Euclid, the great geometrician, was really a Freemason, and that the ancient Egyptians were indebted to him for the establishment of the institution among them. Indeed, the palpable anachronism in the legend which makes Euclid the contemporary of Abraham necessarily prohibits any such belief, and shows that the whole story is a sheer invention. The intelligent Mason, however, will not wholly reject the legend, as ridiculous or absurd; but, with a due sense of the nature and design of our system of symbolism, will rather accept it as what, in the classification laid down on a preceding page, would be called "a philosophical myth"—an ingenious method of conveying, symbolically, a masonic truth.

Euclid is here very appropriately used as a type of geometry, that science of which he was so eminent a teacher, and the myth or legend then symbolizes the fact that there was in Egypt a close connection between that science and the great moral and religious system, which was among the Egyptians, as well as other ancient nations, what Freemasonry is in the present day — a secret institution, established for the inculcation of the same principles, and inculcating them in the same symbolic manner. So interpreted, this legend corresponds to all the developments of Egyptian history, which teach us how close a connection existed in that country between the

all his counsel granted to him alone, and sealed their commission. And then this worthy tooke to him these lords' sonns, and taught them the scyence of Geometrie in practice, for to work in stones all manner of worthy worke that belongeth to buildinge churches, temples, castells, towres, and mannors, and all other manner of buildings."

religious and scientific systems. Thus Kenrick tells us, that "when we read of foreigners [in Egypt] being obliged to submit to painful and tedious ceremonies of initiation, it was not that they might learn the secret meaning of the rites of Osiris or Isis, but that they might partake of the knowledge of astronomy, physic, geometry, and theology."*

Another illustration will be found in the myth or legend of the *Winding Stairs,* by which the Fellow Crafts are said to have ascended to the middle chamber to receive their wages. Now, this myth, taken in its literal sense, is, in all its parts, opposed to history and probability. As a myth, it finds its origin in the fact that there was a place in the temple called the "Middle Chamber," and that there were "winding stairs" by which it was reached; for we read, in the First Book of Kings, that "they went up with winding stairs into the middle chamber."† But we have no historical evidence that the stairs were of the construction, or that the chamber was used for the purpose, indicated in the mythical narrative, as it is set forth in the ritual of the second degree. The whole legend is, in fact, an historical myth, in which the mystic number of the steps, the process of passing to the chamber, and the wages there received, are inventions added to or ingrafted on the fundamental history contained in the sixth chapter of Kings, to inculcate important symbolic instruction relative to the principles of the order. These lessons might, it is true, have been inculcated in a dry, didactic form; but the allegorical and mythical method adopted tends to make a stronger and deeper

* Ancient Egypt under the Pharaohs, vol. i. p. 393.
† I Kings 6:8.

impression on the mind, and at the same time serves more closely to connect the institution of Masonry with the ancient temple.

Again: the myth which traces the origin of the institution of Freemasonry to the beginning of the world, making its commencement coeval with the creation,—a myth which is, even at this day, ignorantly interpreted, by some, as an historical fact, and the reference to which is still preserved in the date of "anno lucis," which is affixed to all masonic documents,—is but a philosophical myth, symbolizing the idea which analogically connects the creation of physical light in the universe with the birth of masonic or spiritual and intellectual light in the candidate. The one is the type of the other When, therefore, Preston says that "from the commencement of the world we may trace the foundation of Masonry," and when he goes on to assert that "ever since symmetry began, and harmony displayed her charms, our order has had a being," we are not to suppose that Preston intended to teach that a masonic lodge was held in the Garden of Eden. Such a supposition would justly subject us to the ridicule of every intelligent person. The only idea intended to be conveyed is this: that the principles of Freemasonry, which, indeed, are entirely independent of any special organization which it may have as a society, are coëval with the existence of the world; that when God said, "Let there be light," the material light thus produced was an antitype of that spiritual light that must burst upon the mind of every candidate when his intellectual world, theretofore "without form and void," becomes adorned and peopled with the living thoughts and divine principles which constitute the great system of Speculative

Masonry, and when the spirit of the institution, brooding over the vast deep of his mental chaos, shall, from intellectual darkness, bring forth intellectual light.*

In the legends of the Master's degree and of the Royal Arch there is a commingling of the historical myth and the mythical history, so that profound judgment is often required to discriminate these differing elements. As, for example, the legend of the third degree is, in some of its details, undoubtedly mythical—in others, just as undoubtedly historical. The difficulty, however, of separating the one from the other, and of distinguishing the fact from the fiction, has necessarily produced a difference of opinion on the subject among masonic writers. Hutchinson, and, after him, Oliver, think the whole legend an allegory or philosophical myth. I am inclined, with Anderson and the earlier writers, to suppose it a mythical history. In the Royal Arch degree, the legend of the rebuilding of the temple is clearly historical; but there are so many accompanying circumstances, which are uncertified, except by oral tradition, as to give to the entire narrative the appearance of a mythical history. The particular legend of the *three weary sojourners* is undoubtedly a myth, and perhaps merely a philosophical one, or the enunciation of an idea —namely, the reward of successful perseverance, through all dangers, in the search for divine truth.

"To form symbols and to interpret symbols," says the learned Creuzer, "were the main occupation of the ancient priesthood." Upon the studious Mason the same task of interpretation devolves. He who desires properly

* An allusion to this symbolism is retained in one of the wellknown mottoes of the order—"*Lux e tenebris.*"

to appreciate the profound wisdom of the institution of which he is the disciple, must not be content, with uninquiring credulity, to accept all the traditions that are imparted to him as veritable histories; nor yet, with unphilosophic incredulity, to reject them in a mass, as fabulous inventions. In these extremes there is equal error. "The myth," says Hermann, "is the representation of an idea." It is for that idea that the student must search in the myths of Masonry. Beneath every one of them there is something richer and more spiritual than the mere narrative.* This spiritual essence he must learn to extract from the ore in which, like a precious metal, it lies imbedded. It is this that constitutes the true value of Freemasonry. Without its symbols, and its myths or legends, and the ideas and conceptions which lie at the bottom of them, the time, the labor, and the expense incurred in perpetuating the institution, would be thrown away. Without them, it would be a "vain and empty show." Its grips and signs are worth nothing, except for social purposes, as mere means of recognition. So, too, would be its words, were it not that they are, for the most part, symbolic. Its social habits and its charities are but incidental points in its constitution

* "An allegory is that in which, under borrowed characters and allusions, is shadowed some real action or moral instruction; or, to keep more strictly to its derivation (ἄλλος, alius, and ἀγορεύω, dico), it is that in which one thing is related and another thing is understood. Hence it is apparent that an allegory must have two senses—the literal and mystical; and for that reason it must convey its instruction under borrowed characters and allusions throughout."—The Antiquity, Evidence, and Certainty of Christianity canvassed, or Dr. Middleton's Examination of the Bishop of London's Discourses on Prophecy. By Anselm Bayly, LL. B., Minor Canon of St. Paul's. Lond. 1751.

of themselves good, it is true, but capable of being attained in a simpler way. Its true value, as a science, consists in its symbolism—in the great lessons of divine truth which it teaches, and in the admirable manner in which it accomplishes that teaching. Every one, therefore, who desires to be a skilful Mason, must not suppose that the task is accomplished by a perfect knowledge of the mere phraseology of the ritual, by a readiness in opening and closing a lodge, nor by an off-hand capacity to confer degrees. All these are good in their places, but without the internal meaning they are but mere child's play. He must study the myths, the traditions, and the symbols of the order, and learn their true interpretation; for this alone constitutes the science and the philosophy— the end, aim, and design of Speculative Masonry.

XXVI.

THE LEGEND OF THE WINDING STAIRS.

BEFORE proceeding to the examination of those more important mythical legends which appropriately belong to the Master's degree, it will not, I think, be unpleasing or uninstructive to consider the only one which is attached to the Fellow Craft's degree—that, namely, which refers to the allegorical ascent of the Winding Stairs to the Middle Chamber, and the symbolic payment of the workmen's wages.

Although the legend of the Winding Stairs forms an important tradition of Ancient Craft Masonry, the only allusion to it in Scripture is to be found in a single verse in the sixth chapter of the First Book of Kings, and is in these words: "The door for the middle chamber was in the right side of the house; and they went up with winding stairs into the middle chamber, and out of the middle into the third." Out of this slender material has been constructed an allegory, which, if properly considered in its symbolical relations, will be found to be of surpassing beauty. But it is only as a symbol that we can regard this whole tradition; for the historical facts and the architectural details alike forbid us for a moment to suppose that the legend, as it is rehearsed in the second degree of Masonry, is anything more than a magnificent philosophical myth.

Let us inquire into the true design of this legend, and learn the lesson of symbolism which it is intended to teach.

In the investigation of the true meaning of every masonic symbol and allegory, we must be governed by the single principle that the whole design of Freemasonry as a speculative science is the investigation of divine truth. To this great object everything is subsidiary. The Mason is, from the moment of his initiation as an Entered Apprentice, to the time at which he receives the full fruition of masonic light, an investigator—a laborer in the quarry and the temple—whose reward is to be Truth. All the ceremonies and traditions of the order tend to this ultimate design. Is there light to be asked for? It is the intellectual light of wisdom and truth. Is there a word to be sought? That word is the symbol of truth. Is there a loss of something that had been promised? That loss is typical of the failure of man, in the infirmity of his nature, to discover divine truth. Is there a substitute to be appointed for that loss? It is an allegory which teaches us that in this world man can only approximate to the full conception of truth.

Hence there is in Speculative Masonry always a progress, symbolized by its peculiar ceremonies of initiation. There is an advancement from a lower to a higher state —from darkness to light—from death to life—from error to truth. The candidate is always ascending; he is never stationary; he never goes back, but each step he takes brings him to some new mental illumination—to the knowledge of some more elevated doctrine. The teaching of the Divine Master is, in respect to this continual progress, the teaching of Masonry—"No man having put his hand to the plough, and looking back, is fit for the kingdom of heaven." And similar to this is the precept of Pythagoras: "When travelling, turn not back, for if you do the Furies will accompany you."

Now, this principle of masonic symbolism is apparent in many places in each of the degrees. In that of the Entered Apprentice we find it developed in the theological ladder, which, resting on earth, leans its top upon heaven, thus inculcating the idea of an ascent from a lower to a higher sphere, as the object of masonic labor. In the Master's degree we find it exhibited in its most religious form, in the restoration from death to life—in the change from the obscurity of the grave to the holy of holies of the Divine Presence. In all the degrees we find it presented in the ceremony of circumambulation, in which there is a gradual inquisition, and a passage from an inferior to a superior officer. And lastly, the same symbolic idea is conveyed in the Fellow Craft's degree in the legend of the Winding Stairs.

In an investigation of the symbolism of the Winding Stairs we shall be directed to the true explanation by a reference to their origin, their number, the objects which they recall, and their termination, but above all by a consideration of the great design which an ascent upon them was intended to accomplish.

The steps of this Winding Staircase commenced, we are informed, at the porch of the temple; that is to say, at its very entrance. But nothing is more undoubted in the science of masonic symbolism than that the temple was the representative of the world purified by the Shekinah, or the Divine Presence. The world of the profane is without the temple; the world of the initiated is within its sacred walls. Hence to enter the temple, to pass within the porch, to be made a Mason, and to be born into the world of masonic light, are all synonymous and convertible terms. Here, then, the symbolism of the Winding Stairs begins.

The Apprentice, having entered within the porch of the temple, has begun his masonic life. But the first degree in Masonry, like the lesser Mysteries of the ancient systems of initiation, is only a preparation and purification for something higher. The Entered Apprentice is the child in Masonry. The lessons which he receives are simply intended to cleanse the heart and prepare the recipient for that mental illumination which is to be given in the succeeding degrees.

As a Fellow Craft, he has advanced another step, and as the degree is emblematic of youth, so it is here that the intellectual education of the candidate begins. And therefore, here, at the very spot which separates the Porch from the Sanctuary, where childhood ends and manhood begins, he finds stretching out before him a winding stair which invites him, as it were, to ascend, and which, as the symbol of discipline and instruction, teaches him that here must commence his masonic labor —here he must enter upon those glorious though difficult researches, the end of which is to be the possession of divine truth. The Winding Stairs begin after the candidate has passed within the Porch and between the pillars of Strength and Establishment, as a significant symbol to teach him that as soon as he has passed beyond the years of irrational childhood, and commenced his entrance upon manly life, the laborious task of self-improvement is the first duty that is placed before him. He cannot stand still, if he would be worthy of his vocation; his destiny as an immortal being requires him to ascend, step by step, until he has reached the summit, where the treasures of knowledge await him.

The number of these steps in all the systems has been odd. Vitruvius remarks—and the coincidence is at least curious—that the ancient temples were always ascended by an odd number of steps; and he assigns as the reason, that, commencing with the right foot at the bottom, the worshipper would find the same foot foremost when he entered the temple, which was considered as a fortunate omen. But the fact is, that the symbolism of numbers was borrowed by the Masons from Pythagoras, in whose system of philosophy it plays an important part, and in which odd numbers were considered as more perfect than even ones. Hence, throughout the masonic system we find a predominance of odd numbers; and while three, five, seven, nine, fifteen, and twenty-seven, are all-important symbols, we seldom find a reference to two, four, six, eight, or ten. The odd number of the stairs was therefore intended to symbolize the idea of perfection, to which it was the object of the aspirant to attain.

As to the particular number of the stairs, this has varied at different periods. Tracing-boards of the last century have been found, in which only *five* steps are delineated, and others in which they amount to *seven.* The Prestonian lectures, used in England in the beginning of this century, gave the whole number as thirty-eight, dividing them into series of one, three, five, seven, nine, and eleven. The error of making an even number, which was a violation of the Pythagorean principle of odd numbers as the symbol of perfection, was corrected in the Hemming lectures, adopted at the union of the two Grand Lodges of England, by striking out the eleven, which was also objectionable as receiving a sectarian explanation. In this country the number was still further reduced to *fifteen,* divided into three series of *three, five,* and *seven.* I shall adopt this American division in explaining the symbolism, although, after all, the particular number of the steps, or the peculiar method of their division into series, will not in any way affect the general symbolism of the whole legend.

The candidate, then, in the second degree of Masonry, represents a man starting forth on the journey of life, with the great task before him of self-improvement. For the faithful performance of this task, a reward is promised, which reward consists in the development of all his intellectual faculties, the moral and spiritual elevation of his character, and the acquisition of truth and knowledge. Now, the attainment of this moral and intellectual condition supposes an elevation of character, an ascent from a lower to a higher life, and a passage of toil and difficulty, through rudimentary instruction, to the full fruition of wisdom. This is therefore beautifully symbolized by the Winding Stairs; at whose foot the aspirant stands ready to climb the toilsome steep, while at its top is placed "that hieroglyphic bright which none but Craftsmen ever saw," as the emblem of divine truth. And hence a distinguished writer has said that "these steps, like all the masonic symbols, are illustrative of discipline and doctrine, as well as of natural, mathematical, and metaphysical science, and open to us an extensive range of moral and speculative inquiry."

The candidate, incited by the love of virtue and the desire of knowledge, and withal eager for the reward of truth which is set before him, begins at once the toilsome ascent. At each division he pauses to gather instruction from the symbolism which these divisions present to his attention.

At the first pause which he makes he is instructed in the peculiar organization of the order of which he has become a disciple. But the information here given, if taken in its naked, literal sense, is barren, and unworthy of his labor. The rank of the officers who govern, and the names of the degrees which constitute the institution, can give him no knowledge which he has not before possessed. We must look therefore to the symbolic meaning of these allusions for any value which may be attached to this part of the ceremony.

The reference to the organization of the masonic institution is intended to remind the aspirant of the union of men in society, and the development of the social state out of the state of nature. He is thus reminded, in the very outset of his journey, of the blessings which arise from civilization, and of the fruits of virtue and knowledge which are derived from that condition. Masonry itself is the result of civilization; while, in grateful return, it has been one of the most important means of extending that condition of mankind.

All the monuments of antiquity that the ravages of time have left, combine to prove that man had no sooner `emerged from the savage into the social state, than he commenced the organization of religious mysteries, and the separation, by a sort of divine instinct, of the sacred from the profane. Then came the invention of architecture as a means of providing convenient dwellings and necessary shelter from the inclemencies and vicissitudes of the seasons, with all the mechanical arts connected with it; and lastly, geometry, as a necessary science to enable the cultivators of land to measure and designate the limits of their possessions. All these are claimed as peculiar characteristics of Speculative Masonry, which may be considered as the type of civilization, the former bearing the same relation to the profane world as the latter does to the savage state. Hence we at once see the fitness of the symbolism which commences the aspirant's upward progress in the cultivation of knowledge and the search after truth, by recalling to his mind the condition of civilization and the social union of mankind as necessary preparations for the attainment of these objects. In the allusions to the officers of a lodge, and the degrees of Masonry as explanatory of the organization of our own society, we clothe in our symbolic language the history of the organization of society.

Advancing in his progress, the candidate is invited to contemplate another series of instructions. The human senses, as the appropriate channels through which we receive all our ideas of perception, and which, therefore, constitute the most important sources of our knowledge, are here referred to as a symbol of intellectual cultivation. Architecture, as the most important of the arts which conduce to the comfort of mankind, is also alluded to here, not simply because it is so closely connected with the operative institution of Masonry, but also as the type of all the other useful arts. In his second pause, in the ascent of the Winding Stairs, the aspirant is therefore reminded of the necessity of cultivating practical knowledge.

So far, then, the instructions he has received relate to his own condition in society as a member of the great social compact, and to his means of becoming, by a knowledge of the arts of practical life, a necessary and useful member of that society.

But his motto will be, "Excelsior." Still must he go onward and forward. The stair is still before him; its summit is not yet reached, and still further treasures of wisdom are to be sought for, or the reward will not be gained, nor the *middle chamber*, the abiding place of truth, be reached.

In his third pause, he therefore arrives at that point in which the whole circle of human science is to be explained. Symbols, we know, are in themselves arbitrary and of conventional signification, and the complete circle of human science might have been as well symbolized by any other sign or series of doctrines as by the seven liberal arts and sciences. But Masonry is an institution of the olden time; and this selection of the liberal arts and sciences as a symbol of the completion of human learning is one of the most pregnant evidences that we have of its antiquity.

In the seventh century, and for a long time afterwards, the circle of instruction to which all the learning of the most eminent schools and most distinguished philosophers was confined, was limited to what were then called the liberal arts and sciences, and consisted of two branches, the *trivium* and the *quadrivium.** The *trivium* included grammar, rhetoric, and logic; the *quadrivium* comprehended arithmetic, geometry, music, and astronomy.

"These seven heads," says Enfield, "were supposed to include universal knowledge. He who was master of these was thought to have no need of a preceptor to explain any books or to solve any questions which lay within the compass of human reason, the knowledge of the *trivium* having furnished him with the key to all language, and that of the *quadrivium* having opened to him the secret laws of nature."†

At a period, says the same writer, when few were instructed in the *trivium,* and very few studied the *quadrivium,* to be master of both was sufficient to complete the character of a philosopher. The propriety, therefore, of adopting the seven liberal arts and sciences as a symbol of the completion of human learning is apparent. The candidate, having reached this point, is now supposed to have accomplished the task upon which he had entered —he has reached the last step, and is now ready to receive the full fruition of human learning.

So far, then, we are able to comprehend the true symbolism of the Winding Stairs. They represent the progress of an inquiring mind with the toils and labors of intellectual cultivation and study, and the preparatory

* The words themselves are purely classical, but the meanings here given to them are of a mediæval or corrupt Latinity. Among the old Romans, a *trivium* meant a place where three ways met, and a *quadrivium* where four, or what we now call a *cross-road.* When we speak of the *paths of learning,* we readily discover the origin of the signification given by the scholastic philosophers to these terms.

† Hist. of Philos. vol. ii. p. 337.

acquisition of all human science, as a preliminary step to the attainment of divine truth, which it must be remembered is always symbolized in Masonry by the WORD.

Here let me again allude to the symbolism of numbers, which is for the first time presented to the consideration of the masonic student in the legend of the Winding Stairs. The theory of numbers as the symbols of certain qualities was originally borrowed by the Masons from the school of Pythagoras. It will be impossible, however, to develop this doctrine, in its entire extent, on the present occasion, for the numeral symbolism of Masonry would itself constitute materials for an ample essay. It will be sufficient to advert to the fact that the total number of the steps, amounting in all to *fifteen*, in the American system, is a significant symbol. For *fifteen* was a sacred number among the Orientals, because the letters of the holy name JAH, יה, were, in their numerical value, equivalent to fiftee n; and hence a figure in which the nine digits were so disposed as to make fifteen either way when added together perpendicularly, horizontally, or diagonally, constituted one of their most sacred talismans.* The fifteen steps in the Winding Stairs are therefore symbolic of the name of God.

* Such a talisman was the following figure:—

8	1	6
3	5	7
4	9	2

But we are not yet done. It will be remembered that a reward was promised for all this toilsome ascent of the Winding Stairs. Now, what are the wages of a Speculative Mason? Not money, nor corn, nor wine, nor oil. All these are but symbols. His wages are TRUTH, or that approximation to it which will be most appropriate to the degree into which he has been initiated. It is one of the most beautiful, but at the same time most abstruse, doctrines of the science of masonic symbolism, that the Mason is ever to be in search of truth, but is never to find it. This divine truth, the object of all his labors, is symbolized by the WORD, for which we all know he can only obtain a *substitute;* and this is intended to teach the humiliating but necessary lesson that the knowledge of the nature of God and of man's relation to him, which knowledge constitutes divine truth, can never be acquired in this life. It is only when the portals of the grave open to us, and give us an entrance into a more perfect life, that this knowledge is to be attained. "Happy is the man," says the father of lyric poetry, "who descends beneath the hollow earth, having beheld these mysteries; he knows the end, he knows the origin of life."

The Middle Chamber is therefore symbolic of this life, where the symbol only of the word can be given, where the truth is to be reached by approximation only, and yet where we are to learn that that truth will consist in a perfect knowledge of the G. A. O. T. U. This is the reward of the inquiring Mason; in this consist the wages of a Fellow Craft; he is directed to the truth, but must travel farther and ascend still higher to attain it.

It is, then, as a symbol, and a symbol only, that we must study this beautiful legend of the Winding Stairs. If we attempt to adopt it as an historical fact, the absurdity of its details stares us in the face, and wise men will wonder at our credulity. Its inventors had no desire thus to impose upon our folly; but offering it to us as a great philosophical myth, they did not for a moment suppose that we would pass over its sublime moral teachings to accept the allegory as an historical narrative, without meaning, and wholly irreconcilable with the records of Scripture, and opposed by all the principles of probability. To suppose that eighty thousand craftsmen were weekly paid in the narrow precincts of the temple chambers, is simply to suppose an absurdity. But to believe that all this pictorial representation of an ascent by a Winding Staircase to the place where the wages of labor were to be received, was an allegory to teach us the ascent of the mind from ignorance, through all the toils of study and the difficulties of obtaining knowledge, receiving here a little and there a little, adding something to the stock of our ideas at each step, until, in the middle chamber of life,—in the full fruition of manhood,—the reward is attained, and the purified and elevated intellect is invested with the reward in the direction how to seek God and God's truth,—to believe this is to believe and to know the true design of Speculative Masonry, the only design which makes it worthy of a good or a wise man's study.

Its historical details are barren, but its symbols and allegories are fertile with instruction.

XXVII.

THE LEGEND OF THE THIRD DEGREE.

T HE most important and significant of the legendary symbols of Freemasonry is, undoubtedly, that which relates to the fate of Hiram Abif, commonly called, "by way of excellence," the Legend of the Third Degree.

The first written record that I have been able to find of this legend is contained in the second edition of Anderson's Constitutions, published in 1738, and is in these words:—

"It (the temple) was finished in the short space of seven years and six months, to the amazement of all the world; when the cape-stone was celebrated by the fraternity with great joy. But their joy was soon interrupted by the sudden death of their dear master, Hiram Abif, whom they decently interred, in the lodge near the temple, according to ancient usage."*

In the next edition of the same work, published in 1756, a few additional circumstances are related, such as

* Anderson's Constitutions, 2d ed. 1738, p. 14.

the participation of King Solomon in the general grief, and the fact that the king of Israel "ordered his obsequies to be conducted with great solemnity and decency."* With these exceptions, and the citations of the same passages, made by subsequent authors, the narrative has always remained unwritten, and descended, from age to age, through the means of oral tradition.

The legend has been considered of so much importance that it has been preserved in the symbolism of every masonic rite. No matter what modifications or alterations the general system may have undergone,—no matter how much the ingenuity or the imagination of the founders of rites may have perverted or corrupted other symbols, abolishing the old and substituting new ones,—the legend of the Temple Builder has ever been left untouched, to present itself in all the integrity of its ancient mythical form.

What, then, is the signification of this symbol, so important and so extensively diffused? What interpretation can we give to it that will account for its universal adoption? How is it that it has thus become so intimately interwoven with Freemasonry as to make, to all appearances, a part of its very essence, and to have been always deemed inseparable from it?

To answer these questions, satisfactorily, it is necessary to trace, in a brief investigation, the remote origin of the institution of Freemasonry, and its connection with the ancient systems of initiation.

It was, then, the great object of all the rites and mysteries which constituted the "Spurious Freemasonry"

* Anderson's Constitutions, 3d ed. 1756, p. 24.

of antiquity to teach the consoling doctrine of the immortality of the soul.* This dogma, shining as an almost solitary beacon-light in the surrounding gloom of pagan darkness, had undoubtedly been received from that ancient people or priesthood† who practised what has been called the system of "Pure Freemasonry," and among whom it probably existed only in the form of an abstract proposition or a simple and unembellished tradition. But in the more sensual minds of the pagan philosophers and mystics, the idea, when presented to the initiates in their Mysteries, was always conveyed in the form of a scenic

* "The hidden doctrines of the unity of the Deity and the immortality of the soul were originally in all the Mysteries, even those of Cupid and Bacchus."—WARBURTON, *in Spence's Anecdotes,* p. 309.

† "The allegorical interpretation of the myths has been, by several learned investigators, especially by Creuzer, connected with the hypothesis of an ancient and highly instructed body of priests, having their origin either in Egypt or in the East, and communicating to the rude and barbarous Greeks religious, physical, and historical knowledge, under the veil of symbols."—GROTE, *Hist. of Greece,* vol. i. ch. xvi. p. 579.—And the Chevalier Ramsay corroborates this theory: "Vestiges of the most sublime truths are to be found in the sages of all nations, times, and religions, both sacred and profane, and these vestiges are emanations of the antediluvian and noevian tradition, more or less disguised and adulterated."— *Philosophical Principles of Natural and Revealed Religion unfolded in a Geometrical Order,* vol. 1, p. iv.

‡ Of this there is abundant evidence in all the ancient and modern writers on the Mysteries. Apuleius, cautiously describing his initiation into the Mysteries of Isis, says, "I approached the confines of death, and having trod on the threshold of Proserpine, I returned therefrom, being borne through all the elements. At midnight I saw the sun shining with its brilliant light; and I approached the presence of the gods beneath, and the gods of heaven, and stood near and worshipped them."—*Metam.* lib. xi. The context shows that all this was a scenic representation.

representation.‡ The influence, too, of the early Sabian worship of the sun and heavenly bodies, in which the solar orb was adored, on its resurrection, each morning, from the apparent death of its evening setting, caused this rising sun to be adopted in the more ancient Mysteries as a symbol of the regeneration of the soul.

Thus in the Egyptian Mysteries we find a representation of the death and subsequent regeneration of Osiris; in the Phoenician, of Adonis; in the Syrian, of Dionysus; in all of which the scenic apparatus of initiation was intended to indoctrinate the candidate into the dogma of a future life.

It will be sufficient here to refer simply to the fact, that through the instrumentality of the Tyrian workmen at the temple of King Solomon, the spurious and pure branches of the masonic system were united at Jerusalem, and that the same method of scenic representation was adopted by the latter from the former, and the narrative of the temple builder substituted for that of Dionysus, which was the myth peculiar to the mysteries practised by the Tyrian workmen.

The idea, therefore, proposed to be communicated in the myth of the ancient Mysteries was the same as that which is now conveyed in the masonic legend of the Third Degree.

Hence, then, Hiram Abif is, in the masonic system, the symbol of human nature, as developed in the life here and the life to come; and so, while the temple was, as I have heretofore shown, the visible symbol of the world, its builder became the mythical symbol of man, the dweller and worker in that world.

Now, is not this symbolism evident to every reflective mind?

Man, setting forth on the voyage of life, with faculties and powers fitting him for the due exercise of the high duties to whose performance he has been called, holds, if he be "a curious and cunning workman,"* skilled in all moral and intellectual purposes (and it is only of such men that the temple builder can be the symbol), within the grasp of his attainment the knowledge of all that divine truth imparted to him as the heirloom of his race—that race to whom it has been granted to look, with exalted countenance, on high;† which divine truth is symbolized by the WORD.

Thus provided with the word of life, he occupies his time in the construction of a spiritual temple, and travels onward in the faithful discharge of all his duties, laying down his designs upon the trestle-board of the future and invoking the assistance and direction of God.

But is his path always over flowery meads and through pleasant groves? Is there no hidden foe to obstruct his progress? Is all before him clear and calm, with joyous sunshine and refreshing zephyrs? Alas! not so. "Man is born to trouble, as the sparks fly upward." At every

---

* *Aish hakam iodea binah,* "a cunning man, endued with understanding," is the description given by the king of Tyre of Hiram Abif. See 2 Chron. 2:13. It is needless to say that "cunning" is a good old Saxon word meaning *skilful.*

> † "Pronaque cum spectent animalia cætera terram;
>   Os homini sublime dedit: cœlumque tueri
>   Jussit, et erectos ad sidera tollere vultus."
>
> OVID, *Met.* i. 84.

"Thus, while the mute creation downward bend
   Their sight, and to their earthly mother tend,
   Man looks aloft, and with erected eyes
   Beholds his own hereditary skies."

DRYDEN.

"gate of life"— as the Orientalists have beautifully called the different ages— he is beset by peril. Temptations allure his youth, misfortunes darken the pathway of his manhood, and his old age is encumbered with infirmity and disease. But clothed in the armor of virtue he may resist the temptation; he may cast misfortunes aside, and rise triumphantly above them; but to the last, the direst, the most inexorable foe of his race, he must eventually yield; and stricken down by death, he sinks prostrate into the grave, *and is buried in the rubbish* of his sin and human frailty.

Here, then, in Masonry, is what was called the *aphanism** in the ancient Mysteries. The bitter but necessary lesson of death has been imparted. The living soul, with the lifeless body which encased it, has disappeared, and *can nowhere be found.* All is darkness—confusion —despair. Divine truth—the WORD—for a time is lost, and the Master Mason may now say, in the language of Hutchinson, "I prepare my sepulchre. I make my grave in the pollution of the earth. I am under the shadow of death."

But if the mythic symbolism ended here, with this lesson of death, then were the lesson incomplete. That teaching would be vain and idle— nay, more, it would be corrupt and pernicious—which should stop short of the conscious and innate instinct for another existence. And hence the succeeding portions of the legend are intended to convey the sublime symbolism of a resurrection from the grave and a new birth into a future life. The discovery

---

* "'Αφανισμὸς, disappearance, destruction, a perishing, death, from ἀφανίζω, to remove from one's view, to conceal," &c. — *Schrevel. Lex.*

of the body, which, in the initiations of the ancient Mysteries, was called the *euresis*,* and its removal, from the polluted grave into which it had been cast, to an honored and sacred place within the precincts of the temple, are all profoundly and beautifully symbolic of that great truth, the discovery of which was the object of all the ancient initiations, as it is almost the whole design of Freemasonry, namely, that when man shall have passed the gates of life and have yielded to the inexorable fiat of death, he shall then (not in the pictured ritual of an earthly lodge, but in the realities of that eternal one, of which the former is but an antitype) be raised, at the omnific word of the Grand Master of the Universe, from time to eternity; from the tomb of corruption to the chambers of hope; from the darkness of death to the celestial beams of life; and that his disembodied spirit shall be conveyed as near to the holy of holies of the divine presence as humanity can ever approach to Deity.

Such I conceive to be the true interpretation of the symbolism of the legend of the Third Degree.

I have said that this mythical history of the temple builder was universal in all nations and all rites, and that in no place and at no time had it, by alteration, diminution, or addition, acquired any essentially new or different form: the myth has always remained the same.

But it is not so with its interpretation. That which I have just given, and which I conceive to be the correct one, has been very generally adopted by the Masons of this country. But elsewhere, and by various writers, other interpretations have been made, very different in their

---

* "Εὔρεσις, a finding, invention, discovery."—*Schrevel. Lex.*

character, although always agreeing in retaining the general idea of a resurrection or regeneration, or a restoration of something from an inferior to a higher sphere or function.

Thus some of the earlier continental writers have supposed the myth to have been a symbol of the destruction of the Order of the Templars, looking upon its restoration to its original wealth and dignities as being prophetically symbolized.

In some of the high philosophical degrees it is taught that the whole legend refers to the sufferings and death, with the subsequent resurrection, of Christ.*

Hutchinson, who has the honor of being the earliest philosophical writer on Freemasonry in England, supposes it to have been intended to embody the idea of the decadence of the Jewish religion, and the substitution of the Christian in its place and on its ruins.†

Dr. Oliver—"clarum et venerabile nomen"—thinks that it is typical of the murder of Abel by Cain, and that it symbolically refers to the universal death of our race through Adam, and its restoration to life in the Redeemer,‡

* A French writer of the last century, speaking of the degree of "Très Parfait Maitre," says, "C'est ici qu'on voit réellement qu'Hiram n'a été que le type de Jésus Christ, que le temple et les autres symboles maçonniques sont des allegories relativesà l'Eglise, à la Foi, et aux bonnes mœurs."—*Originc et Objet de la Franchemaçonnerie, par le F. B.* Paris, 1774.

† "This our order is a positive contradiction to the Judaic blindness and infidelity, and testifies our faith concerning the resurrection of the body."—HUTCHINSON, *Spirit of Masonry,* lect. ix. p. 101.—The whole lecture is occupied in advancing and supporting his peculiar theory.

‡ "Thus, then, it appears that the historical reference of the legend of Speculative Freemasonry, in all ages of the world, was—

according to the expression of the apostle, "As in Adam we all died, so in Christ we all live."

Ragon makes Hiram a symbol of the sun shorn of its vivifying rays and fructifying power by the three winter months, and its restoration to generative heat by the sea. son of spring.*

And, finally, Des Etangs, adopting, in part, the interpretation of Ragon, adds to it another, which he calls the moral symbolism of the legend, and supposes that Hiram is no other than eternal reason, whose enemies are the vices that deprave and destroy humanity.†

To each of these interpretations it seems to me that there are important objections, though perhaps to some less so than to others.

As to those who seek for an astronomical interpretation of the legend, in which the annual changes of the sun are symbolized, while the ingenuity with which they press their argument cannot but be admired, it is evident that, by such an interpretation, they yield all that Masonry has

to our death in Adam and life in Christ. What, then, was the origin of our tradition? Or, in other words, to what particular incident did the legend of initiation refer before the flood? I conceive it to have been the offering and assassination of Abel by his brother Cain; the escape of the murderer; the discovery of the body by his disconsolate parents, and its subsequent interment, under a certain belief of its final resurrection from the dead, and of the detection and punishment of Cain by divine vengeance."— OLIVER, *Historical Landmarks of Freemasonry*, vol. ii. p. 171.

* "Le grade de Maître va donc nous retracer allegoriquement la mort du *dieu-lumière*—mourant en hiver pour reparaître et ressusciter au printemps."—RAGON, *Cours Philos. et Interp. des Init.* p. 158.

† "Dans l'ordre moral, Hiram n'est autre chose que la raison éternelle, par qui tout est pondéré, réglé, conservé."—DES ETANGS, *Œuvres Maçonniques*, p. 90.

gained of religious development in past ages, and fall back upon that corruption and perversion of Sabaism from which it was the object, even of the Spurious Freemasonry of antiquity, to rescue its disciples.

The Templar interpretation of the myth must at once be discarded if we would avoid the difficulties of anachronism, unless we deny that the legend existed before the abolition of the Order of Knights Templar, and such denial would be fatal to the antiquity of Freemasonry.*

And as to the adoption of the Christian reference, Hutchinson, and after him Oliver, profoundly philosophical as are the masonic speculations of both, have, I am constrained to believe, fallen into a great error in calling the Master Mason's degree a Christian institution. It is true that it embraces within its scheme the great truths of Christianity upon the subject of the immortality of the soul and the resurrection of the body; but this was to be presumed, because Freemasonry is truth, and Christianity is truth, and all truth must be identical. But the origin of each is different; their histories are dissimilar. The institution of Freemasonry preceded the advent of Christianity. Its symbols and its legends are derived from the Solomonic temple, and from the people even anterior to that. Its religion comes from the ancient priesthood. Its faith was that primitive one of Noah and his immediate descendants. If Masonry were simply a Christian institution, the Jew and the Moslem, the Brahmin and the Buddhist, could not conscientiously partake of its illumination;

---

* With the same argument would I meet the hypothesis that Hiram was the representative of Charles I. of England—an hypothesis now so generally abandoned, that I have not thought it worth noticing in the text.

but its universality is its boast. In its language citizens of every nation may converse; at its altar men of all religions may kneel; to its creed disciples of every faith may subscribe.

Yet it cannot be denied, that since the advent of Christianity a Christian element has been almost imperceptibly infused into the masonic system, at least among Christian Masons. This has been a necessity; for it is the tendency of every predominant religion to pervade with its influences all that surrounds it, or is about it, whether religious, political, or social. This arises from a need of the human heart. To the man deeply imbued with the spirit of his religion there is an almost unconscious desire to accommodate and adapt all the business and the amusements of life, the labors and the employments of his every-day existence, to the indwelling faith of his soul.

The Christian Mason, therefore, while acknowledging and justly appreciating the great doctrines taught in Masonry, and while grateful that these doctrines were preserved in the bosom of his ancient order at a time when they were unknown to the multitudes of the surrounding nations, is still anxious to give to them a Christian character, to invest them, in some measure, with the peculiarities of his own creed, and to bring the interpretation of their symbolism more nearly home to his own religious sentiments.

The feeling is an instinctive one, belonging to the noblest aspirations of our human nature; and hence we find Christian masonic writers indulging in it almost to an unwarrantable excess, and by the extent of their sectarian interpretations materially affecting the cosmopolitan character of the institution.

This tendency to Christianization has, in some instances, been so universal, and has prevailed for so long a period, that certain symbols and myths have been, in this way, so deeply and thoroughly imbued with the Christian element as to leave those who have not penetrated into the cause of this peculiarity, in doubt whether they should attribute to the symbol an ancient or a modern and Christian origin.

As an illustration of the idea here advanced, and as a remarkable example of the result of a gradually Christianized interpretation of a masonic symbol, I will refer to the subordinate myth (subordinate, I mean, to the great legend of the Builder), which relates the circumstances connected with the grave upon "*the brow of a small hill near Mount Moriah.*"

Now, the myth or legend of a grave is a legitimate deduction from the symbolism of the ancient Spurious Masonry. It is the analogue of the *Pastos, Couch,* or *Coffin,* which was to be found in the ritual of all the pagan Mysteries. In all these initiations, the aspirant was placed in a cell or upon a couch, in darkness, and for a period varying, in the different rites, from the three days of the Grecian Mysteries to the fifty of the Persian. This cell or couch, technically called the "pastos," was adopted as a symbol of the being whose death and resurrection or apotheosis, was represented in the legend.

The learned Faber says that this ceremony was doubtless the same as the descent into Hades,* and that, when the aspirant entered into the mystic cell, he was directed

---

* "The initiation into the Mysteries," he says, "scenically represented the mythic descent into Hades and the return from thence to the light of day; by which was meant the entrance into

to lay himself down upon the bed which shadowed out the tomb of the Great Father, or Noah, to whom, it will be recollected, that Faber refers all the ancient rites. "While stretched upon the holy couch," he continues to remark, "in imitation of his figurative deceased prototype, he was said to be wrapped in the deep sleep of death. His resurrection from the bed was his restoration to life or his regeneration into a new world."

Now, it is easy to see how readily such a symbolism would be seized by the Temple Masons, and appropriated at once to *the grave at the brow of the hill.* At first, the interpretation, like that from which it had been derived, would be cosmopolitan; it would fit exactly to the general dogmas of the resurrection of the body and the immortality of the soul.

But on the advent of Christianity, the spirit of the new religion being infused into the old masonic system, the whole symbolism of the grave was affected by it. The same interpretation of a resurrection or restoration to life, derived from the ancient "pastos," was, it is true, preserved; but the facts that Christ himself had come to promulgate to the multitudes the same consoling dogma, and that Mount Calvary, "the place of a skull," was the spot where the Redeemer, by his own death and resur-

the Ark and the subsequent liberation from its dark enclosure. Such Mysteries were established in almost every part of the pagan world; and those of Ceres were substantially the same as the Orgies of Adonis, Osiris, Hu, Mithras, and the Cabiri. They all equally related to the allegorical disappearance, or death, or descent of the great father at their commencement, and to his invention, or revival, or return from Hades, at their conclusion." —*Origin of Pagan Idolatry,* vol. iv. b. iv. ch. v. p. 384—But this Arkite theory, as it is called, has not met with the general approbation of subsequent writers.

rection, had testified the truth of the doctrine, at once suggested to the old Christian Masons the idea of Christianizing the ancient symbol.

Let us now examine briefly how that idea has been at length developed.

In the first place, it is necessary to identify the spot where the "newly-made grave" was discovered with Mount Calvary, the place of the sepulchre of Christ. This can easily be done by a very few but striking analogies, which will, I conceive, carry conviction to any thinking mind.

1. Mount Calvary was a *small hill.**

2. It was situated in a *westward direction* from the temple, and *near Mount Moriah.*

3. It was on the direct road from Jerusalem to Joppa, and is thus the very spot where a *weary brother,* travelling on that road, would find it convenient to *sit down to rest and refresh himself.*†

* Mount Calvary is a small hill or eminence, situated in a westerly direction from that Mount Moriah on which the temple of Solomon was built. It was originally a hillock of notable eminence, but has, in modern times, been greatly reduced by the excavations made in it for the construction of the Church of the Holy Sepulchre. Buckingham, in his Palestine, p. 283, says, "The present rock, called Calvary, and enclosed within the Church of the Holy Sepulchre, bears marks, in every part that is naked, of its having been a round nodule of rock standing above the common level of the surface."

† Dr. Beard, in the art. "Golgotha," in Kitto's Encyc. of Bib. Lit., reasons in a similar method as to the place of the crucifixion, and supposing that the soldiers, from the fear of a popular tumult, would hurry Jesus to the most convenient spot for execution, says, "Then the road to Joppa or Damascus would be most convenient, and no spot in the vicinity would probably be so suitable as the slight rounded elevation which bore the name of Calvary."

4. It was *outside* the gate of the temple.

5. It has at least *one cleft in the rock,* or cave, which was the place which subsequently became the sepulchre of our Lord. But this coincidence need scarcely to be insisted on, since the whole neighborhood abounds in rocky clefts, which meet at once the conditions of the masonic legend.

But to bring this analogical reasoning before the mind in a more expressive mode, it may be observed that if a party of persons were to start forth from the temple at Jerusalem, and travel in a westward direction towards the port of Joppa, Mount Calvary would be the first hill met with; and as it may possibly have been used as a place of sepulture, which its name of Golgotha* seems to import, we may suppose it to have been the very spot alluded to in the Third Degree, as the place where the craftsmen, on their way to Joppa, discovered the evergreen acacia.

Having thus traced the analogy, let us look a little to the symbolism.

Mount Calvary has always retained an important place in the legendary history of Freemasonry, and there are many traditions connected with it that are highly interesting in their import.

One of these traditions is, that it was the burial-place of Adam, in order, says the old legend, that where he lay, who effected the ruin of mankind, there also might the Savior of the world suffer, die, and be buried. Sir R. Torkington, who published a pilgrimage to Jerusalem in 1517, says that "under the Mount of Calvary is another

* Some have supposed that it was so called because it was the place of public execution. *Gulgoleth* in Hebrew, or *gogultho* in Syriac, means *a skull.*

chapel of our Blessed Lady and St. John the Evangelist, that was called Golgotha; and there, right under the mortise of the cross, was found the head of our forefather, Adam." * Golgotha, it will be remembered, means, in Hebrew, "the place of a skull;" and there may be some connection between this tradition and the name of Golgotha, by which the Evangelists inform us, that in the time of Christ Mount Calvary was known. Calvary, or Calvaria, has the same signification in Latin.

Another tradition states, that it was in the bowels of Mount Calvary that Enoch erected his nine-arched vault, and deposited on the foundation-stone of Masonry that Ineffable Name, whose investigation, as a symbol of divine truth, is the great object of Speculative Masonry.

A third tradition details the subsequent discovery of Enoch's deposit by King Solomon, whilst making excavations in Mount Calvary, during the building of the temple.

On this hallowed spot was Christ the Redeemer slain and buried. It was there that, rising on the third day from his sepulchre, he gave, by that act, the demonstrative evidence of the resurrection of the body and the immortality of the soul.

And it was on this spot that the same great lesson was taught in Masonry—the same sublime truth—the development of which evidently forms the design of the Third or Master Mason's degree.

There is in these analogies a sublime beauty as well as a wonderful coincidence between the two systems of Masonry and Christianity, that must, at an early period, have attracted the attention of the Christian Masons.

* Quoted in Oliver, *Landmarks,* vol. i. p. 587, note.

Mount Calvary is consecrated to the Christian as the place where his crucified Lord gave the last great proof of the second life, and fully established the doctrine of the resurrection which he had come to teach. It was the sepulchre of him

>"Who captive led captivity,
>
>Who robbed the grave of victory,
>
>And took the sting from death."

It is consecrated to the Mason, also, as the scene of the *euresis,* the place of the discovery, where the same consoling doctrines of the resurrection of the body and the immortality of the soul are shadowed forth in profoundly symbolic forms.

These great truths constitute the very essence of Christianity, in which it differs from and excels all religious systems that preceded it; they constitute, also, the end, aim, and object of all Freemasonry, but more especially that of the Third Degree, whose peculiar legend, symbolically considered, teaches nothing more nor less than that there is an immortal and better part within us, which, as an emanation from that divine spirit which pervades all nature, can never die.

The identification of the spot on which this divine truth was promulgated in both systems—the Christian and the Masonic—affords an admirable illustration of the readiness with which the religious spirit of the former may be infused into the symbolism of the latter. And hence Hutchinson, thoroughly imbued with these Christian views of Masonry, has called the Master Mason's order a Christian degree, and thus Christianizes the whole symbolism of its mythical history.

"The Great Father of all, commiserating the miseries of the world, sent his only Son, who was *innocence* itself, to teach the doctrine of salvation—by whom man was raised from the death of sin unto the life of righteousness— from the tomb of corruption unto the chamber of hope— from the darkness of despair to the celestial beams of faith; and not only working for us this redemption, but making with us the covenant of regeneration; whence we are become the children of the Divinity, and inheritors of the realms of heaven.

"We, *Masons,* describing the deplorable estate of religion under the Jewish law, speak in figures: 'Her tomb was in the rubbish and filth cast forth of the temple, and *acacia* wove its branches over her monuments; *akakia* being the Greek word for innocence, or being free from sin; implying that the sins and corruptions of the old law, and devotees of the Jewish altar, had hid Religion from those who sought her, and she was only to be found where *innocence* survived, and under the banner of the Divine Lamb, and, as to ourselves, professing that we were to be distinguished by our *Acacy,* or as true *Acacians* in our religious faiths and tenets.

"The acquisition of the doctrine of redemption is expressed in the typical character of *Huramen* (I have found it.— *Greek*), and by the applications of that name with Masons, it is implied that we have discovered the knowledge of God and his salvation, and have been redeemed from the death of sin and the sepulchre of pollution and unrighteousness.

"Thus the *Master Mason* represents a man, under the Christian doctrine, saved from the grave of iniquity and raised to the faith of salvation."

It is in this way that Masonry has, by a sort of inevitable process (when we look to the religious sentiment of the interpreters), been Christianized by some of the most illustrious and learned writers on masonic science—by such able men as Hutchinson and Oliver in England, and by Harris, by Scott, by Salem Towne, and by several others in this country.

I do not object to the system when the interpretation is not strained, but is plausible, consistent, and productive of the same results as in the instance of Mount Calvary: all that I contend for is, that such interpretations are modern, and that they do not belong to, although they may often be deduced from, the ancient system.

But the true ancient interpretation of the legend,—the universal masonic one,—for all countries and all ages, undoubtedly was, that the fate of the temple builder is but figurative of the pilgrimage of man on earth, through trials and temptations, through sin and sorrow, until his eventual fall beneath the blow of death and his final and glorious resurrection to another and an eternal life.

XXVIII.

THE SPRIG OF ACACIA.

INTIMATELY connected with the legend of the third degree is the mythical history of the Sprig of Acacia, which we are now to consider.

There is no symbol more interesting to the masonic student than the Sprig of Acacia, not only on account of its own peculiar import, but also because it introduces us to an extensive and delightful field of research; that, namely, which embraces the symbolism of sacred plants. In all the ancient systems of religion, and Mysteries of initiation, there was always some one plant consecrated, in the minds of the worshippers and participants, by a peculiar symbolism, and therefore held in extraordinary veneration as a sacred emblem. Thus the ivy was used in the Mysteries of Dionysus, the myrtle in those of Ceres, the erica in the Osirian, and the lettuce in the Adonisian. But to this subject I shall have occasion to refer more fully in a subsequent part of the present investigation.

Before entering upon an examination of the symbolism

of the *Acacia*, it will be, perhaps, as well to identify the true plant which occupies so important a place in the ritual of Freemasonry.

And here, in passing, I may be permitted to say that it is a very great error to designate the symbolic plant of Masonry by the name of "Cassia"—an error which undoubtedly arose, originally, from the very common habit among illiterate people of sinking the sound of the letter *a* in the pronunciation of any word of which it constitutes the initial syllable. Just, for instance, as we constantly hear, in the conversation of the uneducated, the words *pothecary* and *prentice* for *apothecary* and *apprentice,* shall we also find *cassia* used for *acacia.* *
Unfortunately, however, this corruption of *acacia* into *cassia* has not always been confined to the illiterate: but the long employment of the corrupted form has at length introduced it, in some instances, among a few of our writers. Even the venerable Oliver, although well acquainted with the symbolism of the acacia, and having writen most learnedly upon it, has, at times, allowed himself to use the objectionable corruption, unwittingly influenced, in all probability, by the too frequent adoption of the latter word in the English lodges. In America, but few Masons fall into the error of speaking of the *Cassia.* The proper teaching of the *Acacia* is here well understood. †

---

* Oliver's idea(*Landmarks,* ii. 149) that *cassia* has, since the year 1730, been corrupted into *acacia,* is contrary to all etymological experience. Words are corrupted, not by lengthening, but by abbreviating them. The uneducated and the careless are always prone to cut off a syllable, not to add a new one.

† And yet I have been surprised by seeing, once or twice, the word "Cassia" adopted as the name of a lodge. "Cinnamon"

The *cassia* of the ancients was, in fact, an ignoble plant, having no mystic meaning and no sacred character, and was never elevated to a higher function than that of being united, as Virgil informs us, with other odorous herbs in the formation of a garland:—

> " . . . violets pale,
> The poppy's flush, and dill which scents the gale,
> Cassia, and hyacinth, and daffodil,
> With yellow marigold the chaplet fill."*

Alston says that the "Cassia lignea of the ancients was the larger branches of the cinnamon tree, cut off with their bark and sent together to the druggists; their Cassia fistula, or Syrinx, was the same cinnamon in the bark only;" but Ruæus says that it also sometimes denoted the lavender, and sometimes the rosemary.

In Scripture the cassia is only three times mentioned,† twice as the translation of the Hebrew word *kiddah,* and once as the rendering of *ketzioth,* but always as referring to an aromatic plant which formed a constituent portion of some perfume. There is, indeed, strong reason for believing that the cassia is only another name for a coarser preparation of cinnamon, and it is also to be remarked that it did not grow in Palestine, but was imported from the East.

or "sandal wood" would have been as appropriate, for any masonic meaning or symbolism.

* Eclog. ii. 49.

> "Pallentes violas et summa papavera carpens,
> Narcissum et florem jungit benè olentis anethi:
> Turn casia, atque aliis intexens suavibus herbis,
> Mollia luteola pingit vaccinia caltha."

† Exod. 30:24, Ezek. 27:9, and Ps. 45:8.

The *acacia,* on the contrary, was esteemed a sacred tree. It is the *acacia vera* of Tournefort, and the *mimosa nilotica* of Linnæus. It grew abundantly in the vicinity of Jerusalem,* where it is still to be found, and is familiar to us all, in its modern uses at least, as the tree from which the gum arabic of commerce is obtained.

The acacia, which, in Scripture, is always called *shittah,*† and in the plural *shittim,* was esteemed a sacred wood among the Hebrews. Of it Moses was ordered to make the tabernacle, the ark of the covenant, the table for the showbread, and the rest of the sacred furniture. Isaiah, in recounting the promises of God's mercy to the Israelites on their return from the captivity, tells them, that, among other things, he will plant in the wilderness, for their relief and refreshment, the cedar, the acacia (or, as it is rendered in our common version, the *shittah*), the fir, and other trees.

* Oliver, it is true, says, that "there is not the smallest trace of any tree of the kind growing so far north as Jerusalem" (*Landm.* ii. 136); but this statement is refuted by the authority of Lieutenant Lynch, who saw it growing in great abundance at Jericho, and still farther north. —*Exped. to the Dead Sea,* p. 262.—The Rabbi Joseph Schwarz, who is excellent authority, says, "The Acacia (Shittim) Tree, Al Sunt, is found in Palestine of different varieties; it looks like the Mulberry tree, attains a great height, and has a hard wood. The gum which is obtained from it is the gum arabic."—*Descriptive Geography and Historical Sketch of Palestine,* p. 308, Leeser's translation. Phila., 1850.—Schwarz was for sixteen years a resident of Palestine, and wrote from personal observation. The testimony of Lynch and Schwarz should, therefore, forever settle the question of the existence of the acacia in Palestine.

† Calmet, Parkhurst, Gesenius, Clarke, Shaw, and all the best authorities, concur in saying that the *otzi shittim,* or shittim wood of Exodus, was the common acacia or mimosa nilotica of Linnæus.

The first thing, then, that we notice in this symbol of the acacia, is, that it had been always consecrated from among the other trees of the forest by the sacred purposes to which it was devoted. By the Jew the tree from whose wood the sanctuary of the tabernacle and the holy ark had been constructed would ever be viewed as more sacred than ordinary trees. The early Masons, therefore, very naturally appropriated this hallowed plant to the equally sacred purpose of a symbol which was to teach an important divine truth in all ages to come.

Having thus briefly disposed of the natural history of this plant, we may now proceed to examine it in its symbolic relations.

First. The acacia, in the mythic system of Freemasonry, is preëminently the symbol of the IMMORTALITY OF THE SOUL—that important doctrine which it is the great design of the institution to teach. As the evanescent nature of the flower which "cometh forth and is cut down" reminds us of the transitory nature of human life, so the perpetual renovation of the evergreen plant, which uninterruptedly presents the appearance of youth and vigor, is aptly compared to that spiritual life in which the soul, freed from the corruptible companionship of the body, shall enjoy an eternal spring and an immortal youth. Hence, in the impressive funeral service of our order, it is said, "This evergreen is an emblem of our faith in the immortality of the soul. By this we are reminded that we have an immortal part within us, which shall survive the grave, and which shall never, never, never die." And again, in the closing sentences of the monitorial lecture of the Third Degree, the same sentiment is repeated, and we are told that by "the ever green and ever living sprig" the Mason is strengthened "with confidence and composure to look forward to a blessed immortality." Such an interpretation of the symbol is an easy and a natural one; it suggests itself at once to the least reflective mind, and consequently, in some one form or another, is to be found existing in all ages and nations. It was an ancient custom, which is not, even now, altogether disused, for mourners to carry in their hands at funerals a sprig of some evergreen, generally the cedar or the cypress, and to deposit it in the grave of the deceased. According to Dalcho,* the Hebrews always planted a sprig of the acacia at the head of the grave of a departed friend. Potter tells us that the ancient Greeks "had a custom of bedecking tombs with herbs and flowers."† All sorts of purple and white flowers were acceptable to the dead, but principally the amaranth and the myrtle. The very name of the former of these plants, which signifies "never fading," would seem to indicate the true

---

* "This custom among the Hebrews arose from this circumstance. Agreeably to their laws, no dead bodies were allowed to be interred within the walls of the city; and as the Cohens, or priests, were prohibited from crossing a grave, it was necessary to place marks thereon, that they might avoid them. For this purpose the acacia was used."—DALCHO, *Oration,* p. 27, note.—I object to the reason assigned by Dalcho; but of the existence of the custom there can be no question, notwithstanding the denial or doubt of Dr. Oliver. Blount (*Travels in the Levant,* p. 197) says, speaking of the Jewish burial customs, "those who bestow a marble stone over any [grave] have a hole a yard long and a foot broad, in which *they plant an evergreen,* which seems to grow from the body, and is carefully watched." Hasselquist (*Travels,* p. 28) confirms his testimony. I borrow the citations from Brown (*Antiquities of the Jews,* vol. ii. p. 356), but have verified the reference to Hasselquist. The work of Blount I have not been enabled to consult.

† Antiquities of Greece, p. 569.

symbolic meaning of the usage, although archæologists have generally supposed it to be simply an exhibition of love on the part of the survivors. Ragon says, that the ancients substituted the acacia for all other plants because they believed it to be incorruptible, and not liable to injury from the attacks of any kind of insect or other animal—thus symbolizing the incorruptible nature of the soul.

Hence we see the propriety of placing the sprig of acacia, as an emblem of immortality, among the symbols of that degree, all of whose ceremonies are intended to teach us the great truth, that "the life of man, regulated by morality, faith, and justice, will be rewarded at its closing hour by the prospect of eternal bliss."* So, therefore, says Dr. Oliver, when the Master Mason exclaims, "My name is Acacia," it is equivalent to saying, "I have been in the grave,—I have triumphed over it by rising from the dead,—and being regenerated in the process, I have a claim to life everlasting."

The sprig of acacia, then, in its most ordinary signification, presents itself to the Master Mason as a symbol of the immortality of the soul, being intended to remind him, by its evergreen and unchanging nature, of that better and spiritual part within us, which, as an emanation from the Grand Architect of the Universe, can never die. And as this is the most ordinary, the most important; for thus, as the peculiar symbol of immortality, it becomes the most appropriate to an order all of whose teachings are intended to inculcate the great lesson that "life rises out of the grave." But incidental to this the acacia has

* Dr. Crucefix, MS., quoted by Oliver, *Landmarks,* ii. 2.

two other interpretations, which are well worthy of investigation.

Secondly, then, the acacia is a symbol of INNOCENCE. The symbolism here is of a peculiar and unusual character, depending not on any real analogy in the form or use of the symbol to the idea symbolized, but simply on a double or compound meaning of the word. For αχαχια, in the Greek language, signifies both the plant in question and the moral quality of innocence or purity of life. In this sense the symbol refers, primarily, to him over whose solitary grave the acacia was planted, and whose virtuous conduct, whose integrity of life and fidelity to his trusts, have ever been presented as patterns to the craft, and consequently to all Master Masons, who, by this interpretation of the symbol, are invited to emulate his example.

Hutchinson, indulging in his favorite theory of Christianizing Masonry, when he comes to this signification of the symbol, thus enlarges on the interpretation: "We Masons, describing the deplorable estate of religion under the Jewish law, speak in figures: 'Her tomb was in the rubbish and filth cast forth of the temple, and *Acacia* wove its branches over her monument;' *akakia* being the Greek word for innocence, or being free from sin; implying that the sins and corruptions of the old law and devotees of the Jewish altar had hid Religion from those who sought her, and she was only to be found where *innocence* survived, and under the banner of the divine Lamb; and as to ourselves, professing that we were to be distinguished by our *Acacy,* or as true *Acacians* in our religious faith and tenets." *

* Spirit of Masonry, lcct. ix. p. 99.

Among the nations of antiquity, it was common thus by peculiar plants to symbolize the virtues and other qualities of the mind. In many instances the symbolism has been lost to the moderns, but in others it has been retained, and is well understood, even at the present day. Thus the olive was adopted as the symbol of peace, because, says Lee, "its oil is very useful, in some way or other, in all arts manual which principally flourish in times of peace."*

The quince among the Greeks was the symbol of love and happiness;† and hence, by the laws of Solon, in Athenian marriages, the bride and bridegroom were required to eat a quince together.

The palm was the symbol of victory;‡ and hence, in

* The Temple of Solomon, ch. ix. p. 233.

† It is probable that the quince derived this symbolism, like the acacia, from its name; for there seems to be some connection between the Greek word χυδώνιος, which means *a quince,* and the participle χυδίων, which signifies *rejoicing, exulting.* But this must have been an after-thought, for the name is derived from Cydon, in Crete, of which island the quince is a native.

‡ Desprez, speaking of the palm as an emblem of victory, says (*Comment, in Horat. Od.* I. i. 5), "Palma verò signum victoriæ passim apud omnes statuitur, ex Plutarcho, propterea quod ea est ejus natura ligni, ut urgentibus opprimentibusque minimè cedat. Unde est illud Alciati epigramma,—

> 'Nititur in pondus palma, et consurgit in altum:
> Quoque magis premitur, hoc magè tollit onus.'"

It is in the eighth book of his Symposia that Plutarch states this peculiar property of the palm to resist the oppression of any superincumbent weight, and to rise up against it, whence it was adopted as the symbol of victory. Cowley also alludes to it in his *Davideis.*

> "Well did he know how palms by oppression speed
> Victorious, and the victor's sacred meed."

the catacombs of Rome, the burial-place of so many of the early Christians, the palm leaf is constantly found as an emblem of the Christian's triumph over sin and death.

The rosemary was a symbol of remembrance, and hence was used both at marriages and at funerals, the memory of the past being equally appropriate in both rites.*

The parsley was consecrated to grief; and hence all the Greeks decked their tombs with it; and it was used to crown the conquerors in the Nemean games, which were of a funereal character.†

But it is needless to multiply instances of this symbolism. In adopting the acacia as a symbol of innocence, Masonry has but extended the principle of an ancient and universal usage, which thus consecrated particular plants, by a mystical meaning, to the representation of particular virtues.

But lastly, the acacia is to be considered as the symbol of INITIATION. This is by far the most interesting of its interpretations, and was, we have every reason to

---

* "Rosemary was anciently supposed to strengthen the memory, and was not only carried at funerals, but worn at weddings." — STEEVENS, *Notes on Hamlet,* a. iv. s. 5.—Douce(*Illustrations of Shakspeare,* i. 345) gives the following old song in reference to this subject:—

> "Rosemarie is for remembrance
> Betweene us daie and night,
> Wishing that I might always have
> You present in my sight."

† Ste. Croix (*Recherches sur les Mystères,* i. 56) says that in the Samothracian Mysteries it was forbidden to put parsley on the table, because, according to the mystagogues, it had been produced by the blood of Cadmillus, slain by his brothers.

believe, the primary and original, the others being but incidental. It leads us at once to the investigation of that significant fact to which I have already alluded, that in all the ancient initiations and religious mysteries there was some plant, peculiar to each, which was consecrated by its own esoteric meaning, and which occupied an important position in the celebration of the rites; so that the plant, whatever it might be, from its constant and prominent use in the ceremonies of initiation, came at length to be adopted as the symbol of that initiation.

A reference to some of these *sacred plants*—for such was the character they assumed—and an investigation of their symbolism will not, perhaps, be uninteresting or useless, in connection with the subject of the present article.

In the Mysteries of Adonis, which originated in Phœnicia, and were afterwards transferred to Greece, the death and resurrection of Adonis was represented. A part of the legend accompanying these mysteries was, that when Adonis was slain by a wild boar, Venus laid out the body on a bed of lettuce. In memorial of this supposed fact, on the first day of the celebration, when funeral rites were performed, lettuces were carried in the procession, *newly planted* in shells of earth. Hence the lettuce became the sacred plant of the Adonia, or Adonisian Mysteries.

The lotus was the sacred plant of the Brahminical rites of India, and was considered as the symbol of their elemental trinity,—earth, water, and air,—because, as an aquatic plant, it derived its nutriment from all of these elements combined, its roots being planted in the earth, its stem rising through the water, and its leaves exposed to the air.* The Egyptians, who borrowed a large portion of their religious rites from the East, adopted the lotus, which was also indigenous to their country, as a mystical plant, and made it the symbol of their initiation, or the birth into celestial light. Hence, as Champollion observes, they often on their monuments represented the god Phre, or the sun, as borne within the expanded calyx of the lotus. The lotus bears a flower similar to that of the poppy, while its large, tongue-shaped leaves float upon the surface of the water. As the Egyptians had remarked that the plant expands when the sun rises, and closes when it sets, they adopted it as a symbol of the sun; and as that luminary was the principal object of the popular worship, the lotus became in all their sacred rites a consecrated and mystical plant.

The Egyptians also selected the *erica,*† or heath, as a sacred plant. The origin of the consecration of this plant presents us with a singular coincidence, that will be peculiarly interesting to the masonic student. We are informed that there was a legend in the mysteries of Osiris, which related, that Isis, when in search of the body of her murdered husband, discovered it interred at the brow of a hill, near which an erica, or heath plant, grew; and hence, after the recovery of the body and the resurrection

---

* "The Hindoos," says Faber, "represent their mundane lotus, as having four large leaves and four small leaves placed alternately, while from the centre of the flower rises a protuberance. Now, the circular cup formed by the eight leaves they deem a symbol of the earth, floating on the surface of the ocean, and consisting of four large continents and four intermediate smaller islands; while the centrical protuberance is viewed by them as representing their sacred Mount Menu."—*Communication to Gent. Mag.*vol. lxxxvi. p. 408.

†The *erica arborea,* or tree heath.

of the god, when she established the mysteries to commemorate her loss and her recovery, she adopted the erica, as a sacred plant,* in memory of its having pointed out the spot where the *mangled remains* of Osiris were concealed.†

The *mistletoe* was the sacred plant of Druidism. Its consecrated character was derived from a legend of the Scandinavian mythology, and which is thus related in the Edda, or sacred books. the god Balder, the son of Odin, having dreamed that he was in some great danger of life, his mother, Friga, exacted an oath from all the creatures of the animal, the vegetable, and the mineral kingdoms, that they would do no harm to her son. The mistletoe, contemptible from its size and weakness, was alone neglected, and of it no oath of immunity was demanded. Lok, the evil genius, or god of Darkness, becoming acquainted with this fact, placed an arrow made of mistletoe in the hands of Holder, the blind brother of Balder, on a certain day, when the gods were throwing missiles at him in sport, and wondering at their inability to do him injury with any arms with which they could attack him. But, being shot with the mistletoe arrow, it inflicted a fatal wound, and Balder died.

Ever afterwards the mistletoe was revered as a sacred

---

* Ragon thus alludes to this mystical event: "Isis found the body of Osiris in the neighborhood of Biblos, and near a tall plant called the *erica.* Oppressed with grief, she seated herself on the margin of a fountain, whose waters issued from a rock. This rock is the *small hill* mentioned in the ritual; the erica has been replaced by the acacia, and the grief of Isis has been changed for that of the fellow crafts."—*Cours des Initiations,* p. 151.

† It is singular, and perhaps significant, that the word *eriko,* in Greek, ἐρίχω, whence *erica* is probably derived, means *to break in pieces, to mangle.*

plant, consecrated to the powers of darkness; and annually it became an important rite among the Druids to proceed into the forest in search of the mistletoe, which, being found, was cut down by the Arch Druid, and its parts, after a solemn sacrifice, were distributed among the people. Clavel* very ingeniously remarks, that it is evident, in reference to the legend, that as Balder symbolizes the Sun-god, and Lok, Darkness, this search for the mistletoe was intended to deprive the god of Darkness of the power of destroying the god of Light. And the distribution of the fragments of the mistletoe among their pious worshippers, was to assure them that henceforth a similar attempt of Lok would prove abortive, and he was thus deprived of the means of effecting his design.†

The *myrtle* performed the same office of symbolism in the Mysteries of Greece as the lotus did in Egypt, or the mistletoe among the Druids. The candidate, in these initiations, was crowned with myrtle, because, according to the popular theology, the myrtle was sacred to Proserpine, the goddess of the future life. Every classical scholar will remember the golden branch with which Æneas was supplied by the Sibyl, before proceeding on his journey to the infernal regions‡—a voyage which

---

* Histoire Pittoresque des Religions, t. i. p. 217.

† According to Toland (*Works,* i. 74), the festival of searching, cutting, and consecrating the mistletoe, took place on the 10th of March, or New Year's day. "This," he says, "is the ceremony to which Virgil alludes, by his *golden branch,* in the Sixth Book of the Æneid." No doubt of it; for all these sacred plants had a common origin in some ancient and general symbolic idea.

‡ "Under this branch is figured the wreath of myrtle, with which the initiated were crowned at the celebration of the Mysteries."—WARBURTON, *Divine Legation,* vol. i. p. 299.

is now universally admitted to be a mythical representation of the ceremonies of initiation.

In all of these ancient Mysteries, while the sacred plant was a symbol of initiation, the initiation itself was symbolic of the resurrection to a future life, and of the immortality of the soul. In this view, Freemasonry is to us now in the place of the ancient initiations, and the acacia is substituted for the lotus, the erica, the ivy, the mistletoe, and the myrtle. The lesson of wisdom is the same; the medium of imparting it is all that has been changed.

Returning, then, to the acacia, we find that it is capable of three explanations. It is a symbol of immortality, of innoceuce, and of initiation. But these three significations are closely connected, and that connection must be observed, if we desire to obtain a just interpretation of the symbol. Thus, in this one symbol, we are taught that in the initiation of life, of which the initiation in the third degree is simply emblematic, innocence must for a time lie in the grave, at length, however, to be called, by the word of the Grand Master of the Universe, to a blissful immortality. Combine with this the recollection of the place where the sprig of acacia was planted, and which I have heretofore shown to be Mount Calvary, the place of sepulture of Him who "brought life and immortality to light," and who, in Christian Masonry, is designated, as he is in Scripture, as "the lion of the tribe of Judah," and remember, too, that in the mystery of his death, the wood of the cross takes the place of the acacia, and in this little and apparently insignificant symbol, but which is really and truly the most important and significant one in masonic science, we have a beautiful suggestion of all the mysteries of life and death, of time and eternity, of the present and of the future. Thus read (and thus all our symbols should be read), Masonry proves something more to its disciples than a mere social society or a charitable association. It becomes a "lamp to our feet," whose spiritual light shines on the darkness of the deathbed, and dissipates the gloomy shadows of the grave.

XXIX.

THE SYMBOLISM OF LABOR.

IT is one of the most beautiful features of the Masonic Institution, that it teaches not only the necessity, but the nobility, of labor. Among the earliest of the implements in whose emblematic use it instructs its neophytes is the Trestle Board, the acknowledged symbol of the Divine Law, in accordance with whose decree* labor was originally instituted as the common lot of all; and therefore the important lesson that is closely connected with this symbol is, that to labor well and truly, to labor honestly and persistently, is the object and the chief end of all humanity.

To work out well the task that is set before us is our highest duty, and should constitute our greatest happiness. All men, then, must have their trestle boards; for the principles that guide us in the discharge of our duty—the schemes that we devise—the plans that we

---

* "In the sweat of thy face shalt thou eat bread." Gen. 3:19. Bush interprets the decree to mean that "some species of toilsome occupation is the appointed lot of all men."

propose—are but the trestle board, whose designs we follow, for good or for evil, in our labor of life.

Earth works with every coming spring, and within its prolific bosom designs the bursting seed, the tender plant, and the finished tree, upon its trestle board.

Old ocean works forever—restless and murmuring—but still bravely working; and storms and tempests, the purifiers of stagnant nature, are inscribed upon its trestle board.

And God himself, the Grand Architect, the Master Builder of the world, has labored from eternity; and working by his omnipotent will, he inscribes his plans upon illimitable space, for the universe is his trestle board.

There was a saying of the monks of old which is well worth meditation. They taught that "*laborare est orare*"—labor is worship. They did not, it is true, always practise the wise precept. They did not always make labor a part of their religion. Like Onuphrius, who lived threescore years and ten in the desert, without human voice or human sympathy to cheer him, because he had not learned that man was made for man, those old ascetics went into the wilderness, and built cells, and occupied themselves in solitary meditation and profitless thought. They prayed much, but they did no work. And thus they passed their lives, giving no pity, aid, or consolation to their fellow-men, adding no mite to the treasury of human knowledge, and leaving the world, when their selfish pilgrimage was finished, without a single contribution, in labor of mind or body, to its welfare.*

---

* Aristotle says, "He that cannot contract society with others, or who, through his own self-sufficiency [αὐτάρχειαν], does not

And men, seeing the uselessness of these ascetic lives, shrink now from their example, and fall back upon that wiser teaching, that he best does God's will who best does God's work. The world now knows that heaven is not served by man's idleness—that the "*dolce far niente,*" though it might suit an Italian lazzaroni, is not fit for a brave Christian man, and that they who would do rightly, and act well their part, must take this distich for their motto:—

"With this hand work, and with the other pray,

And God will bless them both from day to day.

Now, this doctrine, that labor is worship, is the very doctrine that has been advanced and maintained, from time immemorial, as a leading dogma of the Order of Freemasonry. There is no other human institution under the sun which has set forth this great principle in such bold relief. We hear constantly of Freemasonry as an institution that inculcates morality, that fosters the social feeling, that teaches brotherly love; and all this is well, because it is true; but we must never forget that from its foundation-stone to its pinnacle, all over its vast temple, is inscribed, in symbols of living light, the great truth that *labor is worship.*

It has been supposed that, because we speak of Freemasonry as a speculative system, it has nothing to do with the practical. But this is a most grievous error. Freemasonry is, it is true, and a speculative science, but it is a speculative science based upon an operative art. All its symbols and allegories refer to this connection.

need it, forms no part of the community, but is either a wild beast or a god."

Its very language is borrowed from the art, and it is singularly suggestive that the initiation of a candidate into its mysteries is called, in its peculiar phraseology, *work.*

I repeat that this expression is singularly suggestive. When the lodge is engaged in reading petitions, hearing reports, debating financial matters, it is said to be occupied in *business;* but when it is engaged in the form and ceremony of initiation into any of the degrees, it is said to be at *work.* Initiation is masonic labor. This phraseology at once suggests the connection of our speculative system with an operative art that preceded it, and upon which it has been founded. This operative art must have given it form and features and organization. If the speculative system had been founded solely on philosophical or ethical principles, if it had been derived from some ancient or modern sect of philosophers,— from the Stoics, the Epicureans, or the Platonists of the heathen world, or from any of the many divisions of the scholastics of the middle ages,—this origin would most certainly have affected its interior organization as well as its external form, and we should have seen our modern masonic reunions assuming the style of academies or schools. Its technical language—for, like every institution isolated from the ordinary and general pursuits of mankind, it would have had its own technical dialect—would have been borrowed from, and would be easily traced to, the peculiar phraseology of the philosophic sects which had given it birth. There would have been the *sophists* and the *philosophers;* the *grammatists* and the *grammarians;* the *scholars,* the *masters,* and the *doctors.* It would have had its *trivial* and its *quadrivial* schools; its occupation would have been research, experiment, or investigation; in a word, its whole features would have been colored by a grammatical, a rhetorical, or a mathematical cast, accordingly as it should have been derived from a sect in which any one of these three characteristics was the predominating influence.

But in the organization of Freemasonry, as it now presents itself to us, we see an entirely different appearance. Its degrees are expressive, not of advancement in philosophic attainments, but of progress in a purely mechanical pursuit. Its highest grade is that of *Master of the Work.* Its places of meeting are not schools, but *lodges,* places where the workmen formerly lodged, in the neighborhood of the building on whose construction they were engaged. It does not form theories, but builds temples. It knows nothing of the rules of the dialecticians,—of the syllogism, the dilemma, the enthymeme, or the sorites,—but it recurs to the homely implements of its operative parent for its methods of instruction, and with the plumb-line it inculcates rectitude of conduct, and draws lessons of morality from the workman's square. It sees in the Supreme God that it worships, not a "*numen divinum,*" a divine power, nor a "*moderator rerum omnium,*" a controller of all things, as the old philosophers designated him, but a *Grand Architect of the Universe.* The masonic idea of God refers to Him as the Mighty Builder of this terrestrial globe, and all the countless worlds that surround it. He is not the *ens entium,* or *to theion,* or any other of the thousand titles with which ancient and modern speculation has invested him, but simply the Architect,—as the Greeks have it, the ἀρχὸς τέχτων, the chief workman,—under whom we are all workmen also;* and hence our labor is his worship.

This idea, then, of masonic labor, is closely connected with the history of the organization of the institution. When we say "the lodge is at work," we recognize that it is in the legitimate practice of that occupation for which it was originally intended. The Masons that are in it are not occupied in thinking, or speculating, or reasoning, but simply and emphatically in working. The duty of a Mason as such, in his lodge, is to work. Thereby he accomplishes the destiny of his Order. Thereby he best fulfils his obligation to the Grand Architect, for with the Mason *laborare est orare*—labor is worship.

The importance of masonic labor being thus demonstrated, the question next arises as to the nature of that labor. What is the work that a Mason is called upon to perform?

Temple building was the original occupation of our ancient brethren. Leaving out of view that system of ethics and of religious philosophy, that search after truth, those doctrines of the unity of God and the immortality of the soul, which alike distinguish the ancient Mysteries and the masonic institution, and which both must have derived from a common origin,—most probably from some priesthood of the olden time,—let our attention be exclusively directed, for the present, to that period, so familiar to every Mason, when, under the supposed Grand Mastership

---

* "Der Arbeiter," says Lenning, "ist der symbolische Name eines Freimaurers"—the Workman is the symbolic name of a Freemason.—*Encyclop. der Fraumererei.*

of King Solomon, Freemasonry first assumed "a local habitation and a name" in the holy city of Jerusalem. There the labor of the Israelites and the skill of the Tyrians were occupied in the construction of that noble temple whose splendor and magnificence of decoration made it one of the wonders of the world.

Here, then, we see the two united nations directing their attention, with surprising harmony, to the task of temple building. The Tyrian workmen, coming immediately from the bosom of the mystical society of Dionysian artificers, whose sole employment was the erection of sacred edifices throughout all Asia Minor, indoctrinated the Jews with a part of their architectural skill, and bestowed upon them also a knowledge of those sacred Mysteries which they had practised at Tyre, and from which the present interior form of Freemasonry is said to be derived.

Now, if there be any so incredulous as to refuse their assent to the universally received masonic tradition on this subject, if there be any who would deny all connection of King Solomon with the origin of Freemasonry, except it be in a mythical or symbolical sense, such incredulity will not at all affect the chain of argument which I am disposed to use. For it will not be denied that the corporations of builders in the middle ages, those men who were known as "Travelling Freemasons," were substantial and corporeal, and that the cathedrals, abbeys, and palaces, whose ruins are still objects of admiration to all observers, bear conclusive testimony that their existence was nothing like a myth, and that their labors were not apocryphal. But these Travelling Freemasons, whether led into the error, if error it be, by a mistaken reading of history, or by a superstitious reverence for tradition, always esteemed King Solomon as the founder of their Order. So that the first absolutely historical details that we have of the masonic institution, connect it with the idea of a temple. And it is only for this idea that I contend, for it proves that the first Freemasons of whom we have authentic record, whether they were at Jerusalem or in Europe, and whether they flourished a thousand years before or a thousand years after the birth of Christ, always supposed that temple building was the peculiar specialty of their craft, and that their labor was to be the erection of temples in ancient times, and cathedrals and churches in the Christian age.

So that we come back at last to the proposition with which I had commenced, namely: that temple building was the original occupation of our ancient brethren. And to this is added the fact, that after a long lapse of centuries, a body of men is found in the middle ages who were universally recognized as Freemasons, and who directed their attention and their skill to the same pursuit, and were engaged in the construction of cathedrals, abbeys, and other sacred edifices, these being the Christian substitute for the heathen or the Jewish temple.

And therefore, when we view the history of the Order as thus developed in its origin and its design, we are justified in saying that, in all times past, its members have been recognized as men of labor, and that their labor has been temple building.

But our ancient brethren wrought in both operative and speculative Masonry, while we work only in speculative. They worked with the hand; we work with the brain. They dealt in the material; we in the spiritual. They used in their labor wood and stones; we use thoughts, and feelings, and affections. We both devote ourselves to labor, but the object of the labor and the mode of the labor are different.

The French rituals have given us the key-note to the explanation of what is masonic labor when they say that "Freemasons erect temples for virtue and dungeons for vice."

The modern Freemasons, like the Masons of old, are engaged in the construction of a temple; but with this difference: that the temple of the latter was material, that of the former spiritual. When the operative art was the predominant characteristic of the Order, Masons were engaged in the construction of material and earthly temples. But when the operative art ceased, and the speculative science took its place, then the Freemasons symbolized the labors of their predecessors by engaging in the construction of a spiritual temple in their hearts, which was to be made so pure that it might become the dwelling-place of Him who is all purity. It was to be "a house not made with hands," where the hewn stone was to be a purified heart.

This symbolism, which represents man as a temple, a house, a sacred building in which God is to dwell, is not new, nor peculiar to the masonic science. It was known to the Jewish, and is still recognized by the Christian, system. The Talmudists had a saying that the threefold repetition of the words "Temple of Jehovah," in the seventh chapter and fourth verse of the book of Jeremiah, was intended to allude to the existence of three temples; and hence in one of their treatises it is said,

"Two temples have been destroyed, but the third will endure forever," in which it is manifest that they referred to the temple of the immortal soul in man.

By a similar allusion, which, however, the Jews chose wilfully to misunderstand, Christ declared, "Destroy this temple, and in three days I will raise it up." And the beloved disciple, who records the conversation, does not allow us to doubt of the Saviour's meaning.

"Then said the Jews, Forty and six years was this temple in building, and wilt thou rear it up in three days?

"But he spake of the temple of his body."*

In more than one place the apostle Paul has fondly dwelt upon this metaphor. Thus he tells the Corinthians that they are "God's building," and he calls himself the "wise master builder," who was to lay the foundation in his truthful doctrine, upon which they were to erect the edifice.† And he says to them immediately afterwards, "Know ye not that ye are the temple of God, and that the Spirit of God dwelleth in you?"

In consequence of these teachings of the apostles, the idea that the body was a temple has pervaded, from the earliest times to the present day, the system of Christian or theological symbolism. Indeed, it has sometimes been carried to an almost too fanciful excess. Thus Samuel Lee, in that curious and rare old work, "*The Temple of Solomon, pourtrayed by Scripture Light,*" thus dilates on this symbolism of the temple:—

"The *foundation* of this temple may be laid in humility and contrition of spirit, wherein the inhabiter of eternity delighteth to dwell; we may refer the *porch* to

---

* John 3:19-21.   † 1 Corinth. 3:9.

the mouth of a saint, wherein every holy Jacob erects the *pillars* of God's praise, calling upon and blessing his name for received mercies; when songs of deliverance are uttered from the *doors* of his lips. The *holy place* is the renewed mind, and the *windows* therein may denote divine illumination from above, cautioning a saint lest they be darkened with the smoke of anger, the mist of grief, the dust of vain-glory, or the filthy mire of worldly cares. The *golden candlesticks*, the infused habits of divine knowledge resting within the soul. The *shewbread,* the word of grace exhibited in the promises for the preservation of a Christian's life and glory. The *golden altar* of odors, the breathings, sufferings, and groanings after God, ready to break forth into Abba, Father. The *veiles,* the righteousness of Christ. The *holy of holies* may relate to the conscience purified from dead works and brought into a heavenly frame."* And thus he proceeds, symbolizing every part and utensil of the temple as alluding to some emotion or affection of man, but in language too tedious for quotation.

In a similar vein has the celebrated John Bunyan, the author of the "*Pilgrim's Progress,*" proceeded in his "*Temple of Solomon Spiritualized,*" to refer every part of that building to a symbolic meaning, selecting, however, the church, or congregation of good men, rather than the individual man, as the object of the symbolism.

In the middle ages the Hermetic philosophers seem to have given the same interpretation of the temple, and Swedenborg, in his mystical writings, adopts the idea.

* Orbis Miraculum, or the Temple of Solomon, pourtrayed by Scripture Light, ch. ix. p. 192. London, 1659.

Hitchcock, who has written an admirable little work on Swedenborg considered as a Hermetic Philosopher, thus alludes to this subject, and his language, as that of a learned and shrewd investigator, is well worthy of quotation:—

"With, perhaps, the majority of readers, the Tabernacle of Moses and the Temple of Solomon were mere buildings; very magnificent indeed, but still mere buildings for the worship of God. But some are struck with many portions of the account of their erection, admitting a moral interpretation; and while the buildings are allowed to stand (or to have stood once) visible objects, these interpreters are delighted to meet with indications that Moses and Solomon, in building the temples, were wise in the knowledge of God and of man; from which point it is not difficult to pass on to the moral meaning altogether, and to affirm that the building which was erected without 'the noise of a hammer or axe, or any tool of iron,' was altogether a moral building—a building of God, not made with hands: in short, many see in the story of Solomon's temple a symbolical representation of MAN as the temple of God, with its *holy of holies* deep-seated in the centre of the human heart."*

The French Masons have not been inattentive to this symbolism. Their already quoted expression that the "Freemasons build temples for virtue and dungeons for vice," has very clearly a reference to it, and their most distinguished writers never lose sight of it.

---

* Swedenborg a Hermetic Philosopher, &c., p. 210. The object of the author is to show that the Swedish sage was an adept, and that his writings may be interpreted from the point of view of Hermetic philosophy.

Thus Ragon, one of the most learned of the French historians of Freemasonry, in his lecture to the Apprentice, says that the founders of our Order "called themselves Masons, and proclaimed that they were building a temple to truth and virtue."* And subsequently he addresses the candidate who has received the Master's degree in the following language:—

"Profit by all that has been revealed to you. Improve your heart and your mind. Direct your passions to the general good; combat your prejudices; watch over your thoughts and your actions; love, enlighten, and assist your brethren; and you will have perfected that *temple* of which you are at once the *architect,* the *material,* and the *workman.*"†

Rebold, another French historian of great erudition, says, "If Freemasonry has ceased to erect temples, and by the aid of its architectural designs to elevate all hearts to the Deity, and all eyes and hopes to heaven, it has not therefore desisted from its work of moral and intellectual building;" and he thinks that the success of the institution has justified this change of purpose and the disruption of the speculative from the operative character of the Order.‡

Eliphas Levi, who has written abstrusely and mystically on Freemasonry and its collateral sciences, sees very clearly an allegorical and a real design in the institution, the former being the rebuilding of the temple of Solomon, and the latter the improvement of the human

* Cours Philosophique et Interprétatif des Initiations Anciennes et Modernes, p. 99.

† Ibid., p. 176.

‡ Histoire Générale de la Franc-maçonnerie, p. 52.

race by a reconstruction of its social and religious elements.*

The Masons of Germany have elaborated this idea with all the exhaustiveness that is peculiar to the German mind, and the masonic literature of that country abounds in essays, lectures, and treatises, in which the prominent topic is this building of the Solomonic temple as referring to the construction of a moral temple.

Thus writes Bro. Rhode, of Berlin:—

"So soon as any one has received the consecration of our Order, we say to him that we are building a mystical temple;" and he adds that "this temple which we Masons are building is nothing else than that which will conduce to the greatest possible happiness of mankind."†

And another German brother, Von Wedekind, asserts that "we only labor in our temple when we make man our predominating object, when we unite goodness of heart with polished manners, truth with beauty, virtue with grace."‡

Again we have Reinhold telling us, in true Teutonic expansiveness of expression, that "by the mystical Solomonic temple we are to understand the high ideal or archetype of humanity in the best possible condition of social improvement, wherein every evil inclination is overcome, every passion is resolved into the spirit of

* Histoire de la Magie, liv. v. ch. vii. p. 100.

† Vorlesung aber das Symbol des Tempels, in the "Jarbüchern der Gross. Loge Roy. York zur Freundschaft," cited by Lenning, Encyc., voc. *Tempel.*

‡ In an Essay on the Masonic Idea of Man's Destination, cited by Lenning, *ut supra,* from the Altenburg *Zeitschift der Freimaurcrei.*

love, and wherein each for all, and all for each, kindly strive to work."*

And thus the German Masons call this striving for an almost millennial result *labor in the temple.*

The English Masons, although they have not treated the symbolism of the Order with the same abstruse investigation that has distinguished those of Germany and France, still have not been insensible to this idea that the building of the Solomonic temple is intended to indicate a cultivation of the human character. Thus Hutchinson, one of the earliest of the symbolic writers of England, shows a very competent conception—for the age in which he lived—of the mystical meaning of the temple; and later writers have improved upon his crude views. It must, however, be acknowledged that neither Hutchinson nor Oliver, nor any other of the distinguished masonic writers of England, has dwelt on this peculiar symbolism of a moral temple with that earnest appreciation of the idea that is to be found in the works of the French and German Masons. But although the allusions are rather casual and incidental, yet the symbolic theory is evidently recognized.†

Our own country has produced many students of Masonic symbolism, who have thoroughly grasped this noble thought, and treated it with eloquence and erudition.

Fifty years ago Salem Towne wrote thus: "Speculative

---

* Cited by Lenning, *ut sup.*

† Thus Dr. Oliver, while treating of the relation of the temple to the lodge, thus briefly alludes to this important symbol: "As our ancient brethren erected a material temple, without the use of axe, hammer, or metal tool, so is our moral temple constructed." — *Historical Landmarks,* lect. xxxi.

Masonry, according to present acceptation, has an ultimate reference to that spiritual building erected by virtue in the heart, and summarily implies the arrangement and perfection of those holy and sublime principles by which the soul is fitted for a meet temple of God in a world of immortality."*

Charles Scott has devoted one of the lectures in his "Analogy of Ancient Craft Masonry to Natural and Revealed Religion" to a thorough consideration of this subject. The language is too long for quotation, but the symbol has been well interpreted by him.†

Still more recently, Bro. John A. Lodor has treated the topic in an essay, which I regret has not had a larger circulation. A single and brief passage may show the spirit of the production, and how completely it sustains the idea of this symbolism.

"We may disguise it as we will," says Bro. Lodor, "we may evade a scrutiny of it; but our character, as it is, with its faults and blemishes, its weaknesses and infirmities, its vices and its stains, together with its redeeming traits, its better parts, is our speculative temple." And he goes on to extend the symbolic idea: "Like the exemplar temple on Mount Moriah, it should be preserved as a hallowed shrine, and guarded with the same vigllant care. It should be our pearl of price set round with walls and enclosures, even as was the Jewish temple, and the impure, the vicious, the guilty, and the profane be banished from even its outer courts. A faithful sentinel should be placed at every gate, a watchman on every

* System of Speculative Masonry, ch. vi. p. 63.

† On the Speculative Temple — an essay read in 1861 before the Grand Lodge of Alabama.

wall, and the first approach of a cowan and eavesdropper be promptly met and resisted."

Teachings like this are now so common that every American Mason who has studied the symbolism of his Order believes, with Carlyle, that "there is but one temple in the world, and that is the body of man."

This inquiry into the meaning and object of labor, as a masonic symbol, brings us to these conclusions:—

1. That our ancient brethren worked as long as the operative art predominated in the institution at material temples, the most prominent of these being the temple of King Solomon.

2. That when the speculative science took the place of the operative art, the modern Masons, working no longer at material temples, but holding still to the sacred thought, the reverential idea, of a holy temple, a Lord's house to be built, began to labor at living temples, and to make man, the true house of the Lord, the tabernacle for the indwelling of the Holy Spirit.

And, 3. Therefore to every Freemason who rightly comprehends his art, this construction of a living temple is his labor.

"Labor," says Gadicke, the German masonic lexicographer, "is an important word in Masonry; indeed, we might say the most important. For this, and this alone, does a man become a Freemason. Every other object is secondary or incidental. Labor is the accustomed design of every lodge meeting. But does such meeting always furnish evidence of industry? The labor of an operative mason will be visible, and he will receive his reward for it, even though the building he has constructed may, in the next hour, be overthrown by a tempest. He knows that he has done his labor. And so must the Freemason labor. His labor must be visible to himself and to his brethren, or, at least, it must conduce to his own internal satisfaction. As we build neither a visible Solomonic temple nor an Egyptian pyramid, our industry must become visible in works that are imperishable, so that when we vanish from the eyes of mortals it may be said of us that our labor was well done."

And remembering what the apostle has said, that we are the temple of God, and that the Spirit of God dwelleth in us, we know that our labor is so to build that temple that it shall become worthy of its divine Dweller.

And thus, too, at last, we can understand the saying of the old monks that "labor is worship;" and as Masons we labor in our lodge, labor to make ourselves a perfect building, without blemish, working hopefully for the consummation, when the house of our earthly tabernacle shall be finished, when the LOST WORD of divine truth shall at last be discovered, and when we shall be found by our own efforts at perfection to have done God service. For so truly is the meaning of those noble words—LABOR IS WORSHIP.

XXX.

THE STONE OF FOUNDATION.*

THE Stone of Foundation constitutes one of the most important and abstruse of all the symbols of Freemasonry. It is referred to in numerous legends and traditions, not only of the Freemasons, but also of the Jewish Rabbins, the Talmudic writers, and even the Mussulman doctors. Many of these, it must be confessed, are apparently puerile and absurd; but some of them, and especially the masonic ones, are deeply interesting in their allegorical signification.

The Stone of Foundation is, properly speaking, a symbol of the higher degrees. It makes its first appearance in the Royal Arch, and forms, indeed, the most important symbol of that degree. But it is so intimately connected, in its legendary history, with the construction of the Solomonic temple, that it must be considered as a part of Ancient Craft Masonry, although he who confines the range of his investigations to the first three

---

* A portion of this essay, but in a very abridged form, was used by the author in his work on "Cryptic Masonry."

degrees, will have no means, within that narrow limit, of properly appreciating the symbolism of the Stone of Foundation.

As preliminary to the inquiry which is about to be instituted, it is necessary to distinguish the Stone of Foundation, both in its symbolism and in its legendary history, from other stones which play an important part in the masonic ritual, but which are entirely distinct from it. Such are the *corner-stone,* which was always placed in the north-east corner of the building about to be erected, and to which such a beautiful reference is made in the ceremonies of the first degree; or the *keystone,* which constitutes an interesting part of the Mark Master's degree; or, lastly, the *cape-stone,* upon which all the ritual of the Most Excellent Master's degree is founded. These are all, in their proper places, highly interesting and instructive symbols, but have no connection whatever with the Stone of Foundation or its symbolism. Nor, although the Stone of Foundation is said, for peculiar reasons, to have been of a cubical form, must it be confounded with that stone called by the continental Masons the *cubical stone* — the *pierre cubique* of the French, and the *cubik stein* of the German Masons, but which in the English system is known as the *perfect ashlar.*

The Stone of Foundation has a legendary history and a symbolic signification which are peculiar to itself, and which differ from the history and meaning which belong to these other stones.

Let us first define this masonic Stone of Foundation, then collate the legends which refer to it, and afterwards investigate its significance as a symbol. To the Mason who takes a pleasure in the study of the mysteries of his institution, the investigation cannot fail to be interesting, if it is conducted with any ability.

But in the very beginning, as a necessary preliminary to any investigation of this kind, it must be distinctly understood that all that is said of this Stone of Foundation in Masonry is to be strictly taken in a mythical or allegorical sense. Dr. Oliver, the most learned of our masonic writers, while undoubtedly himself knowing that it was simply a symbol, has written loosely of it, as though it were a substantial reality; and hence, if the passages in his "Historical Landmarks," and in his other works which refer to this celebrated stone are accepted by his readers in a literal sense, they will present absurdities and puerilities which would not occur if the Stone of Foundation was received, as it really is, as a philosophical myth, conveying a most profound and beautiful symbolism. Read in this spirit, as all the legends of Masonry should be read, the mythical story of the Stone of Foundation becomes one of the most important and interesting of all the masonic symbols.

The Stone of Foundation is supposed, by the theory which establishes it, to have been a stone placed at one time within the foundations of the temple of Solomon, and afterwards, during the building of the second temple, transported to the Holy of Holies. It was in form a perfect cube, and had inscribed upon its upper face, within a delta or triangle, the sacred tetragrammaton, or ineffable name of God. Oliver, speaking with the solemnity of an historian, says that Solomon thought that he had rendered the house of God worthy, so far as human adornment could effect, for the dwelling of

God, "when he had placed the celebrated Stone of
Foundation, on which the sacred name was mystically
engraven, with solemn ceremonies, in that sacred
depository on Mount Moriah, along with the foundations
of Dan and Asher, the centre of the Most Holy Place,
where the ark was overshadowed by the shekinah of
God."* The Hebrew Talmudists, who thought as much
of this stone, and had as many legends concerning it as
the masonic Talmudists, called it *eben shatijah,*† or
"Stone of Foundation," because, as they said, it had been
laid by Jehovah as the foundation of the world; and
hence the apocryphal book of Enoch speaks of the
"stone which supports the corners of the earth."

This idea of a foundation stone of the world was most
probably derived from that magnificent passage of the
book of Job, in which the Almighty demands of the
afflicted patriarch,—

> "Where wast thou, when I laid the foundation of the earth?
> Declare, since thou hast such knowledge!
> Who fixed its dimensions, since thou knowest?
> Or who stretched out the line upon it?
> Upon what were its foundations fixed?
> And who laid its corner-stone,
> When the morning stars sang together,
> And all the sons of God shouted for joy?"‡

Noyes, whose beautiful translation I have adopted as
not materially differing from the common version, but
which is far more poetical and more in the strain of the
original, thus explains the allusions to the foundation-
stone:

* Hist. Landmarks, i. 459, note 52.
† אבן שתייה. See the Gemara and Buxtorf Lex. Talm., p. 2541.
‡ Job 38:4-7.

"It was the custom to celebrate the laying of the corner-stone of an important building with music, songs, shouting, &c. Hence the morning stars are represented as celebrating the laying of the corner-stone of the earth."*

Upon this meagre statement have been accumulated more traditions than appertain to any other masonic symbol. The Rabbins, as has already been intimated, divide the glory of these apocryphal histories with the Masons; indeed, there is good reason for a suspicion that nearly all the masonic legends owe their first existence to the imaginative genius of the writers of the Jewish Talmud. But there is this difference between the Hebrew and the masonic traditions, that the Talmudic scholar recited them as truthful histories, and swallowed, in one gulp of faith, all their impossibilities and anachronisms, while the masonic student has received them as allegories, whose value is not in the facts, but in the sentiments which they convey.

With this understanding of their meaning, let us proceed to a collation of these legends.

In that blasphemous work, the "*Toldoth Feshu,*" or *Life of Fesus,* written, it is supposed, in the thirteenth or fourteenth century, we find the following account of this wonderful stone:—

"At that time [the time of Jesus] there was in the House of the Sanctuary [that is, the temple] a Stone of Foundation, which is the very stone that our father Jacob anointed with oil, as it is described in the twentyeighth chapter of the book of Genesis. On that stone the

* A New Translation of the Book of Job, notes, p. 196.

letters of the tetragrammaton were inscribed, and whosoever of the Israelites should learn that name would be able to master the world. To prevent, therefore, any one from learning these letters, two iron dogs were placed upon two columns in front of the Sanctuary. If any person, having acquired the knowledge of these letters, desired to depart from the Sanctuary, the barking of the dogs, by magical power, inspired so much fear, that he suddenly forgot what he had acquired."

This passage is cited by the learned Buxtorf, in his "*Lexicon Talmudicum;*" * but in the copy of the "*Toldoth Feshu,*" which I have the good fortune to possess (for it is among the rarest of books), I find another passage which gives some additional particulars, in the following words:—

"At that time there was in the temple the ineffable name of God, inscribed upon the Stone of Foundation. For when King David was digging the foundation for the temple, he found in the depths of the excavation a certain stone, on which the name of God was inscribed. This stone he removed, and deposited it in the Holy of Holies."†

The same puerile story of the barking dogs is repeated, still more at length. It is not pertinent to the present

---

* In voc. שתייה, where some other curious extracts from the Talmud and Talmudic writers on the subject of the Stone of Foundation are given.

† Sepher Toldoth Jeshu, p. 6. The abominably scurrilous character of this work aroused the indignation of the Christians, who, in the fifteenth century, were not distinguished for a spirit of tolerance, and the Jews, becoming alarmed, made every effort to suppress it. But, in 1681, it was republished by Wagenselius in his "Tela Ignea Satanæ," with a Latin translation.

inquiry, but it may be stated as a mere matter of curious information, that this scandalous book, which is throughout a blasphemous defamation of our Saviour, proceeds to say, that he cunningly obtained a knowledge of the tetragrammaton from the Stone of Foundation, and by its mystical influence was enabled to perform his miracles.

The masonic legends of the Stone of Foundation, based on these and other rabbinical reveries, are of the most extraordinary character, if they are to be viewed as histories, but readily reconcilable with sound sense, if looked at only in the light of allegories. They present an uninterrupted succession of events, in which the Stone of Foundation takes a prominent part, from Adam to Solomon, and from Solomon to Zerubbabel.

Thus the first of these legends, in order of time, relates that the Stone of Foundation was possessed by Adam while in the garden of Eden; that he used it as an altar, and so reverenced it, that, on his expulsion from Paradise, he carried it with him into the world in which he and his descendants were afterwards to earn their bread by the sweat of their brow:

Another legend informs us that from Adam the Stone of Foundation descended to Seth. From Seth it passed by regular succession to Noah, who took it with him into the ark, and after the subsidence of the deluge, made on it his first thank-offering. Noah left it on Mount Ararat, where it was subsequently found by Abraham, who removed it, and consequently used it as an altar of sacrifice. His grandson Jacob took it with him when he fled to his uncle Laban in Mesopotamia, and used it as a pillow when, in the vicinity of Luz, he had his celebrated vision.

Here there is a sudden interruption in the legendary history of the stone, and we have no means of conjecturing how it passed from the possession of Jacob into that of Solomon. Moses, it is true, is said to have taken it with him out of Egypt at the time of the exodus, and thus it may have finally reached Jerusalem. Dr. Adam Clarke * repeats what he very properly calls "a foolish tradition," that the stone on which Jacob rested his head was afterwards brought to Jerusalem, thence carried after a long lapse of time to Spain, from Spain to Ireland, and from Ireland to Scotland, where it was used as a seat on which the kings of Scotland sat to be crowned. Edward I., we know, brought a stone, to which this legend is attached, from Scotland to Westminster Abbey, where, under the name of Jacob's Pillow, it still remains, and is always placed under the chair upon which the British sovereign sits to be crowned, because there is an old distich which declares that wherever this stone is found the Scottish kings shall reign.†

But this Scottish tradition would take the Stone of Foundation away from all its masonic connections, and therefore it is rejected as a masonic legend.

The legends just related are in many respects contradictory and unsatisfactory, and another series, equally as old, are now very generally adopted by masonic scholars, as much better suited to the symbolism by which all these legends are explained.

This series of legends commences with the patriarch Enoch, who is supposed to have been the first consecrator

---

* Comment. on Gen. 28:18.
† " Ni fallit fatum, Scoti quocunque locatum
        Invenient lapidem, regnare tenentur ibidem."

of the Stone of Foundation. The legend of Enoch is so interesting and important in masonic science as to excuse something more than a brief reference to the incidents which it details.

The legend in full is as follows: Enoch, under the inspiration of the Most High, and in obedience to the instructions which he had received in a vision, built a temple under ground on Mount Moriah, and dedicated it to God. His son, Methuselah, constructed the building, although he was not acquainted with his father's motives for the erection. This temple consisted of nine vaults, situated perpendicularly beneath each other, and communicating by apertures left in each vault.

Enoch then caused a triangular plate of gold to be made, each side of which was a cubit long; he enriched it with the most precious stones, and encrusted the plate upon a stone of agate of the same form. On the plate he engraved the true name of God, or the tetragrammaton, and placing it on a cubical stone, known thereafter as the Stone of Foundation, he deposited the whole within the lowest arch.

When this subterranean building was completed, he made a door of stone, and attaching to it a ring of iron, by which it might be occasionally raised, he placed it over the opening of the uppermost arch, and so covered it that the aperture could not be discovered. Enoch himself was not permitted to enter it but once a year, and after the days of Enoch, Methuselah, and Lamech, and the destruction of the world by the deluge, all knowledge of the vault or subterranean temple, and of the Stone of Foundation, with the sacred and ineffable name inscribed upon it, was lost for ages to the world.

At the building of the first temple of Jerusalem, the Stone of Foundation again makes its appearance. Reference has already been made to the Jewish tradition that David, when digging the foundations of the temple, found in the excavation which he was making a certain stone, on which the ineffable name of God was inscribed, and which stone he is said to have removed and deposited in the Holy of Holies. That King David laid the foundations of the temple upon which the superstructure was subsequently erected by Solomon, is a favorite theory of the legend-mongers of the Talmud.

The masonic tradition is substantially the same as the Jewish, but it substitutes Solomon for David, thereby giving a greater air of probability to the narrative; and it supposes that the stone thus discovered by Solomon was the identical one that had been deposited in his secret vault by Enoch. This Stone of Foundation, the tradition states, was subsequently removed by King Solomon, and, for wise purposes, deposited in a secret and safer place.

In this the masonic tradition again agrees with the Jewish, for we find in the third chapter of the "*Treatise on the Temple,*" written by the celebrated Maimonides, the following narrative: —

"There was a stone in the Holy of Holies, on its west side, on which was placed the ark of the covenant, and before it the pot of manna and Aaron's rod. But when Solomon had built the temple, and foresaw that it was, at some future time, to be destroyed, he constructed a deep and winding vault under ground, for the purpose of concealing the ark, wherein Josiah afterwards, as we learn in the Second Book of Chronicles, 35:3, deposited it, with the pot of manna, the rod of Aaron, and the oil of anointing."

The Talmudical book "*Roma*" gives the same tradition, and says that "the ark of the covenant was placed in the centre of the Holy of Holies, upon a stone rising three fingers' breadth above the floor, to be, as it were, a pedestal for it." "This stone," says Prideaux,* "the Rabbins call the Stone of Foundation, and give us a great deal of trash about it."

There is much controversy as to the question of the existence of any ark in the second temple. Some of the Jewish writers assert that a new one was made; others, that the old one was found where it had been concealed by Solomon; and others again contend that there was no ark at all in the temple of Zerubbabel, but that its place was supplied by the Stone of Foundation on which it had originally rested.

Royal Arch Masons well know how all these traditions are sought to be reconciled by the masonic legend, in which the substitute ark and the Stone of Foundation play so important a part.

In the thirteenth degree of the Ancient and Accepted Rite, the Stone of Foundation is conspicuous as the resting-place of the sacred delta.

In the Royal Arch and Select Master's degrees of the Americanized York Rite, the Stone of Foundation constitutes the most important part of the ritual. In both of these it is the receptacle of the ark, on which the ineffable name is inscribed.

Lee, in his "*Temple of Solomon*," has devoted a chapter

* Old and New Testament connected, vol. i. p. 148.

to this Stone of Foundation, and thus recapitulates the Talmudic and Rabbinical traditions on the subject: —

"Vain and futilous are the feverish dreams of the ancient Rabbins concerning the Foundation Stone of the temple. Some assert that God placed this stone in the centre of the world, for a future basis and settled consistency for the earth to rest upon. Others held this stone to be the first matter, out of which all the beautiful visible beings of the world have been hewn forth and produced to light. Others relate that this was the very same stone laid by Jacob for a pillow under his head, in that night when he dreamed of an angelic vision at Bethel, and afterwards anointed and consecrated it to God. Which when Solomon had found (no doubt by forged revelation, or some tedious search, like another Rabbi Selemoh), he durst not but lay it sure, as the principal foundation stone of the temple. Nay, they say further, he caused to be engraved upon it the tetragrammaton, or the ineffable name of Jehovah."*

It will be seen that the masonic traditions on the subject of the Stone of Foundation do not differ very materially from these Rabbinical ones, although they give a few additional circumstances.

In the masonic legend, the Foundation Stone first makes its appearance, as I have already said, in the days of Enoch, who placed it in the bowels of Mount Moriah. There it was subsequently discovered by King Solomon, who deposited it in a crypt of the first temple, where it remained concealed until the foundations of the second temple were laid, when it was discovered and removed

---

* The Temple of Solomon, pourtrayed by Scripture Light, ch. ix. p. 194. Of the Mysteries laid up in the Foundation of the Temple.

to the Holy of Holies. But the most important point of the legend of the Stone of Foundation is its intimate and constant connection with the tetragrammaton, or ineffable name. It is this name, inscribed upon it, within the sacred and symbolic delta, that gives to the stone all its masonic value and significance. It is upon this fact, that it was so inscribed, that its whole symbolism depends.

Looking at these traditions in anything like the light of historical narratives, we are compelled to consider them, to use the plain language of Lee, "but as so many idle and absurd conceits." We must go behind the legend, viewing it only as an allegory, and study its symbolism.

The symbolism of the Foundation Stone of Masonry is therefore the next subject of investigation.

In approaching this, the most abstruse, and one of the most important, symbols of the Order, we are at once impressed with its apparent connection with the ancient doctrine of stone worship. Some brief consideration of this species of religious culture is therefore necessary for a proper understanding of the real symbolism of the Stone of Foundation.

The worship of stones is a kind of fetichism, which in the very infancy of religion prevailed, perhaps, more extensively than any other form of religious culture. Lord Kames explains the fact by supposing that stones erected as monuments of the dead became the place where posterity paid their veneration to the memory of the deceased, and that at length the people, losing sight of the emblematical signification, which was not readily understood, these monumental stones became objects of worship.

Others have sought to find the origin of stone-worship in the stone that was set up and anointed by Jacob at Bethel, and the tradition of which had extended into the heathen nations and become corrupted. It is certain that the Phoenicians worshipped sacred stones under the name of *Bœtylia,* which word is evidently derived from the Hebrew *Bethel;* and this undoubtedly gives some appearance of plausibility to the theory.

But a third theory supposes that the worship of stones was derived from the unskilfulness of the primitive sculptors, who, unable to frame, by their meagre principles of plastic art, a true image of the God whom they adored, were content to substitute in its place a rude or scarcely polished stone. Hence the Greeks, according to Pausanias, originally used unhewn stones to represent their deities, thirty of which that historian says he saw in the city of Pharæ. These stones were of a cubical form, and as the greater number of them were dedicated to the god Hermes, or Mercury, they received the generic name of *Hermœ.* Subsequently, with the improvement of the plastic art, the head was added.*

One of these consecrated stones was placed before the door of almost every house in Athens. They were also placed in front of the temples, in the gymnasia or schools, in libraries, and at the corners of streets, and in the roads. When dedicated to the god Terminus they were used as landmarks, and placed as such upon the concurrent lines of neighboring possessions.

The Thebans worshipped Bacchus under the form of a rude, square stone.

* See Pausanias, lib. iv.

Arnobius* says that Cybele was represented by a small stone of a black color. Eusebius cites Porphyry as saying that the ancients represented the deity by a black stone, because his nature is obscure and inscrutable. The reader will here be reminded of the black stone *Hadsjar el Aswad,* placed in the south-west corner of the Kaaba at Mecca, which was worshipped by the ancient Arabians, and is still treated with religious veneration by the modern Mohammedans. The Mussulman priests, however, say that it was originally white, and of such surprising splendor that it could be seen at the distance of four days' journey, but that it has been blackened by the tears of pilgrims.

The Druids, it is well known, had no other images of their gods but cubical, or sometimes columnar, stones, of which Toland gives several instances.

The Chaldeans had a sacred stone, which they held in great veneration, under the name of *Mnizuris,* and to which they sacrificed for the purpose of evoking the Good Demon.

Stone-worship existed among the early American races. Squier quotes Skinner as asserting that the Peruvians used to set up rough stones in their fields and plantations, which were worshipped as protectors of their crops. And Gama says that in Mexico the presiding god of the spring was often represented without a human body, and in place thereof a pilaster or square column, whose pedestal was covered with various sculptures.

Indeed, so universal was this stone-worship, that Higgins,

* The "Disputationes adversus Gentes" of Arnobius supplies us with a fund of information on the symbolism of the classic mythology.

in his "*Celtic Druids,*" says that, "throughout the world the first object of idolatry seems to have been a plain, unwrought stone, placed in the ground, as an emblem of the generative or procreative powers of nature." And the learned Bryant, in his "*Analysis of Ancient Mythology,*" asserts that "there is in every oracular temple some legend about a stone."

Without further citations of examples from the religious usages of other countries, it will, I think, be conceded that the cubical stone formed an important part of the religious worship of primitive nations. But Cudworth, Bryant, Faber, and all other distinguished writers who have treated the subject, have long since established the theory that the pagan religions were eminently symbolic. Thus, to use the language of Dudley, the pillar or stone "was adopted as a symbol of strength and firmness, — a symbol, also, of the divine power, and, by a ready inference, a symbol or idol of the Deity himself."* And this symbolism is confirmed by Cornutus, who says that the god Hermes was represented without hands or feet, being a cubical stone, because the cubical figure betokened his solidity and stability.†

Thus, then, the following facts have been established, but not precisely in this order: First, that there was a very general prevalence among the earliest nations of antiquity of the worship of stones as the representatives of Deity; secondly, that in almost every ancient temple there was a legend of a sacred or mystical stone; thirdly, that this legend is found in the masonic system; and lastly, that the mystical stone there has received the name of the "Stone of Foundation."

* Naology, ch. iii. p. 119.   † Cornut. de Nat. Deor. c. 16.

Now, as in all the other systems the stone is admitted to be symbolic, and the tradition connected with it mystical, we are compelled to assume the same predicates of the masonic stone. It, too, is symbolic, and its legend a myth or an allegory.

Of the fable, myth, or allegory, Bailly has said that, "subordinate to history and philosophy, it only deceives that it may the better instruct us. Faithful in preserving the realities which are confided to it, it covers with its seductive envelope the lessons of the one and the truths of the other."* It is from this stand-point that we are to view the allegory of the Stone of Foundation, as developed in one of the most interesting and important symbols of Masonry.

The fact that the mystical stone in all the ancient religions was a symbol of the Deity, leads us necessarily to the conclusion that the Stone of Foundation was also a symbol of Deity. And this symbolic idea is strengthened by the tetragrammaton, or sacred name of God, that was inscribed upon it. This ineffable name sanctifies the stone upon which it is engraved as the symbol of the Grand Architect. It takes from it its heathen signification as an idol, and consecrates it to the worship of the true God.

The predominant idea of the Deity, in the masonic system, connects him with his creative and formative power. God is, to the Freemason, *Al Gabil,* as the Arabians called him, that is, *The Builder;* or, as expressed in his masonic title, the *Grand Architect of the Universe,* by common consent abbreviated in the formula G. A. O. T. U. Now, it is evident that no symbol could so appropriately

---

* Essais sur les Fables, t. i. lett. 2. p. 9.

suit him in this character as the Stone of Foundation, upon which he is allegorically supposed to have erected his world. Such a symbol closely connects the creative work of God, as a pattern and exemplar, with the workman's erection of his temporal building on a similar foundation stone.

But this masonic idea is still further to be extended. The great object of all Masonic labor is *divine truth.* The search for the *lost word* is the search for truth. But divine truth is a term synonymous with God. The ineffable name is a symbol of truth, because God, and God alone, is truth. It is properly a scriptural idea. The Book of Psalms abounds with this sentiment. Thus it is said that the truth of the Lord "reacheth unto the clouds," and that "his truth endureth unto all generations." If, then, God is truth, and the Stone of Foundation is the masonic symbol of God, it follows that it must also be the symbol of divine truth.

When we have arrived at this point in our speculations, we are ready to show how all the myths and legends of the Stone of Foundation may be rationally explained as parts of that beautiful "science of morality, veiled in allegory and illustrated by symbols," which is the acknowledged definition of Freemasonry.

In the masonic system there are two temples; the first temple, in which the degrees of Ancient Craft Masonry are concerned, and the second temple, with which the higher degrees, and especially the Royal Arch, are related. The first temple is symbolic of the present life; the second temple is symbolic of the life to come. The first temple, the present life, must be destroyed; on its foundations the second temple, the life eternal, must be built.

But the mystical stone was placed by King Solomon in the foundations of the first temple. That is to say, the first temple of our present life must be built on the sure foundation of divine truth, "for other foundation can no man lay."

But although the present life is necessarily built upon the foundation of truth, yet we never thoroughly attain it in this sublunary sphere. The Foundation Stone is concealed in the first temple, and the Master Mason knows it not. He has not the true word. He receives only a substitute.

But in the second temple of the future life, we have passed from the grave, which had been the end of our labors in the first. We have removed the rubbish, and have found that Stone of Foundation which had been hitherto concealed from our eyes. We now throw aside the substitute for truth which had contented us in the former temple, and the brilliant effulgence of the tetragrammaton and the Stone of Foundation are discovered, and thenceforth we are the possessors of the true word — of divine truth. And in this way, the Stone of Foundation, or divine truth, concealed in the first temple, but discovered and brought to light in the second, will explain that passage of the apostle, "For now we see through a glass darkly, but then face to face: now I know in part; but then shall I know even as also I am known."

And so, the result of this inquiry is, that the masonic Stone of Foundation is a symbol of divine truth, upon which all Speculative Masonry is built, and the legends and traditions which refer to it are intended to describe, in an allegorical way, the progress of truth in the soul, the search for which is a Mason's labor, and the discovery of which is his reward.

XXXI.

THE LOST WORD.

THE last of the symbols, depending for its existence on its connection with a myth to which I shall invite attention, is *the Lost Word, and the search for it.* Very appropriately may this symbol terminate our investigations, since it includes within its comprehensive scope all the others, being itself the very essence of the science of masonic symbolism. The other symbols require for their just appreciation a knowledge of the origin of the order, because they owe their birth to its relationship with kindred and anterior institutions. But the symbolism of the Lost Word has reference exclusively to the design and the objects of the institution.

First, let us define the symbol, and then investigate its interpretation.

The mythical history of Freemasonry informs us that there once existed a WORD of surpassing value, and claiming a profound veneration; that this Word was known to but few; that it was at length lost; and that a temporary substitute for it was adopted. But as the very philosophy of Masonry teaches us that there can be no death without a resurrection,—no decay without a subsequent restoration,—on the same principle it follows that the loss of the Word must suppose its eventual recovery.

Now, this it is, precisely, that constitutes the myth of the Lost Word and the search for it. No matter what was the word, no matter how it was lost, nor why a substitute was provided, nor when nor where it was recovered. These are all points of subsidiary importance, necessary, it is true, for knowing the legendary history, but not necessary for understanding the symbolism. The only term of the myth that is to be regarded in the study of its interpretation, is the abstract idea of a word lost and afterwards recovered.

This, then, points us to the goal to which we must direct our steps in the pursuit of the investigation.

But the symbolism, referring in this case, as I have already said, solely to the great design of Freemasonry, the nature of that design at once suggests itself as a preliminary subject of inquiry in the investigation.

What, then, is the design of Freemasonry? A very large majority of its disciples, looking only to its practical results, as seen in the every-day business of life,—to the noble charities which it dispenses, to the tears of widows which it has dried, to the cries of orphans which it has hushed, to the wants of the destitute which it has supplied,—arrive with too much rapidity at the conclusion that Charity, and that, too, in its least exalted sense of eleemosynary aid, is the great design of the institution.

Others, with a still more contracted view, remembering the pleasant reunions at their lodge banquets, the unreserved communications which are thus encouraged, and the solemn obligations of mutual trust and confidence that are continually inculcated, believe that it was intended solely to promote the social sentiments and cement the bonds of friendship.

But, although the modern lectures inform us that Brotherly Love and Relief are two of "the principal tenets of a Mason's profession," yet, from the same authority, we learn that Truth is a third and not less important one; and Truth, too, not in its old Anglo-Saxon meaning of fidelity to engagements,* but in that more strictly philosophical one in which it is opposed to intellectual and religious error or falsehood.

But I have shown that the Primitive Freemasonry of the ancients was instituted for the purpose of preserving that truth which had been originally communicated to the patriarchs, in all its integrity, and that the Spurious Masonry, or the Mysteries, originated in the earnest need of the sages, and philosophers, and priests, to find again the same truth which had been lost by the surrounding multitudes. I have shown, also, that this same truth continued to be the object of the Temple Masonry, which was formed by a union of the Primitive, or Pure, and the Spurious systems. Lastly, I have endeavored to demonstrate that this truth related to the nature of God and the human soul.

The search, then, after this truth, I suppose to constitute the end and design of Speculative Masonry. From the very commencement of his career, the aspirant is by significant symbols and expressive instructions directed to the

---

* Bosworth *(Aug. Sax. Dict.)* defines *treowth* to signify, troth, truth, treaty, league, pledge, and covenant.

acquisition of this divine truth; and the whole lesson, if not completed in its full extent, is at least well developed in the myths and legends of the Master's degree. *God and the soul*—the unity of the one and the immortality of the other—are the great truths, the search for which is to constitute the constant occupation of every Mason, and which, when found, are to become the chief corner-stone, or the stone of foundation, of the spiritual temple—"the house not made with hands"—which he is engaged in erecting.

Now, this idea of a search after truth forms so prominent a part of the whole science of Freemasonry, that I conceive no better or more comprehensive answer could be given to the question, *What is Freemasonry?* than to say that it is a science which is engaged in the search after divine truth.

But Freemasonry is eminently a system of symbolism, and all its instructions are conveyed in symbols. It is, therefore, to be supposed that so prominent and so prevailing an idea as this,—one that constitutes, as I have said, the whole design of the institution, and which may appropriately be adopted as the very definition of its science,—could not with any consistency be left without its particular symbol.

The WORD, therefore, I conceive to be the symbol of *Divine Truth;* and all its modifications—the loss, the substitution, and the recovery—are but component parts of the mythical symbol which represents a search after truth.

How, then, is this symbolism preserved? How is the whole history of this Word to be interpreted, so as to bear, in all its accidents of time, and place, and circumstance, a patent reference to the substantive idea that has been symbolized?

The answers to these questions embrace what is, perhaps, the most intricate as well as most ingenious and interesting portion of the science of masonic symbolism.

This symbolism may be interpreted, either in an application to a general or to a special sense.

The general application will embrace the whole history of Freemasonry, from its inception to its consummation. The search after the Word is an epitome of the intellectual and religious progress of the order, from the period when, by the dispersion at Babel, the multitudes were enshrouded in the profundity of a moral darkness where truth was apparently forever extinguished. The true name of God was lost; his true nature was not understood; the divine lessons imparted by our father Noah were no longer remembered; the ancient traditions were now corrupted; the ancient symbols were perverted. Truth was buried beneath the rubbish of Sabaism, and the idolatrous adoration of the sun and stars had taken the place of the olden worship of the true God. A moral darkness was now spread over the face of the earth, as a dense, impenetrable cloud, which obstructed the rays of the spiritual sun, and covered the people as with a gloomy pall of intellectual night.

But this night was not to last forever. A brighter dawn was to arise, and amidst all this gloom and darkness there were still to be found a few sages in whom the religious sentiment, working in them with powerful throes, sent forth manfully to seek after truth. There were, even in those days of intellectual and religious darkness, craftsmen who were willing to search for the *Lost Word*. And though they were unable to find it, their approximation to truth was so near that the result of their search may well be symbolized by the *Substitute Word.*

It was among the idolatrous multitudes that the *Word* had been lost. It was among them that the Builder had been smitten, and that the works of the spiritual temple had been suspended; and so, losing at each successive stage of their decline, more and more of the true knowledge of God and of the pure religion which had originally been imparted by Noah, they finally arrived at gross materialism and idolatry, losing all sight of the divine existence. Thus it was that the truth—the Word— was said to have been lost; or, to apply the language of Hutchinson, modified in its reference to the time, "in this situation, it might well be said that the guide to heaven was lost, and the master of the works of righteousness was smitten. The nations had given themselves up to the grossest idolatry, and the service of the true God was effaced from the memory of those who had yielded themselves to the dominion of sin."

And now it was among the philosophers and priests in the ancient Mysteries, or the spurious Freemasonry, that an anxiety to discover the truth led to the search for the Lost Word. These were the craftsmen who saw the fatal blow which had been given, who knew that the Word was now lost, but were willing to go forth, manfully and patiently, to seek its restoration. And there were the craftsmen who, failing to rescue it from the grave of oblivion into which it had fallen, by any efforts of their own incomplete knowledge, fell back upon the dim traditions which had been handed down from primeval times, and through their aid found a substitute for truth in their own philosophical religions.

And hence Schmidtz, speaking of these Mysteries of the pagan world, calls them the remains of the ancient Pelasgian religion, and says that "the associations of persons for the purpose of celebrating them must therefore have been formed at the time when the overwhelming influence of the Hellenic religion began to gain the upper hand in Greece, and when persons who still entertained a reverence for the worship of former times united together, with the intention of preserving and upholding among themselves as much as possible of the religion of their forefathers."

Applying, then, our interpretation in a general sense, the *Word* itself being the symbol of *Divine Truth,* the narrative of its loss and the search for its recovery becomes a mythical symbol of the decay and loss of the true religion among the ancient nations, at and after the dispersion on the plains of Shinar, and of the attempts of the wise men, the philosophers, and priests, to find and retain it in their secret Mysteries and initiations, which have hence been designated as the Spurious Freemasonry of Antiquity.

But I have said that there is a special, or individual, as well as a general interpretation. This compound or double symbolism, if I may so call it, is by no means unusual in Freemasonry. I have already exhibited an illustration of it in the symbolism of Solomon's temple, where, in a general sense, the temple is viewed as a symbol of that spiritual temple formed by the aggregation of the whole order, and in which each mason is considered as a stone; and, in an individual or special sense, the same temple is considered as a type of that spiritual temple which each mason is directed to erect in his heart.

Now, in this special or individual interpretation, the Word, with its accompanying myth of a loss, a substitute, and a recovery, becomes a symbol of the personal progress of a candidate from his first initiation to the completion of his course, when he receives a full development of the Mysteries.

The aspirant enters on this search after truth, as an Entered Apprentice, in darkness, seeking for light—the light of wisdom, the light of truth, the light symbolized by the Word. For this important task, upon which he starts forth gropingly, falteringly, doubtingly, in want and in weakness, he is prepared by a purification of the heart, and is invested with a first substitute for the true Word, which, like the pillar that went before the Israelites in the wilderness, is to guide him onwards in his weary journey. He is directed to take, as a staff and scrip for his journey, all those virtues which expand the heart and dignify the soul. Secrecy, obedience, humility, trust in God, purity of conscience, economy of time, are all inculcated by impressive types and symbols, which connect the first degree with the period of youth.

And then, next in the degree of Fellow Craft, he fairly enters upon his journey. Youth has now passed, and manhood has come on. New duties and increased obligations press upon the individual. The thinking and working stage of life is here symbolized. Science is to be cultivated; wisdom is to be acquired; the lost Word— divine truth—is still to be sought for. But even yet it is not to be found.

And now the Master Mason comes, with all the symbolism around him of old age—trials, sufferings, death. And here, too, the aspirant, pressing onward, *always onward,* still cries aloud for "light, more light." The search is almost over, but the lesson, humiliating to human nature, is to be taught, that in this life—gloomy and dark, earthly and carnal—pure truth has no abiding place; and contented with a substitute, and to that *second temple* of eternal life, for that true Word, that divine Truth, which will teach us all that we shall ever learn of God and his emanation, the human soul.

So, the Master Mason, receiving this substitute for the lost Word, waits with patience for the time when it shall be found, and perfect wisdom shall be attained.

But, work as we will, this symbolic Word—this knowledge of divine Truth—is never thoroughly attained in this life, or in its symbol, the Master Mason's lodge. The corruptions of mortality, which encumber and cloud the human intellect, hide it, as with a thick veil, from mortal eyes. It is only, as I have just said, beyond the tomb, and when released from the earthly burden of life, that man is capable of fully receiving and appreciating the revelation. Hence, then, when we speak of the recovery of the Word, in that higher degree which is a supplement to Ancient Craft Masonry, we intimate that that sublime portion of the masonic system is a symbolic representation of the state after death. For it is only after the decay and fall of this temple of life, which, as masons, we have been building, that from its ruins, deep beneath its foundations, and in the profound abyss of the grave, we find that divine truth, in the search for which life was spent, if not in vain, at least without success, and the mystic key to which death only could supply.

And now we know by this symbolism what is meant

by Masonic *labor,* which, too, is itself but another form of the same symbol. The search for the Word—to find divine Truth—this, and this only, is a mason's work, and the WORD is his reward.

Labor, said the old monks, is worship—*laborare est orare;* and thus in our lodges do we worship, working for the Word, working for the Truth, ever looking forward, casting no glance behind, but cheerily hoping for the consummation and the reward of our labor in the knowledge which is promised to him who plays no laggard's part.

Goethe, himself a mason and a poet, knew and felt all this symbolism of a mason's life and work, when he wrote that beautiful poem, which Carlyle has thus thrown into his own rough but impulsive language.

> "The mason's ways are
> A type of existence,—
> And to his persistence
> Is as the days are
> Of men in this world.
>
> "The future hides in it
> Gladness and sorrow;
> We press still thorow,
> Nought that abides in it
> Daunting us—onward.
>
> "And solemn before us
> Veiled the dark portal,
> Goal of all mortal;
> Stars silent rest o'er us
> Graves under us silent.
>
> "While earnest thou gazest
> Come boding of terror,
> Comes phantasm and error,
> Perplexing the bravest
> With doubt and misgiving.

"But heard are the voices,
　Heard are the sages,
　The worlds and the ages;
　'Choose well; your choice is
　Brief and yet endless.

"'Here eyes do regard you,
　In eternity's stillness;
　Here is all fullness,
　Ye, brave to reward you;
　Work and despair not.'"

* * * *

And now, in concluding this work, so inadequate to the importance of the subjects that have been discussed, one deduction, at least, may be drawn from all that has been said.

In tracing the progress of Freemasonry, and in detailing its system of symbolism, it has been found to be so intimately connected with the history of philosophy, of religion, and of art, in all ages of the world, that the conviction at once forces itself upon the mind, that no mason can expect thoroughly to comprehend its nature, or to appreciate its character as a science, unless he shall devote himself, with some labor and assiduity, to this study of its system. That skill which consists in repeating, with fluency and precision, the ordinary lectures, in complying with all the ceremonial requisitions of the ritual, or the giving, with sufficient accuracy, the appointed modes of recognition, pertains only to the very rudiments of the masonic science.

But there is a far nobler series of doctrines with which Freemasonry is connected, and which it has been my object, in this work, to present in some imperfect way. It is these which constitute the science and the philosophy of Freemasonry, and it is these alone which will return the student who devotes himself to the task, a sevenfold reward for his labor.

Freemasonry, viewed no longer, as too long it has-been, as a merely social institution, has now assumed its original and undoubted position as a speculative science. While the mere ritual is still carefully preserved, as the casket should be which contains so bright a jewel; while its charities are still dispensed as the necessary though incidental result of all its moral teachings; while its social tendencies are still cultivated as the tenacious cement which is to unite so fair a fabric in symmetry and strength, the masonic mind is everywhere beginning to look and ask for something, which, like the manna in the desert, shall feed us, in our pilgrimage, with intellectual food. The universal cry, throughout the masonic world, is for light; our lodges are henceforth to be schools; our labor is to be study; our wages are to be learning; the types and symbols, the myths and allegories, of the institution are beginning to be investigated with reference to their ultimate meaning; our history is now traced by zealous inquiries as to its connection with antiquity; and Freemasons now thoroughly understand that often quoted definition, that "Masonry is a science of morality veiled in allegory and illustrated by symbols."

Thus to learn Masonry is to know our work and to do it well. What true mason would shrink from the task?

SYNOPTICAL INDEX

A

ALLEGORY. A discourse or narrative, in which there is a literal and a figurative sense, a patent and a concealed meaning; the literal or patent sense being intended by analogy or comparison to indicate the figurative or concealed one. Its derivation from the Greek ἀλλος and αγορειν, to *say something different,* that is, to say something where the language is one thing, and the true meaning different, exactly expresses the character of an allegory. It has been said in the text that there is no essential difference between an allegory and a symbol. There is not in design, but there is this in their character: An allegory may be interpreted without any previous conventional agreement, but a symbol cannot. Thus the legend of the third degree is an allegory evidently to be interpreted as teaching a restoration to life; and this we learn from the legend itself, without any previous understanding. The sprig of acacia is a symbol of the immortality of the soul. But this we know only because such meaning had been conventionally determined when the symbol was first established. It is evident, then, that an allegory which is obscure is imperfect. The enigmatical meaning should be easy of interpretation; and hence Lemière, a French poet, has said, "L'allégorie habite un palais diaphane" — *Allegory lives in a transparent palace.* All the legends of Freemasonry are more or less allegorical, and whatever truth there may be in some of them in an historical point of view, it is only as allegories, or legendary symbols, that they are important. 75

ALL-SEEING EYE. A symbol of the third degree, of great antiquity. See *Eye.*

ANCIENT CRAFT MASONRY. The first three degrees of Freemasonry; viz., Entered Apprentice, Fellow Craft, and Master Mason. They are so called because they alone are supposed to have been practised by the ancient craft. In the agreement between the two grand lodges of England in 1813, the definition was made to include the Royal Arch degree. Now if by the "ancient craft" are meant the workmen at the first temple, the definition will be wrong, because the Royal Arch degree could have had no existence until the time of the building of the second temple. But if by the "ancient craft" is meant the body of workmen who introduced the rites of Masonry into Europe in the early ages of the history of the Order, then it will be correct; because the Royal Arch degree always, from its origin until the middle of the eighteenth century, formed a part of the Master's. "Ancient Craft Masonry," however, in this country, is generally understood to embrace only the first three degrees. 124

ANDERSON. James Anderson, D. D., is celebrated as the compiler and editor of "The Constitutions of the Freemasons," published by order of the Grand Lodge of England, in 1723. A second edition was published by him in 1738. Shortly after, Anderson died, and the subsequent editions, of which there are several, have been edited by other persons. The edition of 1723 has become exceedingly rare, and copies of it bring fancy prices among the collectors of old masonic books. Its intrinsic value is derived only from the fact that it contains the first printed copy of the "Old Charges," and also the "General Regulations." The history of Masonry which precedes these, and constitutes the body of the work, is fanciful, unreliable, and pretentious to a degree that often leads to absurdity. The craft are greatly indebted to Anderson for his labors in reorganizing the institution, but doubtless it would have been better if he had contented himself with giving the records of the Grand Lodge from 1717 to 1738 which are contained in his second edition, and with preserving for us the charges and regulations, which without his industry might have been lost. No masonic writer would now venture to quote Anderson as authority for the history of the Order anterior to the eighteenth century. It must also be added that in the republication of the old charges in the edition of 1738, he made several important alterations and interpolations, which justly gave some offence to the Grand Lodge, and which render the second edition of no authority in this respect. 228

ANIMAL WORSHIP. The worship of animals is a species of idolatry that was especially practised by the ancient Egyptians. Temples were erected by this people in their honor, in which they were fed and cared for during life; to kill one of them was a crime punishable with death; and after death, they were embalmed, and interred in the catacombs. This worship was derived first from the earlier adoration of the stars, to certain constellations of which the names of animals had been given; next, from an Egyptian tradition that the gods, being pursued by Typhon, had concealed themselves under the forms of animals; and lastly, from the doctrine of the

is drawn from the art of architecture. While the
improvements of Greek and Roman architecture are
recognized in Freemasonry, the three ancient orders, the
Doric, Ionic, and Corinthian are alone symbolized. No
symbolism attaches to the Tuscan and Composite............... 222

ARK OF THE COVENANT. One of the most sacred objects among
the Israelites. It was a chest made of shittim wood, or
acacia, richly decorated, forty-five inches long, and
eighteen inches wide, and contained the two tables of stone
on which the ten commandments were engraved, the
golden pot that held manna, and Aaron's rod. It was placed
in the holy of holies, first of the tabernacle, and then of the
temple. Such is its masonic and scriptural history. The idea
of this ark was evidently borrowed from the Egyptians, in
whose religious rites a similar chest or coffer is to be found.
Herodotus mentions several instances. Speaking of the
festival of Papremis, he says (ii. 63) that the image of the
god was kept in a small wooden shrine covered with plates
of gold, which shrine was conveyed in a procession of the
priests and people from the temple into a second sacred
building. Among the sculptures are to be found bass reliefs
of the ark of Isis. The greatest of the religious ceremonies
of the Egyptians was the procession of the shrines
mentioned in the Rosetta stone, and which is often found
depicted on the sculptures. These shrines were of two kinds,
one a canopy, but the other, called the great shrine, was an
ark or sacred boat. It was borne on the shoulders of priests
by means of staves passing through rings in its sides, and
was taken into the temple and deposited on a stand. Some
of these arks contained, says Wilkinson *(Notes to Herod.* II.
58, n. 9), the elements of life and stability, and others the
sacred beetle of the sun, overshadowed by the wings of two
figures of the goddess Thmei. In all this we see the type of
the Jewish ark. The introduction of the ark into the
ceremonies of Freemasonry evidently is in reference to its
loss and recovery; and hence its symbolism is to be
interpreted as connected with the masonic idea of loss and
recovery, which always alludes to a loss of life and a
recovery of immortality. In the first temple of this life the
ark is lost; in the second temple of the future life it is
recovered. And thus the ark of the covenant is one of the
many masonic symbols of the resurrection............................ 81

ARTS AND SCIENCES, LIBERAL. In the seventh century, and

for many centuries afterwards, all learning was limited to and comprised in what were called the seven liberal arts and sciences; namely, grammar, rhetoric, logic, arithmetic, geometry, music, and astronomy. The epithet "liberal" is a fair translation of the Latin "ingenuus," which means "free-born;" thus Cicero speaks of the "artes ingenuæ," or the arts befitting a free-born man; and Ovid says in the well-known lines, —

"Ingenuas didicisse fideliter artes
Emollit mores nec sinit esse feros,"—

To have studied carefully the liberal arts refines the manners, and prevents us from being brutish. And Phillips, in his "New World of Words" (1706), defines the liberal arts and sciences to be "such as are fit for gentlemen and scholars, as mechanic trades and handicrafts for meaner people." As Freemasons are required by their landmarks to be *free-born,* we see the propriety of incorporating the arts of free-born men among their symbols. As the system of Masonry derived its present form and organization from the times when the study of these arts and sciences constituted the labors of the wisest men, they have very appropriately been adopted as the symbol of the completion of human learning. 223

ASHMOLE, ELIAS. A celebrated antiquary of England, who was born in 1617. He has written an autobiography, or rather diary of his life, which extends to within eight years of his death. Under the date of October 16, 1646, he has made the following entry: "I was made a Free-Mason at Warrington, in Lancashire, with Col. Henry Mainwaring, of Carticham, in Cheshire; the names of those that were then at the lodge: Mr. Richard Penket, warden; Mr. James Collier, Mr. Richard Sankey, Henry Littler, John Ellam and Hugh Brewer." Thirty-six years afterwards, under date of March 10, 1682, he makes the following entry: "I received a summons to appear at a lodge to be held the next day at Masons' Hall, in London. 11. Accordingly I went, and about noon was admitted into the fellowship of Freemasons by Sir William Wilson, Knight, Captain Richard Borthwick, Mr. William Woodman, Mr. William Grey, Mr. Samuel Taylour, and Mr. William Wise. I was the senior fellow among them (it being thirty-five years since I was admitted); there was present beside myself the fellows after named: Mr. Thomas Wise, master of the Masons' Company this year; Mr. Thomas Shorthose, Mr. Thomas Shadbolt,——Waidsfford, Esq., Mr. Nicholas Young, Mr. John Shorthose, Mr. William Hamon, Mr. John Thompson, and Mr. William Stanton. We all dined at the Half-Moon Tavern, in Cheapside, at a noble dinner prepared at the charge of the new-accepted Masons." The titles of some of the persons named in these two receptions confirm what is said in the text, that the operative was at that time being superseded by the speculative element. It is deeply to be regretted that Ashmole did not carry out his projected design of writing a history of Freemasonry, for which it is said that he had collected abundant materials. His History of the Order of the Garter shows what we might have expected from his treatment of the Masonic institution......... 66

ASPIRANT. One who aspires to or seeks after the truth. The title given to the candidate in the ancient Mysteries. 43

ATHELSTAN. King of England, who ascended the throne in 924. Anderson cites the old constitutions as saying that he encouraged the Masons, and brought many over from France and elsewhere. In his reign, and in the year 926, the celebrated General Assembly of the Craft was held in the city of York, with Prince Edward, the king's brother, for Grand

B

Now there was in the old rituals a formula in the third degree, preserved in some places to the present day, which teaches that the candidate has come *from the tower of Babel, where language was confounded and Masonry lost,* and that he is travelling *to the* threshing-*floor of Ornan the Jebusite, where language was restored and Masonry found.* An attentive perusal of the nineteen propositions set forth in the preliminary chapter of this work will furnish the reader with a key for the interpretation of this formula. The principles of the Primitive Freemasonry of the early priesthood were corrupted or lost at Babel by the defection of a portion of mankind from Noah, the conservator of those principles. Long after, the descendants of this people united with those of Noah at the temple of Solomon, whose site was the threshing-floor of Ornan the Jebusite, from whom it had been bought by David; and here the lost principles were restored by this union of the Spurious Freemasons of Tyre with the Primitive Freemasons of Jerusalem. And this explains the latter clause of the formula.. 28

BABYLONISH CAPTIVITY. When the city and temple of Jerusalem were destroyed by the army of Nebuchadnezzar, and the inhabitants conveyed as captives to Babylon, we have a right to suppose, — that is to say, if there be any truth in masonic history, the deduction is legitimate, — that among these captives were many of the descendants of the workmen at the temple. If so, then they carried with them into captivity the principles of Masonry which they had acquired at home, and the city of Babylon became the great seat of Speculative Masonry for many years. It was during the captivity that the philosopher Pythagoras, who was travelling as a seeker after knowledge, visited Babylon. With his ardent thirst for wisdom, he would naturally hold frequent interviews with the leading Masons among the Jewish captives. As he suffered himself to be initiated into the Mysteries of Egypt during his visit to that country, it is not unlikely that he may have sought a similar initiation into the masonic Mysteries. This would account for the many analogies and resemblances to Masonry that we find in the moral teachings, the symbols, and the peculiar organization of the school of Pythagoras — resemblances so extraordinary as to have justified, or at least excused, the rituals for calling the sage of Samos "our ancient brother.".... 54

BACCHUS. One of the appellations of the "many-named" god Dionysus. The son of Jupiter and Semele was to the Greeks Dionysus, to the Romans Bacchus.. 46

BARE FEET. A symbol of reverence when both feet are uncovered. Otherwise the symbolism is modern; and from the ritualistic explanation which is given in the first degree, it would seem to require that the single bare foot should be interpreted as the symbol of a covenant............................... 125

BLACK. Pythagoras called this color the symbol of the evil principle in nature. It was equivalent to darkness, which is the antagonist of light. But in masonic symbolism the interpretation is different. There, black is a symbol of grief, and always refers to the fate of the temple-builder. 154

BRAHMA. In the mythology of the Hindoos there is a trimurti, or trinity, the Supreme Being exhibiting himself in three manifestations; as, Brahma the Creator, Vishnu the Preserver, and Siva the Destroyer, — the united godhead being a symbol of the sun. 28

Brahma was a symbol of the rising sun, Siva of the sun at meridian, and Vishnu of the setting sun. 108

BRUCE. The introduction of Freemasonry into Scotland has been attributed by some writers to King Robert Bruce, who is said to have established in 1314 the Order of Herodom, for the reception of those Knights Templars who had taken refuge in his dominions from the persecutions of the Pope and the King of France. Lawrie, who is excellent authority for Scottish Masonry, does not appear, however, to give any credit to the narrative. Whatever Bruce may have done for the higher degrees, there is no doubt that Ancient Craft Masonry was introduced into Scotland at an earlier period. See *Kilwinning.* Yet the text is right in making Bruce one of the patrons and encouragers of Scottish Freemasonry. 64

BRYANT. Jacob Bryant, frequently quoted in this work, was a distinguished English antiquary, born in the year 1715, and deceased in 1804. His most celebrated work is "A New System of Ancient Mythology," which appeared in 1773-76. Although objectionable on account of its too conjectural character, it contains a fund of details on the subject of symbolism, and may be consulted with advantage by the masonic student. 41

BUILDER. The chief architect of the temple of Solomon is often called "the Builder." But the word is also applied generally to the craft; for every Speculative Mason is as much a builder as was his operative predecessor. An American writer (F. S. Wood, of Arkansas) thus alludes to this symbolic idea. "Masons are called moral builders. In their rituals, they declare that a more noble and glorious purpose than squaring stones and hewing timbers is theirs, fitting immortal nature for that spiritual building not made with hands, eternal in the heavens." And he adds, "The builder builds for a century; masons for eternity." In this sense, "the builder" is the noblest title that can be bestowed upon a mason. 52

BUNYAN, JOHN. Familiar to every one as the author of the "Pilgrim's Progress." He lived in the seventeenth century, and was the most celebrated allegorical writer of England. His work entitled "Solomon's Temple Spiritualized" will supply the student of masonic symbolism with many valuable suggestions. 87

C

CABALA. The mystical philosophy of the Jews. The word which is derived from a Hebrew root, signifying *to receive,* has sometimes been used in an enlarged sense, as comprehending all the explanations, maxims, and ceremonies which have been traditionally handed down to the Jews; but in that more limited acceptation, in which it is intimately connected with the symbolic science of Freemasonry, the cabala may be defined to be a system of philosophy which embraces certain mystical interpretations of Scripture, and metaphysical speculations concerning the Deity, man, and spiritual beings. In these interpretations and speculations, according to the Jewish doctors, were enveloped the most profound truths of religion, which, to be comprehended by finite beings, are obliged to be revealed through the medium of symbols and allegories. Buxtorf (Lex. Talm.) defines the Cabala to be a secret science, which treats in a mystical and enigmatical manner of things divine, angelical, theological, celestial, and metaphysical, the subjects being enveloped in striking symbols and secret modes of teaching. 154

CABALIST. A Jewish philosopher. One who understands and teaches the doctrines of the Cabala, or the Jewish philosophy... 154

CABIRI. Certain gods, whose worship was first established in the Island of Samothrace, where the Cabiric Mysteries were practised until the beginning of the Christian era. They were four in number, and by some are supposed to have referred to Noah and his three sons. In the Mysteries there was a legend of the death and restoration to life of Atys, the son of Cybele. The candidate represented Cadmillus, the youngest of the Cabiri, who was slain by his three brethren. The legend of the Cabiric Mysteries, as far as it can be understood from the faint allusions of ancient authors, was in spirit and design very analogous to that of the third degree of Masonry. 256

CADMILLUS. One of the gods of the Cabiri, who was slain by his brothers, on which circumstance the legend of the Cabiric or Samothracian Mysteries is founded. He is the analogue of the Builder in the Hiramic legend of Freemasonry... 256

CAIRNS. Heaps of stones of a conical form, erected by the Druids. Some suppose them to have been sepulchral monuments, others altars. They were undoubtedly of a religious

The myths and traditions of this ancient people were adopted by Hesiod, Homer, and the later poets, although not without some misunderstanding of them, and they were finally preserved in the Mysteries, and became subjects of investigation for the philosophers. This theory Creuzer has developed in his most important work, entitled "Symbolik und Mythologie der alten Völker, besonders der Greichen," which was published at Leipsic in 1819. There is no translation of this work into English, but Guigniaut published at Paris, in 1824, a paraphrastic translation of it, under the title of "Religions de l'Antiquité considérées principalement dans leur Formes Symboliques et Mythologiques." Creuzer's views throw much light on the symbolic history of Freemasonry... 37

CROSS. No symbol was so universally diffused at an early period as the cross. It was, says Faber (Cabir. ii. 390), a symbol throughout the pagan world long previous to its becoming an object of veneration to Christians. In ancient symbology it was a symbol of eternal life. M. de Mortillet, who in 1866 published a work entitled "Le Signe de la Croix avant le Christianisme," found in the very earliest epochs three principal symbols of universal occurrences; viz., the *circle,* the *pyramid,* and the *cross.* Leslie (Man's Origin and Destiny, p. 312), quoting from him in reference to the ancient worship of the cross, says "It seems to have been a worship of such a peculiar nature as to exclude the worship of idols." This sacredness of the crucial symbol may be one reason why its form was often adopted, especially by the Celts in the construction of their temples, though I have admitted in the text the commonly received opinion that in cross-shaped temples the four limbs of the cross referred to the four elements. But in a very interesting work lately published — "The Myths of the New World" (N. Y., 1863) — Mr. Brinton assigns another symbolism. "The symbol," says this writer, "that beyond all others has fascinated the human mind, THE CROSS, finds here its source and meaning. Scholars have pointed out its sacredness in many natural religions, and have reverently accepted it as a mystery, or offered scores of conflicting, and often debasing, interpretations. *It is but another symbol of the four cardinal points, the four winds of heaven.* This will luminously appear by a study of its use and meaning in America." (p. 95.) And Mr. Brinton gives many instances of the religious use

D

E

ELEPHANTA. An island in the Bay of Bombay, celebrated for the stupendous caverns artificially excavated out of the solid rock, which were appropriated to the initiations in the ancient Indian Mysteries. 108

ELEUSINIAN MYSTERIES. Of all the Mysteries of the ancients these were the most popular. They were celebrated at the village of Eleusis, near Athens, and were dedicated to Demeter. In them the loss and the restoration of Persephone were scenically represented, and the doctrines of the unity of God and the immortality of the soul were taught. See *Demeter*. 36

ENTERED APPRENTICE. The first degree of Ancient Craft Masonry, analogous to the aspirant in the Lesser Mysteries... 93
It is viewed as a symbol of childhood, and is considered as a preparation and purification for something higher. 218

EPOPT. (From the Greek ἐπόπτης, an eye witness.) One who, having been initiated in the Greater Mysteries of paganism, has seen the aporrheta. 44

ERA OF MASONRY. The legendary statement that the origin of Masonry is coeval with the beginning of the world, is only a philosophical myth to indicate the eternal nature of its principles. 211

ERICA. The tree heath; a sacred plant among the Egyptians, and used in the Osirian Mysteries as the symbol of immortality, and the analogue of the masonic acacia. 258

ESSENES. A society or sect of the Jews, who combined labor with religious exercises, whose organization partook of a secret character, and who have been claimed to be the descendants of the builders of the temple of Solomon............ 18

EUCLID. The masonic legend which refers to Euclid is altogether historically untrue. It is really a philosophical myth intended to convey a masonic truth. 208

EURESIS. (From the Greek εὕρεσις, *a discovery*.) That part of the initiation in the ancient Mysteries which represented the finding of the body of the god or hero whose death was the subject of the initiation.. 44
The euresis has been adopted in Freemasonry, and forms an essential part of the ritual of the third degree. 234

EVERGREEN. A symbol of the immortality of the soul. 251
Planted by the Hebrews and other ancient peoples at the heads of graves. 252
For this purpose the Hebrews preferred the acacia, because its wood was incorruptible, and because, as the material of the ark, it was already considered as a sacred plant. 253

F

contain the right angle. It is said to have been discovered by Pythagoras while in Egypt, but was most probably taught to him by the priests of that country, in whose rites he had been initiated; it is a symbol of the production of the world by the generative and prolific powers of the Creator; hence the Egyptians made the perpendicular and base the representatives of Osiris and Isis, while the hypothenuse represented their child Horus. Dr. Lardner says (*Com. on Euclid,* p. 60) of this problem, "Whether we consider the forty-seventh proposition with reference to the peculiar and beautiful relation established by it, or to its innumerable uses in every department of mathematical science, or to its fertility in the consequences derivable from it, it must certainly be esteemed the most celebrated and important in the whole of the elements, if not in the whole range of mathematical science.".. 193

FOURTEEN. Some symbologists have referred the fourteen pieces into which the mutilated body of Osiris was divided, and the fourteen days during which the body of the builder was buried, to the fourteen days of the disappearance of the moon. The Sabian worshippers of "the hosts of heaven" were impressed with the alternate appearance and disappearance of the moon, which at length became a symbol of death and resurrection. Hence fourteen was a sacred number. As such it was viewed in the Osirian Mysteries, and may have been introduced into Freemasonry with other relies of the old worship of the sun and planets..... 40

FREEMASONRY, DEFINITION OF. See *Definition.*

FREEMASONS, TRAVELLING. The travelling Freemasons were a society existing in the middle ages, and consisting of learned men and prelates, under whom were operative masons. The operative masons performed the labors of the craft, and travelling from country to country, were engaged in the construction of cathedrals, monasteries, and castles. "There are few points in the history of the middle ages," says Godwin, "more pleasing to look back upon than the existence of the associated masons; they are the bright spot in the general darkness of that period; the patch of verdure when all around is barren." *The Builder,* ix. 463. 62

G

H

HIEROPHANT. (From the Greek ἱερὸς, *holy, sacred,* and φαίνω, *to show.*) One who instructs in sacred things; the explainer of the aporrheta, or secret doctrines, to the initiates in the ancient Mysteries. He was the presiding officer, and his rank and duties were analogous to those of the master of a masonic lodge.

HIRAM ABIF. The architect of Solomon's temple. The word "Abif" signifies in Hebrew "his father," and is used by the writer of Second Chronicles (4:16) when he says, "These things did *Hiram his father* [in the original *Hiram Abif*] do for King Solomon.".. 56

The legend relating to him is of no value as a mere narrative, but of vast importance in a symbolical point of view, as illustrating a great philosophical and religious truth; namely, the dogma of the immortality of the soul................ 207

Hence, Hiram Abif is the symbol of man in the abstract sense, or human nature, as developed in the life here and in the life to come... 231

HIRAM OF TYRE. The king of Tyre, the friend and ally of King Solomon, whom he supplied with men and materials for building the temple. In the recent, or what I am inclined to call the grand lecturer's symbolism of Masonry (a sort of symbolism for which I have very little veneration), Hiram of Tyre is styled the symbol of strength, as Hiram Abif is of beauty. But I doubt the antiquity or authentieity of any such symbolism. Hiram of Tyre can only be considered, historically, as being necessary to complete the myth and symbolism of Hiram Abif. The king of Tyre is an historical personage, and there is no necessity for transforming him into a symbol, while his historical character lends credit and validity to the philosophical myth of the third degree of Masonry. 51

HIRAM THE BUILDER. An epithet of Hiram Abif. For the full significance of the term, see the word *Builder*........................ 55

HO-HI. A cabalistic pronunciation of the tetragrammaton, or ineffable name of God; it is most probably the true one; and as it literally means HE-SHE, it is supposed to denote the hermaphroditic essence of Jehovah, as containing within himself the male and the female principle, — the generative and the prolific energy of creation........................ 187

HC. The sacred name of God among the Druids. Bryant supposes that by it they intended the Great Father Noah; but it is very possible that it was a modification of the Hebrew tetragrammaton, being the last syllable read cabalistically (see *ho-hi*); if so, it signified the great male principle of nature. But Hu, in Hebrew הוא, is claimed by Talmudic writers to be one of the names of God; and the passage in Isaiah 42:8, in the original *ani Jehovah, Hu shemi,* which is in the common version "I am the LORD; that is my name," they interpret, "I am Jehovah; my name is Hu." 185

HUTCHINSON, WILLIAM. A distinguished masonic writer of England, who lived in the eighteenth century. He is the author of "The Spirit of Masonry," published in 1775. This was the first English work of any importance that sought to give a scientific interpretation of the symbols of Freemasonry; it is, in fact, the earliest attempt of any kind to treat Freemasonry as a science of symbolism. Hutchinson, however, has to some extent impaired the value of his labors by contending that the institution is exclusively Christian in its character and design. 235

I

IH-HO. See *Ho-hi.*

IMMORTALITY OF THE SOUL. This is one of the two religious dogmas which have always been taught in Speculative Masonry. 22

It was also taught in all the Rites and Mysteries of antiquity.. 229

The doctrine was taught as an abstract proposition by the ancient priesthood of the Pure or Primitive Freemasonry of antiquity, but was conveyed to the mind of the initiate, and impressed upon him by a scenic representation in the ancient Mysteries, or the Spurious Freemasonry of the ancients... 230

INCOMMUNICABLE NAME. The tetragrammaton, so called because it was not common to, and could not be bestowed upon, nor shared by, any other being. It was proper to the true God alone. Thus Drusius (Tetragrammaton, sive de Nomine Dei proprio, p. 108) says, "Nomen quatuor literarum proprie et absolute non tribui nisi Deo vero. Unde doctores catholici dicunt *incommunicabile* [not common] esse creaturæ" 175

INEFFABLE NAME. The tetragrammaton. So called because it is *ineffabile,* or unpronounceable. See *Tetragrammaton.* 175

INTRUSTING, RITE OF. That part of the ceremony of initiation which consists in communicating to the aspirant or candidate the aporrheta, or secrets of the mystery. 147

J

L

"Our name of Mason, and our emblems, distinctly announce that our object is the elevation of labor.

"We do not, as masons, consider labor as a punishment inflicted on man; but on the contrary, we elevate it in our thought to the height of a religious act, which is the most acceptable to God because it is the most usefnl to man and to society.

"We decorate ourselves with the emblems of labor to affirm that our doctrine is an incessant protest against the stigma branded on the law of labor, and which an error of apprehension, proceeding from the ignorance of men in primitive times has erected into a dogma; an error that has resulted in the production of this anti-social phenomenon which we meet with every day; namely, that the degradation of the workman is the greater as his labor is more severe, and the elevation of the idler is higher as his idleness is more complete. But the study of the laws which maintain order in nature, released from the fetters of preconceived ideas, has led the Freemasons to that doctrine, far more moral than the contrary belief, that labor is not an expiation, but a law of harmony, from the subjection to which man cannot be released without impairing his own happiness, and deranging the order of creation. The design of Freemasons is, then, the rehabilitation of labor, which is indicated by the apron which we wear, and the gavel, the trowel, and the level, which are found among our symbols."

LEGEND. A narrative, whether true or false, that has been traditionally preserved from the time of its first oral communication. Such is the definition of a masonic legend. The authors of the Conversations-Lexicon, referring to the monkish Lives of the Saints which originated in the twelfth and thirteenth centuries, say that the title *legend* was given to all fictions which make pretensions to truth. Such a remark, however correct it may be in reference to these monkish narratives, which were often invented as ecclesiastical exercises, is by no means applicable to the legends of Freemasonry. These are not necessarily fictitious, but are either based on actual and historical facts which have been but slightly modified, or they are the offspring and expansion of some symbolic idea, in which latter respect they differ entirely from the monastic legends, which often have only the fertile imagination of some studious monk for the basis of their construction 198

M

N

or character of the persons receiving them. Camden says that the same custom prevailed among all the nations of antiquity. So important has this subject been considered, that "Onomastica," or treatises on the signification of names have been written by Eusebius and St. Jerome, by Simonis and Hillerus, and by several other scholars, of whom Eusebe Salverte is the most recent and the most satisfactory. Shuckford (Connect. ii. 377) says that the Jewish Rabbins thought that the true knowledge of names was a science preferable to the study of the written law. 187

NAME OF GOD. The true pronunciation, and consequently the signification, of the name of God can only be obtained through a cabalistical interpretation. 187

It is a symbol of divine truth. None but those who are familiar with the subject can have any notion of the importance bestowed on this symbol by the Orientalists. The Arabians have a science called *Ism Allah,* or the *science of the name of God;* and the Talmudists and Rabbins have written copiously on the same subject. The Mussulmans, says Salverte (Essai sur les Noms, ii. 7), have one hundred names of God, which they repeat while counting the beads of a rosary. 197

NEOPHYTE. (From the Greek νέον and φυιὸν, *a new plant.)* One who has been recently initiated in the Mysteries. St. Paul uses the same word (1 Tim. 3:6) to denote one who had been recently converted to the Christian faith. 162

NOACHIDÆ. The descendants of Noah, and the transmitters of his religious dogmas, which were the unity of God and the immortality of the soul. The name has from the earliest times been bestowed upon the Freemasons, who teach the same doctrines. Thus in the "old charges," as quoted by Anderson (Const. edit. 1738, p. 143), it is said, "A mason is obliged by his tenure to observe the moral law as a true Noachidæ." 22

NOACHITES. The same as *Noachidæ,* which see.

NORTH. That part of the earth which, being most removed from the influence of the sun at his meridian height, is in Freemasonry called "a place of darkness." Hence it is a symbol of the profane world 167

NORTH-EAST CORNER. An important ceremony of the first degree, which refers to the north-east corner of the lodge, is explained by the symbolism of the corner-stone. 159

The corner-stone of a building is always laid in the north-east corner, for symbolic reasons. 165

O

To the author of this work the recollection will ever be most grateful that he enjoyed the friendship of so good and so great a man; one of whom we may testify, as Johnson said of Goldsmith, that "nihil quod tetigit non ornavit." In his writings he has traversed the whole field of masonic literature and science, and has treated, always with great ability and wonderful research, of its history, its antiquities, its rites and ceremonies, its ethics, and its symbols. Of all his works, his "Historical Landmarks," in two volumes, is the most important, the most useful, and the one which will perhaps the longest perpetuate his memory. In the study of his works, the student must be careful not to follow too implicitly all his conclusions. These were in his own mind controlled by the theory which he had adopted, and which he continuously maintained, that Freemasonry was a Christian institution, and that the connection between it and the Christian religion was absolute and incontrovertible. He followed in the footsteps of Hutchinson, but with a far more expanded view of the masonic system.

OPERATIVE MASONRY. Masonry considered merely as a useful art, intended for the protection and the convenience of man by the erection of edifices which may supply his intellectual, religious, and physical wants.............................. 83
In contradistinction to Speculative Masonry, therefore, it is said to be engaged in the construction of a material temple. 161

ORAL LAW. The oral law among the Jews was the commentary on and the interpretation of the written contained in the Pentateuch; and the tradition is, that it was delivered to Moses at the same time, accompanied by the divine command, "Thou shalt not divulge the words which I have said to thee out of my mouth." The oral law was, therefore, never intrusted to books; but being preserved in the memories of the judges, prophets, priests, and wise men, was handed down from one to the other through a long succession of ages. But after the destruction of Jerusalem by the Romans under Adrian, A. D. 135, and the final dispersion of the Jews, fears being entertained that the oral law would be lost, it was then committed to writing, and now constitutes the text of the Talmud.

ORMUZD. Worshipped by the disciples of Zoroaster as the principle of good, and symbolized by light. See *Ahriman.* ... 153

OSIRIS. The chief god of the ancient Egyptians, and worshipped as a symbol of the sun, and more philosophically as the male or generative principle. Isis, his wife, was the

P

R

S

T

possession; and Oliver descants on Tubal Cain as a symbol of worldly possessions. As to the identity of Vulcan with Tubal Cain, we may learn something from the definition of the offices of the former, as given by Diodorus Siculus: "Vulcan was the first founder of works in iron, brass, gold, silver, and all fusible metals; and he taught the uses to which fire can be applied in the arts." See Genesis: "Tubal Cain, an instructor of every artificer in brass and iron."

U

W

Y

Z

Stone Guild Publishing

Look for these and other great titles at:
http://www.stoneguildpublishing.com

CPSIA information can be obtained
at www.ICGtesting.com
Printed in the USA
LVHW011531010620
657133LV00033B/1923